OXFORD PAPERBACK REFERENCE

The Concise Oxford Dictionary of
Literary Terms

Chris Baldick is Professor of English at Goldsmiths'
College, University of London. He edited *The Oxford
Book of Gothic Tales* (1992), and is the author of *In
Frankenstein's Shadow* (1987), *Criticism and Literary
Theory 1890 to the Present* (1996), and other works of
literary history. He has edited, with Rob Morrison,
Tales of Terror from Blackwood's Magazine, and *The
Vampyre and Other Tales of the Macabre,* and has
written an introduction to Charles Maturin's
Melmoth the Wanderer (all available in the Oxford
World's Classics series).

Oxford Paperback Reference

The most authoritative and up-to-date reference books for both students and the general reader.

ABC of Music
Accounting
Allusions
Archaeology
Architecture
Art and Artists
Art Terms
Astronomy
Better Wordpower
Bible
Biology
British History
British Place-Names
Buddhism*
Business
Card Games
Catchphrases
Celtic Mythology
Chemistry
Christian Art
Christian Church
Chronology of English
  Literature*
Classical Literature
Classical Myth and Religion*
Computing
Contemporary World History
Dance
Dates
Dynasties of the World
Earth Sciences
Ecology
Economics
Encyclopedia
Engineering*
English Etymology
English Folklore
English Grammar
English Language
English Literature
Euphemisms
Everyday Grammar
Finance and Banking
First Names
Food and Drink
Food and Nutrition
Foreign Words and Phrases
Geography
Handbook of the World
Humorous Quotations
Idioms
Internet
Islam
Irish Literature

Jewish Religion
Kings and Queens of Britain
Language Toolkit
Law
Linguistics
Literary Quotations
Literary Terms
Local and Family History
London Place-Names
Mathematics
Medical
Medicinal Drugs
Modern Design*
Modern Slang
Music
Musical Terms
Musical Works
Nursing
Ologies and Isms
Philosophy
Phrase and Fable
Physics
Plant Sciences
Plays*
Pocket Fowler's Modern
  English Usage
Political Quotations
Politics
Popes
Proverbs
Psychology
Quotations
Quotations by Subject
Reverse Dictionary
Rhyming Slang
Saints
Science
Shakespeare
Slang
Sociology
Statistics
Synonyms and Antonyms
Twentieth-Century Art
Weather
Weights, Measures, and Units
Word Histories
World History
World Mythology
World Place-Names*
World Religions
Zoology

*forthcoming

The Concise
Oxford Dictionary of

Literary
Terms

CHRIS BALDICK

OXFORD
UNIVERSITY PRESS

OXFORD
UNIVERSITY PRESS

Great Clarendon Street, Oxford OX2 6DP

Oxford University Press is a department of the University of Oxford.
It furthers the University's objective of excellence in research, scholarship,
and education by publishing worldwide in

Oxford New York

Auckland Bangkok Buenos Aires Cape Town Chennai
Dar es Salaam Delhi Hong Kong Istanbul Karachi Kolkata
Kuala Lumpur Madrid Melbourne Mexico City Mumbai
Nairobi São Paulo Shanghai Taipei Tokyo Toronto

Oxford is a registered trade mark of Oxford University Press
in the UK and in certain other countries

Published in the United States
by Oxford University Press Inc., New York

First published 1990
First issued as an Oxford University Press paperback 1991
Reissued in new covers 1996
Second edition published 2001
Reissued with new covers 2004

British Library Cataloguing in Publication Data
Data available

Library of Congress Cataloging in Publication Data
Data available

ISBN 0-19-860883-7

2

Typeset in Swift and Frutiger by Kolam Information Services Pvt. Ltd, Pondicherry, India
Printed in Great Britain by
Clays Ltd, St Ives plc

For Steve, and Oriel Jane

Preface

This is a book of hard words alphabetically arranged and briefly explained. It cannot purport to fulfil the functions of a balanced expository guide to literary criticism or literary concepts, nor does it attempt to catalogue the entire body of literary terms in use. It offers instead to clarify those thousand terms that are most likely to cause the student or general reader some doubt or bafflement in the context of literary criticism and other discussion of literary works. Rather than include for the sake of encyclopaedic completeness all the most common terms found in literary discussion, I have set aside several that I have judged to be sufficiently well understood in common speech (*anagram*, *biography*, *cliché* and many more), or virtually self-explanatory (*detective story*, *psychological criticism*), along with a broad category of general concepts such as *art*, *belief*, *culture*, etc., which may appear as literary-critical problems but which are not specifically literary terms. This policy has allowed space for the inclusion of many terms generated by the growth of academic literary theory in recent years, and for adequate attention to the terminology of classical rhetoric, now increasingly revived. Along with these will be found hundreds of terms from literary criticism, literary history, prosody, and drama. The selection is weighted towards literature and criticism in English, but there are many terms taken from other languages, and many more associated primarily with other literatures. Many of the terms that I have omitted from this dictionary are covered by larger or more specialist works; a brief guide to these appears on page 279.

In each entry I have attempted to explain succinctly how the term is or has been used, with a brief illustrative example wherever possible, and to clarify any relevant distinctions of sense. Related terms are indicated by cross-reference, using an asterisk (*) before a term explained elsewhere in the dictionary, or the instruction *see*. I have chosen not to give much space to questions of etymology, and to discuss a term's origin only when this seems genuinely necessary to clarify its current sense. My attention has been devoted more to helping readers to use the terms confidently for themselves. To this end I have displayed the plural forms, adjectival forms, and other derived words relevant to each entry, and have provided pronunciation guides for more than two hundred potentially troublesome terms. The simplified pronunciation system used, closely based on the system devised by Joyce M. Hawkins for the *Oxford Paperback Dictionary*, offers a basic but sufficient indication of the essential features of stress-placing and vowel quality. One of its advantages is that it requires very little checking against the pronunciation key on page ix.

In compiling this dictionary, the principal debt I have incurred is to my predecessors in the vexed business of literary definition and distinction, from Aristotle to the editors of the *Princeton Encyclopedia of Poetry and Poetics*. If the following entries make sense, it is very often because those who have gone before have cleared the ground and mapped its more treacherous sites. My thanks are owed also to Joyce Hawkins and Michael Ockenden for their help with pronunciations; to Kim Scott Walwyn of Oxford University Press for her constant encouragement; to Peter Currie, Michael Hughes, Colin Pickthall, and Hazel Richardson for their advice on particular entries; to my students for giving me so much practice; and especially to Harriet Barry, Pamela Jackson, and John Simons for giving up their time to scrutinize the typescript and for the valuable amendments they suggested.

C.B.

Acknowledgement
I am grateful to David Higham Associates Limited on behalf of Muriel Spark for permission to quote from *The Prime of Miss Jean Brodie* published by Macmillan Publishers Ltd.

Preface to the Second Edition

For this edition I have added new entries expanding the dictionary's coverage of terms from rhetoric, theatre history, textual criticism, and other fields; and introduced further terms that have arrived or become more prominent in literary usage in the last ten years. I have also updated many of the existing entries along with the appendix on general further reading, and more extensively attached additional recommendations for further reading to several of the longer or more complex entries. For advice on some of this additional material I am indebted to my colleagues Alcuin Blamires, Michael Bruce, Hayley Davis, and Philip McGowan.

C.B.

Pronunciation

Where a term's pronunciation may not be immediately obvious from its spelling, a guide is provided in square brackets following the word or phrase. Words are broken up into small units, usually of one syllable. The syllable that is spoken with most stress in a word of two or more syllables is shown in **bold type**.

The pronunciations given follow the standard speech of southern England. However, since this system is based on analogies rather than on precise phonetic description, readers who use other varieties of spoken English will rarely need to make any conscious adjustment to suit their own forms of pronunciation.

The sounds represented are as follows:

a	*as in* cat	i	*as in* pin	s	*as in* sit
ă	*as in* ago	ĭ	*as in* pencil	sh	*as in* shop
ah	*as in* calm	I	*as in* eye	t	*as in* top
air	*as in* hair	j	*as in* jam	th	*as in* thin
ar	*as in* bar	k	*as in* kind	*th*	*as in* this
aw	*as in* law	l	*as in* leg	u	*as in* cup
ay	*as in* say	m	*as in* man	ŭ	*as in* focus
b	*as in* bat	n	*as in* not	uu	*as in* book
ch	*as in* chin	ng	*as in* sing, finger	v	*as in* voice
d	*as in* day	nk	*as in* thank	w	*as in* will
e	*as in* bed	o	*as in* top	y	*as in* yes
ĕ	*as in* taken	ŏ	*as in* lemon		*or when preceded by*
ee	*as in* meet	oh	*as in* most		*a consonant* = I *as in*
eer	*as in* beer	oi	*as in* join		cry, realize
er	*as in* her	oo	*as in* soon	yoo	*as in* unit
ew	*as in* few	oor	*as in* poor	yoor	*as in* Europe
ewr	*as in* pure	or	*as in* for	yr	*as in* fire
f	*as in* fat	ow	*as in* cow	z	*as in* zebra
g	*as in* get	p	*as in* pen	zh	*as in* vision
h	*as in* hat	r	*as in* red		

The raised n (ⁿ) is used to indicate the nasalizing of the preceding vowel sound in some French words, as in *baton* or in *Chopin*. In several French words no syllable is marked for stress, the distribution of stress being more even than in English.

A consonant is sometimes doubled, especially to help show that the vowel before it is short, or when without this the combination of letters might suggest a wrong pronunciation through looking misleadingly like a familiar word.

absurd, the, a term derived from the *existentialism of Albert Camus, and often applied to the modern sense of human purposelessness in a universe without meaning or value. Many 20th-century writers of prose fiction have stressed the absurd nature of human existence: notable instances are the novels and stories of Franz Kafka, in which the characters face alarmingly incomprehensible predicaments. The critic Martin Esslin coined the phrase **theatre of the absurd** in 1961 to refer to a number of dramatists of the 1950s (led by Samuel Beckett and Eugène Ionesco) whose works evoke the absurd by abandoning logical form, character, and dialogue together with realistic illusion. The classic work of **absurdist** theatre is Beckett's *En attendant Godot* (*Waiting for Godot*, 1952), which revives some of the conventions of clowning and *farce to represent the impossibility of purposeful action and the paralysis of human aspiration. Other dramatists associated with the theatre of the absurd include Edward Albee, Jean Genet, Harold Pinter, and Václav Havel. For a fuller account, consult Arnold P. Hinchliffe, *The Absurd* (1969).

academic drama (also called school drama), a dramatic tradition which arose from the *Renaissance, in which the works of Plautus, Terence, and other ancient dramatists were performed in schools and colleges, at first in Latin but later also in *vernacular adaptations composed by schoolmasters under the influence of *humanism. This tradition produced the earliest English comedies, notably *Ralph Roister Doister* (*c*.1552) by the schoolmaster Nicholas Udall.

acatalectic, possessing the full number of syllables in the final *foot (of a metrical verse line); not *catalectic. *Noun:* **acatalexis.**

accent, the emphasis placed upon a syllable in pronunciation. The term is often used as a synonym for *stress, although some theorists prefer to use 'stress' only for metrical accent. Three kinds of accent may be distinguished, according to the factor that accounts for each: etymological accent (or 'word accent') is the emphasis normally given to a syllable according to the word's derivation or *morphology; rhetorical accent (or 'sense accent') is allocated according to the relative importance of the word in the context of a sentence or question; metrical accent (or stress) follows a recurrent pattern of stresses in a verse line (*see* metre). Where metrical accent overrides etymological or rhetorical accent, as it often does in *ballads and songs (Coleridge: 'in a far coun-*tree*'), the effect is known as a **wrenched accent.** *See also* ictus, recessive accent.

accentual verse, verse in which the *metre is based on counting only the number of stressed syllables in a line, and in which the number of unstressed syllables in the line may therefore vary. Most verse in Germanic languages (including Old English) is accentual, and much English poetry of later periods has been written in accentual verse, especially in the popular tradition of songs, *ballads, nursery rhymes, and hymns. The predominant English metrical system in the 'high' literary tradition since Chaucer, however, has been that of **accentual-syllabic** verse, in which both stressed and unstressed syllables are counted: thus an iambic *pentameter should normally have five stresses distributed among its ten syllables (or, with a *feminine ending, eleven syllables). *See also* alliterative metre

acephalous [a-**sef**-ăl-ŭs], the Greek word for 'headless', applied to a metrical verse line that lacks the first syllable expected according to regular *metre; e.g. an iambic *pentameter missing the first unstressed syllable, as sometimes in Chaucer:

> Twenty bookès, clad in blak or reed

Noun: **acephalexis.** *See also* truncation.

Acmeism, a short-lived (*c.*1911–1921) but significant movement in early 20th-century Russian poetry, aiming for precision and clarity in opposition to the alleged vagueness of the preceding *Symbolist movement. Its leaders, Nikolai Gumilev and Sergei Gorodetsky, founded an Acmeist 'Poets' Guild' in 1911, and propounded its principles in the magazine *Apollon*. The principal poetic luminaries of this school were Anna Akhmatova (1889–1966) and Osip Mandelstam (1891–1938).

acrostic, a poem in which the initial letters of each line can be read down the page to spell either an alphabet, a name (often that of the author, a patron, or a loved one), or some other concealed message.

Variant forms of acrostic may use middle letters or final letters of lines or, in prose acrostics, initial letters of sentences or paragraphs.

act, a major division in the action of a play, comprising one or more *scenes. A break between acts often coincides with a point at which the plot jumps ahead in time.

actant, in the *narratology of A. J. Greimas, one of six basic categories of fictional role common to all stories. The actants are paired in *binary opposition: Subject/Object, Sender/Receiver, Helper/Opponent. A character (or *acteur*) is an individualized manifestation of one or more actants; but an actant may be realized in a non-human creature (e.g. a dragon as Opponent) or inanimate object (e.g. magic sword as Helper, or Holy Grail as Object), or in more than one *acteur*, *Adjective*: **actantial.**

adynaton, a *figure of speech related to *hyperbole that emphasizes the inexpressibility of some thing, idea, or feeling, either by stating that words cannot describe it, or by comparing it with something (e.g. the heavens, the oceans) the dimensions of which cannot be grasped.

Aestheticism, the doctrine or disposition that regards beauty as an end in itself, and attempts to preserve the arts from subordination to moral, *didactic, or political purposes. The term is often used synonymously with the **Aesthetic Movement,** a literary and artistic tendency of the late 19th century which may be understood as a further phase of *Romanticism in reaction against *philistine bourgeois values of practical efficiency and morality. Aestheticism found theoretical support in the *aesthetics of Immanuel Kant and other German philosophers who separated the sense of beauty from practical interests. Elaborated by Théophile Gautier in 1835 as a principle of artistic independence, aestheticism was adopted in France by Baudelaire, Flaubert, and the *Symbolists, and in England by Walter Pater, Oscar Wilde, and several poets of the 1890s, under the slogan *l'art pour l'art* (*'art for art's sake'). Wilde and other devotees of pure beauty—like the artists Whistler and Beardsley—were sometimes known as **aesthetes.** *See also* decadence, *fin de siècle*. For a fuller account, consult R. V. Johnson, *Aestheticism* (1969).

aesthetics (*US* **esthetics**), philosophical investigation into the nature of beauty and the perception of beauty, especially in the arts; the theory of art or of artistic taste. *Adjective*: **aesthetic** or **esthetic.**

affective, pertaining to emotional effects or dispositions (known in psychology as 'affects'). Affective criticism or **affectivism** evaluates literary works in terms of the feelings they arouse in audiences or readers (*see* e.g. catharsis). It was condemned in an important essay by W. K. Wimsatt and Monroe C. Beardsley (in *The Verbal Icon*, 1954) as the **affective fallacy,** since in the view of these *New Critics such affective evaluation confused the literary work's objective qualities with its subjective results. The American critic Stanley Fish has given the name **affective stylistics** to his form of *reader-response criticism. *See also* intentional fallacy.

afflatus, a Latin term for poetic inspiration.

agitprop [aj-it-prop], a Russian abbreviation of 'agitation and propaganda', applied to the campaign of cultural and political propaganda mounted in the years after the 1917 revolution. The term is sometimes applied to the simple form of *didactic drama which the campaign employed, and which influenced the *epic theatre of Piscator and Brecht in Germany.

agon [a-gohn] (plural **agones** [ă-goh-niz]), the contest or dispute between two characters which forms a major part of the action in the Greek *Old Comedy of Aristophanes, e.g. the debate between Aeschylus and Euripides in his play *The Frogs* (405 BCE). The term is sometimes extended to formal debates in Greek tragedies. *Adjective:* **agonistic.**

alba, *see* aubade.

Alcaics, a Greek verse form using a four-line *stanza in which the first two lines have eleven syllables each, the third nine, and the fourth ten. The *metre, predominantly *dactylic, was used frequently by the Roman poet Horace, and later by some Italian and German poets, but its *quantitative basis makes it difficult to adapt into English—although Tennyson and Clough attempted English Alcaics, and Peter Reading has experimented with the form in *Ukelele Music* (1985) and other works.

aleatory [ayl-eer-tri] or **aleatoric,** dependent upon chance. Aleatory writing involves an element of randomness either in composition, as in *automatic writing and the *cut-up, or in the reader's selection and ordering of written fragments, as in B. S. Johnson's novel *The Unfortunates* (1969), a box of loose leaves which the reader could shuffle at will.

Alexandrianism, the works and styles of the Alexandrian school of

Greek poets in the *Hellenistic age (323 BCE–31 BCE), which included
Callimachus, Apollonius Rhodius, and Theocritus. The Alexandrian style
was marked by elaborate artificiality, obscure mythological *allusion,
and eroticism. It influenced Catullus and other Roman poets.

alexandrine, a verse line of twelve syllables adopted by poets since the
16th century as the standard verse-form of French poetry, especially
dramatic and narrative. It was first used in 12th-century *chansons de
geste*, and probably takes its name from its use in Lambert le Tort's *Roman
d'Alexandre* (*c.*1200). The division of the line into two groups of six
syllables, divided by a *caesura, was established in the age of Racine, but
later challenged by Victor Hugo and other 19th-century poets, who
preferred three groups of four. The English alexandrine is an iambic
*hexameter (and thus has six stresses, whereas the French line usually
has four), and is found rarely except as the final line in the *Spenserian
stanza, as in Keats's 'The Eve of St Agnes':

> She knelt, so pure a thing, so free from mortal taint.

alienation effect or **A-effect,** the usual English translation of the
German *Verfremdungseffekt* or *V-effekt*, a major principle of Bertolt Brecht's
theory of *epic theatre. It is a dramatic effect aimed at encouraging an
attitude of critical detachment in the audience, rather than a passive
submission to realistic illusion; and achieved by a variety of means, from
allowing the audience to smoke and drink to interrupting the play's
action with songs, sudden scene changes, and switches of role. Actors are
also encouraged to distance themselves from their characters rather
than identify with them; ironic commentary by a narrator adds to this
'estrangement'. By reminding the audience of the performance's
artificial nature, Brecht hoped to stimulate a rational view of history as a
changeable human creation rather than as a fated process to be accepted
passively. Despite this theory, audiences still identify emotionally with
the characters in *Mother Courage* (1941) and Brecht's other plays. The
theory was derived partly from the *Russian Formalists' concept of
*defamiliarization.

allegory, a story or visual image with a second distinct meaning
partially hidden behind its literal or visible meaning. The principal
technique of allegory is *personification, whereby abstract qualities
are given human shape—as in public statues of Liberty or Justice. An
allegory may be conceived as a *metaphor that is extended into a
structured system. In written narrative, allegory involves a continuous

parallel between two (or more) levels of meaning in a story, so that its persons and events correspond to their equivalents in a system of ideas or a chain of events external to the tale: each character and episode in John Bunyan's *The Pilgrim's Progress* (1678), for example, embodies an idea within a pre-existing Puritan doctrine of salvation. Allegorical thinking permeated the Christian literature of the Middle Ages, flourishing in the *morality plays and in the *dream visions of Dante and Langland. Some later allegorists like Dryden and Orwell used allegory as a method of *satire; their hidden meanings are political rather than religious. In the medieval discipline of biblical *exegesis, allegory became an important method of interpretation, a habit of seeking correspondences between different realms of meaning (e.g. physical and spiritual) or between the Old Testament and the New (*see* typology). It can be argued that modern critical interpretation continues this allegorizing tradition. *See also* anagogical, emblem, exemplum, fable, parable, psychomachy, symbol. For a fuller account, consult Angus Fletcher, *Allegory* (1964).

alliteration (also known as 'head rhyme' or 'initial rhyme'), the repetition of the same sounds—usually initial consonants of words or of stressed syllables—in any sequence of neighbouring words: 'Landscape-lover, lord of language' (Tennyson). Now an optional and incidental decorative effect in verse or prose, it was once a required element in the poetry of Germanic languages (including Old English and Old Norse) and in Celtic verse (where alliterated sounds could regularly be placed in positions other than the beginning of a word or syllable). Such poetry, in which alliteration rather than *rhyme is the chief principle of repetition, is known as **alliterative verse**; its rules also allow a vowel sound to **alliterate** with any other vowel. *See also* alliterative metre, alliterative revival, assonance, consonance.

alliterative metre, the distinctive verse form of Old Germanic poetry, including Old English. It employed a long line divided by a *caesura into two balanced half-lines, each with a given number of stressed syllables (usually two) and a variable number of unstressed syllables. These half-lines are linked by *alliteration between both (sometimes one) of the stressed syllables in the first half and the first (and sometimes the second) stressed syllable in the second half. In Old English, the lines were normally unrhymed and not organized in *stanzas, although some works of the later Middle English *alliterative revival used both stanzaic patterns and rhyme. This *metre was the standard form of verse in English until the 11th century, and was still important in the 14th, but

declined under the influence of French *syllabic verse. W. H. Auden
revived its use in *The Age of Anxiety* (1948). These lines from the 14th-
century poem *Piers Plowman* illustrate the alliterative metre:

> Al for love of oure Lord livede wel straite,
> In hope for to have hevene-riche blisse.

See also accentual verse.

alliterative revival, a term covering the group of late 14th-century
English poems written in an *alliterative metre similar to that of Old
English verse but less regular (notably in Langland's *Piers Plowman*) and
sometimes—as in the anonymous *Pearl* and *Sir Gawain and the Green
Knight*—using rhyme and elaborate *stanza structure. This group may
represent more a continuation than a revival of the alliterative tradition.

allusion, an indirect or passing reference to some event, person, place,
or artistic work, the nature and relevance of which is not explained by
the writer but relies on the reader's familiarity with what is thus
mentioned. The technique of allusion is an economical means of calling
upon the history or the literary tradition that author and reader are
assumed to share, although some poets (notably Ezra Pound and T. S.
Eliot) allude to areas of quite specialized knowledge. In his poem 'The
Statues'—

> When Pearse summoned Cuchulain to his side
> What stalked through the Post Office?

—W. B. Yeats **alludes** both to the hero of Celtic legend (Cuchulain) and to
the new historical hero (Patrick Pearse) of the 1916 Easter Rising, in
which the revolutionaries captured the Dublin Post Office. In addition to
such *topical* allusions to recent events, Yeats often uses *personal* allusions
to aspects of his own life and circle of friends. Other kinds of allusion
include the *imitative* (as in *parody), and the *structural*, in which one work
reminds us of the structure of another (as Joyce's *Ulysses* refers to Homer's
Odyssey). Topical allusion is especially important in *satire. *Adjective*:
allusive.

ambiguity, openness to different interpretations; or an instance in
which some use of language may be understood in diverse ways.
Sometimes known as 'plurisignation' or 'multiple meaning', ambiguity
became a central concept in the interpretation of poetry after William
Empson, in *Seven Types of Ambiguity* (1930), defended it as a source of
poetic richness rather than a fault of imprecision. Ambiguities in

everyday speech are usually resolved by their context, but isolated statements ('they are hunting dogs') or very compressed phrases like book titles (*Scouting for Boys*) and newspaper headlines (GENERALS FLY BACK TO FRONT) can remain ambiguous. The verbal compression and uncertain context of much poetry often produce ambiguity: in the first line of Keats's 'Ode on a Grecian Urn',

> Thou still unravish'd bride of quietness,

'still' may mean 'even yet' or 'immobile', or both. The simplest kind of ambiguity is achieved by the use of *homophones in the *pun. On a larger scale, a character (e.g. Hamlet, notoriously) or an entire story may display ambiguity. See also *double entendre*, equivoque, multi-accentuality, polysemy.

American Renaissance, the name sometimes given to a flourishing of distinctively American literature in the period before the Civil War. As described by F. O. Matthiessen in his influential critical work *American Renaissance* (1941), this renaissance is represented by the work of Ralph Waldo Emerson, H. D. Thoreau, Nathaniel Hawthorne, Herman Melville, and Walt Whitman. Its major works are Hawthorne's *The Scarlet Letter* (1850), Melville's *Moby-Dick* (1851), and Whitman's *Leaves of Grass* (1855). The American Renaissance may be regarded as a delayed manifestation of *Romanticism, especially in Emerson's philosophy of *Transcendentalism.

amoebean verses [a-mě-**bee**-ăn], a poetic form in which two characters chant alternate lines, *couplets, or *stanzas, in competition or debate with one another. This form is found in the *pastoral poetry of Theocritus and Virgil, and was imitated by Spenser in his *Shepheardes Calender* (1579); it is similar to the *débat*, and sometimes resembles *stichomythia. *See also* flyting.

amphibrach [am-fib-rak], a metrical *foot consisting of one stressed syllable between two unstressed syllables, as in the word 'confession' (or, in *quantitative verse, one long syllable between two shorts). It is the opposite of the *amphimacer. It was rarely used in classical verse, but may occur in English in combination with other feet.

amphimacer [am-**fim**-ăsě], a Greek metrical *foot, also known as the cretic foot. The opposite of the *amphibrach, it has one short syllable between two long ones (thus in English verse, one unstressed syllable between two stressed, as in the phrase 'bowing down'). Sometimes used

in Roman comedy, it occurs rarely in English verse. Blake's 'Spring' is an
example:

> Sound the flute! / Now it's mute; / Birds delight / Day and night.

anachronism, the misplacing of any person, thing, custom, or event
outside its proper historical time. Performances of Shakespeare's
plays in modern dress use deliberate anachronism, but many fictional
works based on history include unintentional examples, the most
famous being the clock in Shakespeare's *Julius Caesar*. *Adjective*:
anachronistic.

anachrony [an-ak-rŏni], a term used in modern *narratology to
denote a discrepancy between the order in which events of the
*story occur and the order in which they are presented to us in the
*plot. Anachronies take two basic forms: 'flashback' or *analepsis,
and 'flashforward' or *prolepsis. *Adjective*: **anachronic.** See also *in
medias res*.

anacoluthon [an-ă-kŏ-**loo**-thon], a grammatical term for a change of
construction in a sentence that leaves the initial construction
unfinished: 'Either you go—but we'll see.' *Adjective*: **anacoluthic.**

Anacreontics [ă-nayk-ri-**on**-tiks], verses resembling, either metrically
or in subject-matter, those of the Greek poet Anacreon (6th century BCE)
or of his later imitators in the collection known as the *Anacreontea*.
Metrically, the original Anacreontic line combined long (−) and short (◡)
syllables in the pattern ◡ ◡ − ◡ − ◡ − −. It was imitated in English by
Sir Philip Sidney. More often, though, the term refers to the subject-
matter: the celebration of love and drinking. Anacreontics in this sense
are usually written in short *trochaic lines, as in Tom Moore's translated
Odes of Anacreon (1800):

> Hither haste, some cordial soul!
> Give my lips the brimming bowl.

anacrusis (plural **-uses**), the appearance of an additional unstressed
syllable or syllables at the beginning of a verse line, before the regular
metrical pattern begins.

anadiplosis [an-ă-di-**ploh**-sis] (plural **-oses**), a *rhetorical figure of
repetition in which a word or phrase appears both at the end of one
clause, sentence, or stanza, and at the beginning of the next, thus linking
the two units, as in the final line of Shakespeare's 36th sonnet:

As thou being mine, mine is thy good report.

See also climax.

anagnorisis [an-ag-**nor**-ĭs-is] (plural **-ises**), the Greek word for 'recognition' or 'discovery', used by Aristotle in his *Poetics* to denote the turning point in a drama at which a character (usually the *protagonist) recognizes the true state of affairs, having previously been in error or ignorance. The classic instance is Oedipus' recognition, in *Oedipus Tyrannus*, that he himself has killed his own father Laius, married his mother Jocasta, and brought the plague upon Thebes. The anagnorisis is usually combined with the play's *peripeteia or reversal of fortunes, in comedy as in tragedy. Similarly, the plots of many novels involve crucial anagnorises, e.g. Pip's discovery, in *Great Expectations*, that Magwitch rather than Miss Havisham has been his secret benefactor. *See also* dénouement. For a fuller account, consult Terence Cave, *Recognitions* (1988).

anagogical [an-ă-**goj**-ik-ăl], revealing a higher spiritual meaning behind the literal meaning of a text. Medieval Christian *exegesis of the Bible (*see* typology) reinterpreted many episodes of Hebrew scripture according to four levels of meaning: the literal, the allegorical, the moral, and the anagogical. Of these, the anagogical sense was seen as the highest, relating to the ultimate destiny of humanity according to the Christian scheme of universal history, whereas the allegorical and moral senses refer respectively to the Church and to the individual soul. **Anagogy** or **anagoge** is thus a specialized form of allegorical interpretation, which reads texts in terms of *eschatology. *See also* allegory.

analepsis (plural **-pses**), a form of *anachrony by which some of the events of a story are related at a point in the narrative after later story-events have already been recounted. Commonly referred to as retrospection or flashback, analepsis enables a storyteller to fill in background information about characters and events. A narrative that begins *in medias res* will include an **analeptic** account of events preceding the point at which the tale began. *See also* prolepsis.

analogy, illustration of an idea by means of a more familiar idea that is similar or parallel to it in some significant features, and thus said to be **analogous** to it. Analogies are often presented in the form of an extended *simile, as in Blake's *aphorism: 'As the caterpillar chooses

the fairest leaves to lay her eggs on, so the priest lays his curse on the
fairest joys.' In literary history, an **analogue** is another story or plot
which is parallel or similar in some way to the story under discussion.
Verb: **analogize**.

anapaest (*US* **anapest**) [an-ă-pest], a metrical *foot made up of
two unstressed syllables followed by a stressed syllable, as in the word
'interrupt' (or, in *quantitative verse, two short syllables followed by
a long one). Originally a Greek marching beat, adopted by some Greek
and Roman dramatists, the *rising rhythm of **anapaestic** (or **anapestic**)
verse has sometimes been used by poets in English to echo energetic
movement, notably in Robert Browning's 'How they Brought the Good
News from Ghent to Aix' (1845):

> Not a word to each other; we kept the great pace
> Neck by neck, stride by stride, never changing our place.

Others have used anapaestic verse for tones of solemn complaint, as in
this famous line from Swinburne's 'Hymn to Proserpine' (1866):

Thou hast conquered, O pale Galilean; the world has grown grey from thy breath.

Lines made up of anapaests alone are rare in English verse, though; more
often they are used in combination with other feet. The commonest
anapaestic verse form in English, the *limerick, usually omits the first
syllable in its first, second, and fifth lines. *See also* metre, triple metre.

anaphora [a-naf-ō-ră], a rhetorical *figure of repetition in which the
same word or phrase is repeated in (and usually at the beginning of)
successive lines, clauses, or sentences. Found very often in both verse
and prose, it was a device favoured by Dickens and used frequently in the
*free verse of Walt Whitman. These lines by Emily Dickinson illustrate
the device:

> Mine—by the Right of the White Election!
> Mine—by the Royal Seal!
> Mine—by the Sign in the Scarlet prison
> Bars—cannot conceal!

Adjective: **anaphoral** or **anaphoric**. *See also* epistrophe.

anatomy, a written analysis of some subject, which purports to be
thorough and comprehensive. The famous model for this literary form
is Robert Burton's *Anatomy of Melancholy* (1621). The Canadian critic
Northrop Frye, in *Anatomy of Criticism* (1957), discusses the anatomy
as an important category of fiction similar to the *Menippean satire.

A humorous display of extensive and detailed knowledge, as in Melville's account of whaling in *Moby-Dick* (1851) or Thomas Pynchon's rocket-lore in *Gravity's Rainbow* (1973), is characteristic of this *genre.

Angry Young Men, a term applied by journalists in the 1950s to the authors and *protagonists of some contemporary novels and plays that seemed to sound a note of protest or resentment against the values of the British middle class. The most striking example of the angry young man was Jimmy Porter, the ranting protagonist of John Osborne's play *Look Back in Anger* (1956). Other works then taken to express 'angry' attitudes included Kingsley Amis's *campus novel *Lucky Jim* (1954), and John Braine's novel of social ambition, *Room at the Top* (1957), but the label is more appropriate to the *anti-heroes of these works than to the authors, whose views were hastily misinterpreted as being socially radical.

Angst, the German word for 'anxiety' or 'dread', used by the philosophers of *existentialism—notably the Danish theologian Søren Kierkegaard in *Begrebet Angst* (*The Concept of Dread*, 1844)—to denote a state of anguish that we feel as we are confronted by the burden of our freedom and the accompanying responsibility to impose values and meanings on an *absurd universe.

antagonist, the most prominent of the characters who oppose the *protagonist or hero(ine) in a dramatic or narrative work. The antagonist is often a villain seeking to frustrate a heroine or hero; but in those works in which the protagonist is represented as evil, the antagonist will often be a virtuous or sympathetic character, as Macduff is in *Macbeth*.

antanaclasis, a *figure of speech that makes a *pun by repeating the same word, or two words sounding alike (*see* homophone), but with differing senses.

anthem, originally an *antiphon; Wilfred Owen's 'Anthem for Doomed Youth' and W. H. Auden's 'Anthem for St Cecilia's Day' both preserve something of this antiphonal sense. The term is now used more often to denote a song in which the words affirm a collective identity, usually expressing attachment to some nation, institution, or cause. Anthems have been adopted, formally or informally, by states, schools, sports clubs, and social movements of all kinds. A significant modern example is Tom Robinson's 'Glad to be Gay' (1977).

anticlimax, an abrupt lapse from growing intensity to triviality in any
passage of dramatic, narrative, or descriptive writing, with the effect of
disappointed expectation or deflated suspense. Where the effect is
unintentionally feeble or ridiculous it is known as *bathos; but
anticlimactic descent from the sublime to the ludicrous can also be used
deliberately for comic effect. Byron employs comic anticlimax
repeatedly in *Don Juan*, as in these lines from Canto II (1819), which
describe the survivors of a shipwreck:

> Though every wave roll'd menacing to fill,
>   And present peril all before surpass'd,
> They grieved for those who perished with the cutter
> And also for the biscuit-casks and butter.

anti-hero or **anti-heroine,** a central character in a dramatic or
narrative work who lacks the qualities of nobility and magnanimity
expected of traditional heroes and heroines in *romances and *epics.
Unheroic characters of this kind have been an important feature of the
Western *novel, which has subjected idealistic heroism to *parody
since Cervantes's *Don Quixote* (1605). Flaubert's Emma Bovary (in *Madame
Bovary*, 1857) and Joyce's Leopold Bloom (in *Ulysses*, 1922) are outstanding
examples of this antiheroic ordinariness and inadequacy. The anti-hero
is also an important figure in modern drama, both in the theatre of the
*absurd and in the *tragedies of Arthur Miller, notably *Death of a
Salesman* (1949). In these plays, as in many modern novels, the
*protagonist is an ineffectual failure who succumbs to the pressure of
circumstances. The anti-hero should not be confused with the
*antagonist or the *villain.

anti-masque, a comic and grotesque piece of clowning that sometimes
preceded the performance of a *masque (hence the alternative spelling,
antemasque). Ben Jonson introduced this farcical prelude to some of his
masques from 1609 onwards, using it as a kind of *burlesque of the main
action.

antimetabole [anti-me-**tab**-oli], a *figure of speech in which a pair of
words is repeated in reverse order: 'All for one, and one for all'. This
figure is a sub-type of *chiasmus.

anti-novel, a form of experimental fiction that dispenses with certain
traditional elements of novel-writing like the analysis of characters'
states of mind or the unfolding of a sequential *plot. The term is usually
associated with the French *nouveau roman* of Alain Robbe-Grillet,

Nathalie Sarraute, and Michel Butor in the 1950s, but has since been extended to include other kinds of fictional experiment that disrupt conventional *narrative expectations, as in some works in English by Flann O'Brien, Vladimir Nabokov, B. S. Johnson, and Christine Brooke-Rose. Antecedents of the anti-novel can be found in the blank pages and comically self-defeating digressions of Sterne's *Tristram Shandy* (1759–67) and in some of the innovations of *modernism, like the absence of narration in Virginia Woolf's *The Waves* (1931). See also *avant-garde*, postmodernism.

antiphon, a song, hymn, or poem in which two voices or choruses respond to one another in alternate verses or *stanzas, as is common in verses written for religious services. *Adjective*: **antiphonal** [an-**tif**-ŏn-ăl]. *See also* amoebean verses, anthem.

antiphrasis [an-**tif**-ră-sis], a *figure of speech in which a single word is used in a sense directly opposite to its usual meaning, as in the naming of a giant as 'Tiny' or of an enemy as 'friend'; the briefest form of *irony. *Adjective*: **antiphrastic.**

antistrophe [an-**tis**-trŏ-fi], (1) the returning movement of the Greek dramatic *chorus of dancers, after their first movement or *strophe; hence also the accompanying verse lines recited by the chorus in a *stanza matching exactly the *metre of the preceding strophe. The *odes of Pindar and his imitators conform to a triple structure of strophe, antistrophe, and *epode. (2) In *rhetoric, antistrophe is also the name given to two rhetorical *figures of repetition: in the first, the order of terms in one clause is reversed in the next ('All for one, and one for all'); in the second (also known as *epistrophe), a word or phrase is repeated at the end of several successive clauses, lines, or sentences ('the truth, the whole truth, and nothing but the truth'). *Adjective*: **antistrophic.**

antithesis [an-**tith**-ĕsis] (plural -**theses**), a contrast or opposition, either rhetorical or philosophical. In *rhetoric, any disposition of words that serves to emphasize a contrast or opposition of ideas, usually by the balancing of connected clauses with parallel grammatical constructions. In Milton's *Paradise Lost* (1667), the characteristics of Adam and Eve are contrasted by antithesis:

> For contemplation he and valour formed,
> For softness she and sweet attractive grace;
> He for God only, she for God in him.

Antithesis was cultivated especially by Pope and other 18th-century poets. It is also a familiar device in prose, as in John Ruskin's sentence, 'Government and cooperation are in all things the laws of life; anarchy and competition the laws of death.' In philosophy, an antithesis is a second argument or principle brought forward to oppose a first proposition or *thesis (*see* dialectic). *Adjective*: **antithetical.**

antonomasia [an-ton-ŏ-may-ziă], a *figure of speech that replaces a proper name with an *epithet (*the Bard* for Shakespeare), official address (*His Holiness* for a pope), or other indirect description; or one that applies a famous proper name to a person alleged to share some quality associated with it, e.g. *a Casanova*, *a little Hitler*. Antonomasia is common in *epic poetry: Homer frequently refers to Achilles as Pelides (i.e. son of Peleus). *Adjective*: **antonomastic.** *See also* metonymy.

anxiety of influence, in the unusual view of literary history offered by the critic Harold Bloom, a poet's sense of the crushing weight of poetic tradition which he has to resist and challenge in order to make room for his own original vision. Bloom has in mind particularly the mixed feelings of veneration and envy with which the English Romantic poets regarded Milton, as a 'father' who had to be displaced by his 'sons'. This theory represents the development of poetic tradition as a masculine battle of wills modelled on Freud's concept of the Oedipus complex: the 'belated' poet fears the emasculating dominance of the 'precursor' poet and seeks to occupy his position of strength through a process of misreading or *misprision of the parent-poem in the new poem, which is always a distortion of the original. Thus Shelley's 'Ode to the West Wind' is a powerful misreading of Wordsworth's 'Ode: Intimations of Immortality', through which the younger poet seeks to free himself from the hold of his predecessor. Bloom's theory is expounded in *The Anxiety of Influence* (1973), in which he claims that 'the covert subject of most poetry for the last three centuries has been the anxiety of influence, each poet's fear that no proper work remains for him to perform'.

aperçu [ap-air-soo], an insight. The French word for a 'glimpse', often used to refer to a writer's formulation or discovery of some truth. Also an outline or summary of a story or argument.

aphorism, a statement of some general principle, expressed memorably by condensing much wisdom into few words: 'Give a man a mask and he will tell you the truth' (Wilde); 'The road of excess leads to the palace of wisdom' (Blake). Aphorisms often take the form of a definition: 'Hypocrisy is a homage paid by vice to virtue' (La Rochefoucauld). An author who composes aphorisms is an **aphorist**. *Adjective*: **aphoristic**. *See also* apophthegm, maxim, proverb.

apocalyptic, revealing the secrets of the future through prophecy; or having the character of an **apocalypse** or world-consuming holocaust. Apocalyptic writing is usually concerned with the coming end of the world, seen in terms of a visionary scheme of history, as in Yeats's poem 'The Second Coming'. *See also* eschatology.

Apollonian and Dionysian, terms for the twin principles which the German philosopher Friedrich Nietzsche detected in Greek civilization in his early work *Die Geburt der Tragödie* (*The Birth of Tragedy*, 1872). Nietzsche was challenging the usual view of Greek culture as ordered and serene, emphasizing instead the irrational element of frenzy found in the rites of Dionysus (the god of intoxication known to the Romans as Bacchus). He associated the Apollonian tendency with the instinct for form, beauty, moderation, and symmetry, best expressed in Greek sculpture, while the Dionysian (or **Dionysiac**) instinct was one of irrationality, violence, and exuberance, found in music. This opposition has some resemblance to that between *classicism and *Romanticism. In Nietzsche's theory of drama, the Apollonian (in dialogue) and the Dionysian (in choric song) are combined in early Greek tragedy, but then split apart in the work of Euripides; he hoped at first that Wagner's operas would reunite them.

apologue, another word for a *fable, usually a *beast fable.

apology, in the literary sense, a justification or defence of the writer's opinions or conduct, not usually implying (as in the everyday sense) any admission of blame. The major classical precedent is the *Apologia* of Socrates as recorded by Plato (4th century BCE), in which the philosopher defends himself unsuccessfully against the capital charge of impiety before the Athenian court, justifying his role as 'gadfly' to the state. Later writers adopted the title for various kinds of work from literary theory, as in Sidney's *An Apologie for Poetry* (1595), to autobiography, as in *An Apology for the Life of Mr Colley Cibber, Comedian* (1740) by the much-mocked poet laureate. John Henry Newman's *Apologia Pro Vita Sua* ('apology for his life', 1864) has a greater element of *polemic, justifying his adoption of Roman Catholicism against aspersions cast by Charles Kingsley. An apology is sometimes called an **apologetic**. An **apologist** is more often a defender of some other person's actions, works, or beliefs.

apophthegm [ap-ŏ-them] or **apothegm,** an *aphorism or *maxim, especially one of the pithiest kind. Boswell refers to Johnson's famous saying, 'Patriotism is the last refuge of a scoundrel', as an apophthegm. A person who composes apophthegms is an **apophthegmatist.** *Adjective*: **apophthegmatic** or **apothegmatic.**

aporia, in *rhetoric, a *figure of speech in which a speaker deliberates, or purports to be in doubt about a question, e.g. 'Well, what can one say?', or 'I hardly know which of you is the worse.' Hamlet's famous 'To be or not to be' soliloquy is an extended example. In the critical terminology of *deconstruction, the term is frequently used in the sense of a final impasse or *paradox: a point at which a *text's self-contradictory meanings can no longer be resolved, or at which the text undermines its own most fundamental presuppositions. It is this aporia that deconstructive readings set out to identify in any given work or passage, leading to the claim that the text's meanings are finally 'un-decidable'. *Adjective*: **aporetic.**

aposiopesis [ap-ŏ-syr-**pee**-sis] (plural **-peses**), a *rhetorical device in which the speaker suddenly breaks off in the middle of a sentence, leaving the sense unfinished. The device usually suggests strong emotion that makes the speaker unwilling or unable to continue. The common threat 'get out, or else—' is an example. *Adjective*: **aposiopetic.** *See also* anacoluthon.

apostrophe [ă-**pos**-trŏ-fi], a rhetorical *figure in which the speaker addresses a dead or absent person, or an abstraction or inanimate object. In classical *rhetoric, the term could also denote a speaker's turning to address a particular member or section of the audience. Apostrophes are found frequently among the speeches of Shakespeare's characters, as when Elizabeth in *Richard III* addresses the Tower of London:

> Pity, you ancient stones, those tender babes
> Whom envy hath immured within your walls.

The figure, usually employed for emotional emphasis, can become ridiculous when misapplied, as in Wordsworth's line

> Spade! with which Wilkinson hath tilled his lands

The apostrophe is one of the *conventions appropriate to the *ode and to the *elegy. The poet's *invocation of a *muse in *epic poetry is a special form of apostrophe. *Verb*: **apostrophize.** *See also* prosopopoeia.

apparatus, a collective term (sometimes given in Latin as *apparatus* *criticus*) for the textual notes, glossary, lists of variant readings, appendices, introductory explanations and other aids to the study of a *text, provided in scholarly editions of literary works or historical documents.

arbitrary, lacking any natural basis or substantial justification. In the theory of the *sign elaborated by the Swiss linguist Ferdinand de Saussure, the relationship between the *signifier (the sound-image or written mark) and its *signified (or concept) is described as 'unmotivated' or arbitrary because there is no natural or necessary bond between them, only the convention of a given language. The same applies to the relationship between the sign and the object to which it refers. The **arbitrariness** of these relationships can be shown by comparing the ways in which different languages allocate signifiers to signifieds. Some theorists point out that the sense of randomness attached to the term is misleading, and that the term 'conventional' is preferable.

Arcadia or **Arcady,** an isolated mountainous region of Greece in the central Peloponnese, famed in the ancient world for its sheep and as the home of the god Pan. It was imagined by Virgil in his *Eclogues* (42–37 BCE), and by later writers of *pastorals in the *Renaissance, as an ideal world of rural simplicity and tranquillity. The adjective **Arcadian** can be applied to any such imagined pastoral setting. *See also* idyll.

archaism [ark-ay-izm], the use of words or constructions that have passed out of the language before the time of writing; or a particular example of such an obsolete word or expression. A common feature of much English poetry from Spenser to Hardy, it rarely appears in prose or in modern verse. Archaism may help to summon up a nostalgic flavour of the past, as in Spenser's use of Chaucerian expressions and in Coleridge's 'Rime of the Ancient Mariner', which imitates old ballads:

> 'There was a ship,' quoth he.
> 'Hold off! unhand me, greybeard loon!'
> Eftsoons his hand dropped he.

Or it may help to maintain metrical regularity, as in the frequent use of the monosyllable *morn* for 'morning'. Keats combines both motives in this line from 'The Eve of St Agnes':

> Though thou forsakest a deceivèd thing

Here the archaic pronunciation maintains the *metre, and supports (with the 'thou') the poem's medieval setting and atmosphere. *See also* diction, poeticism.

archetype [ar-ki-typ], a *symbol, theme, setting, or character-type that recurs in different times and places in *myth, *literature, *folklore, dreams, and rituals so frequently or prominently as to suggest (to certain speculative psychologists and critics) that it embodies some essential element of 'universal' human experience. Examples offered by the advocates of *myth criticism include such recurrent symbols as the rose, the serpent, and the sun; common themes like love, death, and conflict; mythical settings like the paradisal garden; *stock characters like the *femme fatale*, the hero, and the magician; and some basic patterns of action and plot such as the quest, the descent to the underworld, or the feud. The most fundamental of these patterns is often said to be that of death and rebirth, reflecting the natural cycle of the seasons: the Canadian critic Northrop Frye put forward an influential model of literature based on this proposition in *Anatomy of Criticism* (1957). **Archetypal** criticism originated in the early 20th century from the speculations of the British anthropologist J. G. Frazer in *The Golden Bough* (1890–1915)—a comparative study of mythologies—and from those of the Swiss psychologist C. G. Jung, who in the 1920s proposed that certain symbols in dreams and myths were residues of ancestral memory preserved in the *collective unconscious. More recently, critics have been wary of the *reductionism involved in the application of such unverified hypotheses to literary works, and more alert to the cultural differences that the archetypal approach often overlooks in its search for universals.

architectonics, the principle of structure and governing design in an artistic work, as distinct from its *texture or stylistic details of execution.

argument, in the specialized literary sense, a brief summary of the *plot or subject-matter of a long poem (or other work), such as those prefixed to the books of Milton's *Paradise Lost*; or, in a sense closer to everyday usage, the set of opinions expounded in a work (especially in *didactic works) and capable of being *paraphrased as a logical sequence of propositions.

Aristotelian [a-ris-tŏ-tee-li-ăn], belonging to or derived from the works of the Greek philosopher Aristotle (384–322 BCE), the most important of all ancient philosophers in his influence on medieval science and logic, and on literary theory since the *Renaissance. In his *Poetics*, Aristotle saw poetry in terms of the imitation or *mimesis of human actions, and accordingly regarded the *plot or *mythos* as the basic principle of coherence in any literary work, which must have a beginning, a middle, and an end. Since the Renaissance, his name has been associated most often with his concepts of tragic *catharsis, *anagnorisis, and unity of action (*see* unities). The *Chicago critics have been regarded as Aristotelian in the renewed emphasis they gave to the importance of plot in literature.

art for art's sake, the slogan of *Aestheticism in the 19th century, often given in its French form as *l'art pour l'art*. The most important early manifesto for the idea, Théophile Gautier's preface to his novel *Mademoiselle de Maupin* (1835), does not actually use the phrase itself, which is a simplified expression of the principle adopted by many leading French authors and by Walter Pater, Oscar Wilde, and Arthur Symons in England.

Asclepiad [as-**klee**-pi-ad], a Greek poetic *metre named after Asclepiades of Samos (*c.*300 BCE), although it was used earlier in *lyrics and *tragedies. It consists of two or three *choriambs preceded by a *spondee and followed by an *iamb. Employed frequently by Horace and later adopted by the German poet Hölderlin, it is rarely found in English. *Adjective*: **Asclepiadean.**

aside, a short speech or remark spoken by a character in a drama, directed either to the audience or to another character, which by *convention is supposed to be inaudible to the other characters on stage. *See also* soliloquy.

assonance [ass-ŏn-ăns], the repetition of identical or similar vowel sounds in the stressed syllables (and sometimes in the following unstressed syllables) of neighbouring words; it is distinct from *rhyme in that the consonants differ although the vowels or *diphthongs match: sweet dreams, hit or miss. As a substitute for rhyme at the ends of verse lines, assonance (sometimes called vowel rhyme or vocalic rhyme) had a significant function in early Celtic, Spanish, and French *versification (notably in the *chansons de geste*), but in English it has been an optional poetic device used within and between lines of verse for emphasis or musical effect, as in these lines from Tennyson's 'The Lotos-Eaters':

And round about the keel with faces pale,
Dark faces pale against that rosy flame,
The mild-eyed melancholy Lotos-eaters came.

Adjective: **assonantal.** *See also* alliteration, consonance, half-rhyme.

asyndeton [a-**sin**-dĕt-on] (plural **-deta**), a form of verbal compression which consists of the omission of connecting words (usually conjunctions) between clauses. The most common form is the omission of 'and', leaving only a sequence of phrases linked by commas, as in these sentences from Conrad's *Heart of Darkness*: 'An empty stream, a great silence, an impenetrable forest. The air was thick, warm, heavy, sluggish.' The most famous example is Julius Caesar's boast, *Veni, vidi, vici* ('I came, I saw, I conquered'). Less common is the omission of pronouns, as in Auden's early poem 'The Watershed': 'two there were / Cleaned out a damaged shaft by hand'. Here the relative pronoun 'who' is omitted. *Adjective*: **asyndetic.** *See also* ellipsis, paratactic.

Attic style or **Atticism,** the style of *oratory or prose writing associated with the speeches of the great Attic (i.e. Athenian) orators of the 5th and 4th centuries BCE, including Lysias and Demosthenes. Later Roman writers distinguished the purity and simplicity of these Attic models from the excessive artifice and ornamentation of the 'Asiatic' style that had since developed among the Greeks in Asia Minor.

aubade [oh-**bahd**], also known by its Provençal name *alba* and in German as *Tagelied* (plural *-lieder*), a song or lyric poem lamenting the arrival of dawn to separate two lovers. The form, which has no fixed metrical pattern, flourished in the late Middle Ages in France; it was adopted in Germany by Wolfram von Eschenbach and in England by Chaucer, whose *Troilus and Criseyde* includes a fine aubade. Later English examples include Donne's 'The Sunne Rising' and Act III scene v of Shakespeare's *Romeo and Juliet*.

Aufklärung, the German term for the *Enlightenment.

Augustan Age, the greatest period of Roman literature, adorned by the poets Virgil, Ovid, Horace, and Propertius. It is named after the reign (27 BCE–14 CE) of the emperor Augustus, but many literary historians prefer to date the literary period from the death of Julius Caesar in 44 CE, thus including the early works of Virgil and Horace. In English literary history, the term is usually applied to the period from the accession of Queen Anne (1702) to the deaths of Pope and Swift (1744–5), although

John Dryden, whose major translation of Virgil's works appeared in 1697, may also be regarded as part of the English phenomenon known as **Augustanism**. The Augustans, led by Pope and Swift, wrote in conscious emulation of the Romans, adopted their literary forms (notably the *epistle and the *satire), and aimed to create a similarly sophisticated urban literary milieu: a characteristic preference in Augustan literature, encouraged by the periodicals of Addison and Steele, was for writing devoted to the public affairs and coffee-house gossip of the imperial capital, London. *See also* neoclassicism.

aureate diction, a highly ornate ('gilded') poetic *diction favoured by the *Scottish Chaucerians and some English poets in the 15th century, notably John Lydgate. The aureate style, perfected by William Dunbar, is notable for its frequent use of *internal rhyme and of *coinages adapted from Latin. *Noun*: **aureation**.

automatic writing, a method of composition that tries to dispense with conscious control or mental censorship, transcribing immediately the promptings of the unconscious mind. Some writers in the early days of *Surrealism attempted it, notably André Breton and Philippe Soupault in their work *Les Champs Magnétiques* (1919). W. B. Yeats had earlier conducted similar experiments with Georgie Hyde-Lees after their marriage in 1917; these séances influenced the mystical system of his prose work *A Vision* (1925).

autotelic, having, as an artistic work, no end or purpose beyond its own existence. The term was used by T. S. Eliot in 1923 and adopted by *New Criticism to distinguish the self-referential nature of literary art from *didactic, philosophical, critical, or biographical works that involve practical reference to things outside themselves: in the words of the American poet Archibald MacLeish, 'A poem should not mean / But be'. A similar idea is implied in the theory of the 'poetic function' put forward in *Russian Formalism.

auxesis, a *figure of speech that lists a series of things in ascending order of importance, as in this line from Shakespeare's *Richard II*:

> O'erthrows thy joys, friends, fortune, and thy state

See also climax.

avant-garde, the French military and political term for the vanguard of an army or political movement, extended since the late 19th century to that body of artists and writers who are dedicated to the idea of art as experiment and revolt against tradition. Ezra Pound's view, that 'Artists are the antennae of the race', is a distinctly modern one, implying a duty to stay ahead of one's time through constant innovation in forms and subjects.

ballad, a *folk song or orally transmitted poem telling in a direct and dramatic manner some popular story usually derived from a tragic incident in local history or legend. The story is told simply, impersonally, and often with vivid dialogue. Ballads are normally composed in *quatrains with alternating four-stress and three-stress lines, the second and fourth lines rhyming (*see* ballad metre); but some ballads are in *couplet form, and some others have six-line *stanzas. Appearing in many parts of Europe in the late Middle Ages, ballads flourished particularly strongly in Scotland from the 15th century onward. Since the 18th century, educated poets outside the folk-song tradition—notably Coleridge and Goethe—have written imitations of the popular ballad's form and style: Coleridge's 'Rime of the Ancient Mariner' (1798) is a celebrated example.

ballad metre or **ballad stanza,** the usual form of the folk ballad and its literary imitations, consisting of a *quatrain in which the first and third lines have four stresses while the second and fourth have three stresses. Usually only the second and fourth lines rhyme. The rhythm is basically *iambic, but the number of unstressed syllables in a line may vary, as in this *stanza from the traditional 'Lord Thomas and Fair Annet':

> 'O art thou blind, Lord Thomas?' she said,
> 'Or canst thou not very well see?
> Or dost thou not see my own heart's blood
> Runs trickling down my knee?'

This *metre may also be interpreted (and sometimes printed) as a couplet of seven-stress lines, as in Kipling's 'Ballad of East and West' (1889):

> The Colonel's son has taken horse, and a raw rough dun was he,
> With the mouth of a bell and the heart of Hell and the head of a gallows-tree.

See also common measure.

ballade [bal-**ahd**], a form of French *lyric poem that flourished in the

14th and 15th centuries, notably in the work of François Villon. It normally consists of three *stanzas of eight lines rhyming *ababbcbc*, with an *envoi (i.e. a final half-stanza) of four lines rhyming *bcbc*. The last line of the first stanza forms a *refrain which is repeated as the final line of the subsequent stanzas and of the *envoi*. Conventionally, the *envoi* opens with an address to a prince or lord. Variant forms include the ballade with ten-line stanzas and a five-line *envoi*, and the double ballade with six stanzas and an optional *envoi*. Poets who have used this very intricate form in English include Chaucer and Swinburne.

bard, a poet who was awarded privileged status in ancient Celtic cultures, and who was charged with the duty of celebrating the laws and heroic achievements of his people. In modern Welsh usage, a bard is a poet who has participated in the annual poetry festival known as the Eisteddfod. The nostalgic mythology of *Romanticism tended to imagine the bards as solitary visionaries and prophets. Since the 18th century, the term has often been applied more loosely to any poet, and as a fanciful title for Shakespeare in particular. *Adjective*: **bardic**.

bardolatry [bar-**dol**-ătri], excessive veneration of Shakespeare. Ben Jonson said of Shakespeare, 'I loved the man, and do honour his memory, on this side idolatry, as much as any.' A **bardolater** is one who goes even further in revering 'the Bard'. *Adjective*: **bardolatrous**.

baroque [bă-**rok**], eccentric or lavishly ornate in style. The term is used more precisely in music and in art history than it is in literary history, where it usually refers to the most artificial poetic styles of the early 17th century, especially those known as Gongorism and Marinism after the Spanish poet Luis de Góngora and the Italian poet Giovanni Battista Marini. In English, the ornate prose style of Sir Thomas Browne may be called baroque, as may the strange *conceits of the *metaphysical poets, especially Richard Crashaw. Some critics have tried to extend the term to Milton and the later works of Shakespeare as well. *See also* mannerism, rococo.

bathos [**bay**-thos], a lapse into the ridiculous by a poet aiming at elevated expression. Whereas *anticlimax can be a deliberate poetic effect, bathos is an unintended failure. Pope named this stylistic blemish from the Greek word for 'depth', in his *Peri Bathous, or the Art of Sinking in Poetry* (1727). This example comes from Dryden's *Annus Mirabilis* (1667):

> The Eternal heard, and from the heavenly quire
> Chose out the Cherub with the flaming sword
> And bad him swiftly drive the approaching fire
> From where our naval magazines were stored.

Wordsworth, Whitman, and other poets who seek to dignify humble subjects are especially vulnerable to such lapses. *Adjective*: **bathetic**.

beast fable, the commonest type of *fable, in which animals and birds speak and behave like human beings in a short tale usually illustrating some moral point. The fables attributed to Aesop (6th century BCE) and those written in verse by Jean de la Fontaine (from 1668) are the best known, along with the fables of Brer Rabbit adapted by the American journalist Joel Chandler Harris from black *folklore in his 'Uncle Remus' stories (from 1879). A related form is the **beast epic**, which is usually a longer tale written in pseudo-*epic style. Pierre de Saint-Cloud's *Roman de Renart* (1173) was an influential beast epic containing the Chanticleer story later adapted by Chaucer in the *Nun's Priest's Tale*. There were many other beast epics of Reynard the Fox in late-medieval France and Germany.

Beat writers, a group of American writers in the late 1950s, led by the poet Allen Ginsberg and the novelist Jack Kerouac. Writers of the 'beat generation' dropped out of middle-class society in search of 'beatific' ecstasy through drugs, sex, and Zen Buddhism. Their loose styles favour spontaneous self-expression and recitation to jazz accompaniment. The principal works of the group are Ginsberg's *Howl* (1956) and Kerouac's *On the Road* (1957). Significant contributions in poetry were Gregory Corso's *Gasoline* (1958) and Gary Snyder's *Riprap* (1959); while in prose, the group's mentor William S. Burroughs published *The Naked Lunch* in 1959. The poet Lawrence Ferlinghetti was another leading figure. The Beats had a strong influence on the 'counter-culture' of the 1960s.

belatedness, in Harold Bloom's theory of literary history (*see* anxiety of influence), the predicament of the poet who feels that previous poets have already said all that there is to say, leaving no room for new creativity.

belles-lettres [bel-**letr**], the French term for 'fine writing', originally used (as in 'fine art') to distinguish artistic literature from scientific or philosophical writing. Since the 19th century, though, the term has more often been used dismissively to denote a category of elegant essay-writing and lightweight literary chatter, of which much was published in

Britain in the late 19th and early 20th centuries: Max Beerbohm's essays and Andrew Lang's *Letters to Dead Authors* (1896) are examples. An author of such elegant trifles is a **belletrist**. *Adjective*: **belletristic**.

bestiary, a description of animal life in verse or prose, in which the characteristics of real and fabulous beasts (like the phoenix or the unicorn) are given edifying religious meanings. This kind of *allegory was popular in the Middle Ages, and survives in some later children's books. *See also* beast fable, emblem.

bibliography, the description of books: (i) a systematic list of writings by a given author or on a given subject; (ii) the study of books as material objects, involving technical analysis of paper, printing methods, bindings, page-numbering, and publishing history. A compiler of bibliographies or a student of bibliography is a **bibliographer**.

Bildungsroman [bil-duungz-raw-mahn] (plural *-ane*), a kind of novel that follows the development of the hero or heroine from childhood or adolescence into adulthood, through a troubled quest for identity. The term ('formation-novel') comes from Germany, where Goethe's *Wilhelm Meisters Lehrjahre* (1795–6) set the pattern for later *Bildungsromane*. Many outstanding novels of the 19th and early 20th centuries follow this pattern of personal growth: Dickens's *David Copperfield* (1849–50), for example. When the novel describes the formation of a young artist, as in Joyce's *A Portrait of the Artist as a Young Man* (1916), it may also be called a *Künstlerroman. For a fuller account, consult Franco Moretti, *The Way of the World* (1987).

binary opposition, the principle of contrast between two mutually exclusive terms: on/off, up/down, left/right etc; an important concept of *structuralism, which sees such distinctions as fundamental to all language and thought. The theory of *phonology developed by Roman Jakobson uses the concept of 'binary features', which are properties either present or absent in any *phoneme: voicing, for example is present in /z/ but not in /s/. This concept has been extended to anthropology by Claude Lévi-Strauss (in such oppositions as nature/culture, raw/cooked, inedible/edible), and to *narratology by A. J. Greimas (*see* actant).

black comedy, a kind of drama (or, by extension, a non-dramatic work) in which disturbing or sinister subjects like death, disease, or warfare, are treated with bitter amusement, usually in a manner calculated to offend and shock. Prominent in the theatre of the *absurd, black comedy is also a feature of Joe Orton's *Loot* (1965). A similar **black humour** is strongly evident in modern American fiction from Nathanael West's *A Cool Million* (1934) to Joseph Heller's *Catch-22* (1961) and Kurt Vonnegut's *Slaughterhouse-Five* (1969).

blank verse, unrhymed lines of iambic *pentameter, as in these final lines of Tennyson's 'Ulysses' (1842):

> One equal temper of heroic hearts,
> Made weak by time and fate, but strong in will
> To strive, to seek, to find, and not to yield.

Blank verse is a very flexible English verse form which can attain rhetorical grandeur while echoing the natural rhythms of speech and allowing smooth *enjambment. First used (*c*.1540) by Henry Howard, Earl of Surrey, it soon became both the standard *metre for dramatic poetry and a widely used form for *narrative and meditative poems. Much of the finest verse in English—by Shakespeare, Milton, Wordsworth, Tennyson, and Stevens—has been written in blank verse. In other languages, notably Italian (in *hendecasyllables) and German, blank verse has been an important medium for poetic drama. Blank verse should not be confused with *free verse, which has no regular metre.

blazon or **blason,** a poetic catalogue of a woman's admirable physical features, common in Elizabethan *lyric poetry: an extended example is Sidney's 'What tongue can her perfections tell?' The *Petrarchan conventions of the blazon include a listing of parts from the hair down, and the use of *hyperbole and *simile in describing lips like coral, teeth like pearls, and so on. These conventions are mocked in Shakespeare's famous sonnet, 'My mistress' eyes are nothing like the sun'.

Bloomsbury group, a loose *coterie of writers linked by friendship to the homes of Vanessa Stephen (from 1907 Vanessa Bell) and her sister Virginia (from 1912 Virginia Woolf) in Bloomsbury—the university quarter of London near the British Museum—from about 1906 to the late 1930s. In addition to the sisters and their husbands—Clive Bell, the art critic, and Leonard Woolf, a political journalist—the group included the novelist E. M. Forster, the biographer Lytton Strachey, the economist John Maynard Keynes, and the art critic Roger Fry. It had no doctrine or aim, despite a shared admiration for the moral philosophy of G. E. Moore, but the group had some importance as a centre of modernizing liberal opinion in the 1920s, and later as the subject of countless memoirs and biographies.

bob and wheel, a short sequence of rhymed lines that concludes the larger unrhymed *strophes of *Sir Gawain and the Green Knight* and some other Middle English *romances. It consists of one short line (the bob) with a single stress, followed by four three-stress lines (the wheel) of which the second and fourth lines rhyme with the bob.

bodice-ripper, a popular modern variety of *romance that emphasizes the sexual excitement of seduction and 'ravishment', usually in colourful settings based on the conventions of the *historical novel and peopled by pirates, highwaymen, wenches etc. A classic example is Kathleen Winsor's best-selling romance, *Forever Amber* (1944). *See also* S & F.

bombast, extravagantly inflated and grandiloquent *diction, disproportionate to its subject. It was a common feature of English drama of Shakespeare's age, and of later *heroic drama. Marlowe is known especially for the bombastic ranting of his *Tamburlaine the Great* (1590):

> Our quivering lances, shaking in the air,
> And bullets, like Jove's dreadful thunderbolts,
> Enroll'd in flames and fiery smouldering mists,
> Shall threat the gods more than Cyclopean wars;
> And with our sun-bright armour, as we march,
> We'll chase the stars from heaven, and dim their eyes
> That stand and muse at our admired arms.

See also fustian, hyperbole, rodomontade.

bovarysme [bohv-ar-eezm], a disposition towards escapist day dreaming in which one imagines oneself as a heroine or hero of a *romance and refuses to acknowledge everyday realities. This condition (a later version of Don Quixote's madness) can be found in fictional characters before Emma Bovary, the *protagonist of Gustave Flaubert's novel *Madame Bovary* (1857), gave it her name: for example, Catherine Morland in Jane Austen's *Northanger Abbey* (1818) makes similar confusions between fiction and reality. Novelists have often exposed *bovarysme* to ironic analysis, thus warning against the delusive enchantments of the romance tradition.

bowdlerize, to censor or expurgate from a literary work those passages considered to be indecent or blasphemous. The word comes from Dr

Thomas Bowdler, who published in 1818 *The Family Shakespeare*, 'in which those words or expressions are omitted which cannot with propriety be read aloud in a family'. Many oaths and sexually suggestive speeches were cut, and even entire characters like Doll Tearsheet in *Henry IV, Part One*. Similarly bowdlerized editions of *Gulliver's Travels* and *Moby-Dick* have been produced for children. *Nouns*: **bowdlerization, bowdlerism.**

braggadocio [brag-ă-**doh**-chi-oh], a cowardly but boastful man who appears as a *stock character in many comedies; or the empty boasting typical of such a braggart. This sort of character was known in Greek comedy as the *alazon*. When he is a soldier, he is often referred to as the *miles gloriosus* ('vainglorious soldier') after the title of a comedy by the Roman dramatist Plautus. The most famous example in English drama is Shakespeare's Falstaff.

Brechtian, belonging to or derived from the work of Bertolt Brecht (1898–1956), German poet, playwright, and dramatic theorist. When applied to the work of other dramatists, the term usually indicates their use of the techniques of *epic theatre, especially the disruption of realistic illusion known as the *alienation effect.

bricolage [brik-ō-lah*zh*], a French term for improvisation or a piece of makeshift handiwork. It is sometimes applied to artistic works in a sense similar to *collage: an assemblage improvised from materials ready to hand, or the practice of transforming 'found' materials by incorporating them in a new work. Verb: *bricoler*.

broadside, a large sheet of paper printed on one side only, often containing a song or *ballad, and sold by wandering pedlars in Britain from the 16th century until the beginning of the 20th century, when they were superseded by mass-circulation newspapers; they also appeared in the USA in the late 19th century. The broadside ballads were intended to be sung to a well-known tune; often they related topical events, and some were adopted as *folk songs. Broadsides are sometimes called broadsheets.

broken rhyme, the splitting of a word (not in fact of the rhyme) at the end of a verse line, to allow a rhyme on a syllable other than the final one, which is transferred to the following line. It is a liberty taken for comic effect in light verse, and more rarely used in serious works. Hopkins employed it frequently: the first line of 'The Windhover' ends with the first syllable of 'king/dom' to rhyme with 'wing' in line four.

bucolic poetry or **bucolics** [bew-**kol**-ik], another term for *pastoral poetry, especially for Virgil's *Eclogues* (42–37 BCE) and later imitations. More loosely, any verse on rustic subjects. *See also* eclogue, idyll.

burden, the *refrain or chorus of a song; or the main theme of a song, poem, or other literary work. A burden is sometimes distinguished from a refrain in that it starts the song or poem, and stands separate from the *stanzas (as in many medieval *carols), whereas a refrain usually appears as the final part of each stanza.

burlesque [ber-**lesk**], a kind of *parody that ridicules some serious literary work either by treating its solemn subject in an undignified style (*see* travesty), or by applying its elevated style to a trivial subject, as in Pope's *mock-epic poem *The Rape of the Lock* (1712–14). Often used in the theatre, burlesque appears in Shakespeare's *A Midsummer Night's Dream* (in the Pyramus and Thisbe play, which mocks the tradition of *interludes), while *The Beggar's Opera* (1728) by John Gay burlesques Italian opera. An early form of burlesque is the Greek *satyr play. In the USA, though, burlesque is also a disreputable form of comic entertainment with titillating dances or striptease. *See also* extravaganza, satire.

Burns stanza or **Burns metre,** a six-line *stanza rhyming *aaabab*, the first three lines and the fifth having four *stresses, and the fourth and sixth having two stresses. Although it was used much earlier in medieval English *romances and Provençal poetry, it is named after the Scottish poet Robert Burns (1759–96), who used it frequently, as in 'A Poet's Welcome to his love-begotten Daughter':

> Welcome! My bonie, sweet, wee dochter!
> Though ye come here a wee unsought for;
> And though your comin I hae fought for,
>   Baith Kirk and Queir;
> Yet by my faith, ye're no unwrought for,
>   That I shall swear!

Byronic, belonging to or derived from Lord Byron (1788–1824) or his works. The **Byronic hero** is a character-type found in his celebrated narrative poem *Childe Harold's Pilgrimage* (1812–18), his verse drama *Manfred* (1817), and other works; he is a boldly defiant but bitterly self-tormenting outcast, proudly contemptuous of social norms but suffering for some unnamed sin. Emily Brontë's Heathcliff in *Wuthering Heights* (1847) is a later example. See also *poète maudit*.

cacophony [kǎ-ko-fŏni], harshness or discordancy of sound; the opposite of *euphony. Usually the result of awkward *alliteration as in tongue-twisters, it is sometimes used by poets for deliberate effect, as in these lines from Robert Browning's 'Caliban upon Setebos':

> And squared and stuck there squares of soft white chalk,
> And, with a fish-tooth, scratched a moon on each,
> And set up endwise certain spikes of tree,
> And crowned the whole with a sloth's skull a-top.

Adjective: **cacophonous** or **cacaphonic**. *See also* dissonance.

cadence [kay-děns], the rising and falling *rhythm of speech, especially that of the balanced phrases in *free verse or in prose, as distinct from the stricter rhythms of verse *metre. Also the fall or rise in pitch at the end of a phrase or sentence. *Adjective*: **cadent**.

caesura [si-zew-rǎ] (plural **-as** or **-ae**), a pause in a line of verse, often coinciding with a break between clauses or sentences. It is usually placed in the middle of the line ('medial caesura'), but may appear near the beginning ('initial') or towards the end ('terminal'). In *scansion, a caesura is normally indicated by the symbol ‖. If it follows a stressed syllable, it is known as a 'masculine' caesura, while if it follows an unstressed syllable, it is 'feminine'. The regular placing of the caesura was an important metrical requirement in much Greek and Latin verse, in the Old English and Middle English *alliterative metre, and in the French *alexandrine; but in the English iambic *pentameter there is scope for artful variation between medial, initial, and terminal positions, and a line may have more than one caesura, or none. In Greek and Latin *prosody, the term is also applied to a break between words within a *foot: the opposite of *diaeresis. *Adjective*: **caesural**.

Cambridge school, the name sometimes given to an influential group of English critics associated with the University of Cambridge in the 1920s and 1930s. The leading figures were I. A. Richards, F. R. Leavis, Q. D. Leavis, and William Empson. Influenced by the critical writings of

Coleridge and of T. S. Eliot, they rejected the prevalent biographical and historical modes of criticism in favour of the 'close reading' of texts. They saw poetry in terms of the reintegration of thought and feeling (*see* dissociation of sensibility), and sought to demonstrate its subtlety and complexity, notably in Empson's *Seven Types of Ambiguity* (1930). The Leavises achieved great influence through the journal *Scrutiny* (1932–53), judging literary works according to their moral seriousness and 'life-enhancing' tendency. *See also* Leavisites, practical criticism.

campus novel, a novel, usually comic or satirical, in which the action is set within the enclosed world of a university (or similar seat of learning) and highlights the follies of academic life. Many novels have presented nostalgic evocations of college days, but the campus novel in the usual modern sense dates from the 1950s: Mary McCarthy's *The Groves of Academe* (1952) and Kingsley Amis's *Lucky Jim* (1954) began a significant tradition in modern fiction including John Barth's *Giles Goat-Boy* (1966), David Lodge's *Changing Places* (1975), and Robertson Davies's *The Rebel Angels* (1982).

canon, a body of writings recognized by authority. Those books of holy scripture which religious leaders accept as genuine are **canonical,** as are those works of a literary author which scholars regard as authentic. The canon of a national literature is a body of writings especially approved by critics or anthologists and deemed suitable for academic study. **Canonicity** is the quality of being canonical. *Verb*: **canonize**. *See also* corpus, *oeuvre*.

canto, a subdivision of an *epic or other narrative poem, equivalent to a chapter in a prose work.

canzone [can-tsoh-ni] (plural *-oni*), a term covering various kinds of medieval Provençal and Italian *lyric poem. The most influential form was the *Petrarchan *canzone*, which has five or six *stanzas and a shorter concluding *envoi (or half-stanza); the lengths of the stanzas (equal in each poem) ranged from seven to twenty lines. See also *chanson*.

carnivalization, the liberating and subversive influence of popular humour on the literary tradition, according to the theory propounded by the Russian linguist Mikhail Bakhtin in his works *Problems of Dostoevsky's Poetics* (1929) and *Rabelais and his World* (1965). Bakhtin argued that the overturning of hierarchies in popular carnival—its mingling of the sacred with the profane, the sublime with the ridiculous—lies behind the most 'open' (*dialogic or *polyphonic) literary *genres, notably *Menippean satire and the *novel, especially since the *Renaissance. Carnivalized literary forms allow alternative voices to dethrone the authority of official culture: Rabelais, for example, subverts the asceticism of the medieval Church by giving free rein to the bodily profanity of folk festivities. *Adjective*: **carnivalistic** or **carnivalesque**.

carol, a song of religious rejoicing, usually associated with Christmas or Easter in the Christian calendar. In the Middle Ages, however, a carol could be a purely secular song of love or *satire. A carol in this earlier sense is a song appropriate for a round dance, composed in regular rhyming *stanzas with a *refrain or *burden: a common form was the four-line stanza rhyming *aaab* with a two-line burden rhyming *bb*.

Caroline, belonging to the period 1625–49, when Charles I (Latin, *Carolus*) reigned as king of England, Scotland, and Ireland. This period includes the later *metaphysical poets, the early work of Milton, and the so-called 'cavalier poets' Thomas Carew, Robert Herrick, Richard Lovelace, and Sir John Suckling.

carpe diem [**kar**-pe **dee**-em], a quotation from Horace's *Odes* (I, xi) meaning 'seize the day', in other words 'make the best of the present moment'. A common theme or *motif in European *lyric poetry, in which the speaker of a poem argues (often to a hesitant virgin) that since life is short, pleasure should be enjoyed while there is still time. The most celebrated examples in English are Marvell's 'To His Coy Mistress' (1681) and Herrick's 'To the Virgins, To Make Much of Time' (1648), which begins 'Gather ye rosebuds while ye may'. In some Christian poems and sermons, the *carpe diem* motif warns us to prepare our souls for death, rather than our bodies for bed.

catachresis [kat-ă-**kree**-sis], the misapplication of a word (e.g. *disinterested* for 'uninterested'), or the extension of a word's meaning in a surprising but strictly illogical *metaphor. In the second sense, a well-known example from *Hamlet* is 'To take arms against a sea of troubles'. *Adjective*: **catachretic**.

catalectic, lacking the final syllable or syllables expected in the regular pattern of a metrical verse line (*see* metre). The term is most often used of the common English *trochaic line in which the optional final unstressed syllable (or *feminine ending) is not used. Of these lines from Shelley's 'To a Skylark', the second and fourth are catalectic:

> In the golden lightning
>> Of the sunken sun,
> O'er which clouds are bright'ning,
>> Thou dost float and run

The first and third lines, which have the full number of syllables, are **acatalectic**. Unlike most English adjectives, 'catalectic' and its opposite 'acatalectic' usually follow the nouns they qualify: thus the last of Shelley's lines quoted above would be called a trochaic *trimeter catalectic. A line which is short by more than one syllable is **brachycatalectic,** while a line with one syllable too many is **hypercatalectic**. *Noun*: **catalexis**. *See also* acephalous, defective foot, truncation.

catalogue verse, verse that records the names of several persons, places, or things in the form of a list. It is common in *epic poetry, where the heroes involved in a battle are often enumerated. Other types of catalogue verse record genealogical or geographical information. Walt Whitman created a new kind of catalogue verse in his *Song of Myself* (1855), which celebrates the huge variety of peoples, places, and occupations in the United States in the form of long lists.

catastrophe, the final resolution or *dénouement of the plot in a *tragedy, usually involving the death of the *protagonist.

catharsis, the effect of 'purgation' or 'purification' achieved by tragic drama, according to Aristotle's argument in his *Poetics* (4th century BCE). Aristotle wrote that a *tragedy should succeed 'in arousing pity and fear in such a way as to accomplish a catharsis of such emotions'. There has been much dispute about his meaning, but Aristotle seems to be rejecting Plato's hostile view of poetry as an unhealthy emotional stimulant. His metaphor of emotional cleansing has been read as a solution to the puzzle of audiences' pleasure or relief in witnessing the disturbing events enacted in tragedies. Another interpretation is that it is the *protagonist's guilt that is purged, rather than the audience's feeling of terror. *Adjective*: **cathartic**.

causerie, the French word for a chat, sometimes used to denote an informal literary essay or article, after the *Causeries du lundi*—the famous weekly articles by the French literary critic Sainte-Beuve published in Parisian newspapers from 1849 to 1869.

Celtic Revival, a term sometimes applied to the period of Irish literature in English (*c*.1885–1939) now more often referred to as the Irish Literary Revival or Renaissance. There are other similar terms: Celtic Renaissance, Celtic Dawn, and Celtic Twilight (the last famously mocked by James Joyce as the 'cultic twalette'). These Celtic titles are misleading as descriptions of the broader Irish Revival, but they indicate a significant factor in the early phase of the movement: **Celticism** involves an idea of Irishness based on fanciful notions of innate racial character outlined by the English critic Matthew Arnold in *On the Study of Celtic Literature* (1866), in which Celtic traits are said to include delicacy, charm, spirituality, and ineffectual sentimentality. This image of Irishness was adopted in part by W. B. Yeats in his attempt to create a distinctively Irish literature with his dreamy early verse and with *The Celtic Twilight* (1893), a collection of stories based on Irish folklore and fairy-tales. Apart from the poet 'AE' (George Russell), the other major figures in the Irish Literary Revival—Synge, O'Casey, and Joyce—had little or nothing to do with such Celticism.

cénacle [say-**nahkl**], a clique or *coterie of writers that assembles around a leading figure. A characteristic of the hero-worshipping culture of *Romanticism, *cénacles* appeared in Paris from the 1820s onwards around Charles Nodier and, most famously, Victor Hugo.

chanson [shah^n-so^n], the French word for a song, also applied specifically to the kind of love song composed by the Provençal *troubadours of the late Middle Ages. This usually has five or six matching *stanzas and a concluding *envoi (or half-stanza), and its subject is *courtly love. The *metres and *rhyme schemes vary greatly, as the form was seen as a test of technical skills. See also *canzone*.

chanson de geste [shah^n-so^n dĕ zhest] ('song of deeds'), a kind of shorter *epic poem in Old French, composed between the late 11th century and the early 14th century, celebrating the historical and legendary exploits of Charlemagne (late 8th century) and other Frankish nobles in holy wars against the Saracens or in internal rebellions. The *chansons de geste* were sung by *jongleurs in *strophes of varying length known as *laisses*, usually composed of 10-syllable lines linked by *assonance (or by rhyme in later examples). About 80 of these poems survive, of which the most celebrated is the *Chanson de Roland* (late 11th century). Some similar *Cantares de gesta* appeared in Spain, notably the *Cantar de mio Cid*, a Castilian epic of the 12th or 13th century.

chant royal [shah^n rwa-yal], a French verse form normally consisting of five *stanzas of eleven 10-syllable lines rhyming *ababccddede*, followed by an *envoi* (or half-stanza) rhyming *ddede*. The last line of the first stanza is repeated as a *refrain at the end of the succeeding stanzas and of the *envoi*. The pattern is similar to that of the *ballade, but even more demanding. Most *chants royaux* were *allegories on dignified subjects. They appeared in France from the time of Eustache Deschamps (late 14th century) to that of Clément Marot (early 16th century), but very rarely in English.

chapbook, the name given since the 19th century to a kind of small, cheaply printed book or pamphlet hawked by chapmen (i.e. pedlars) from the 16th century to the early 19th century, and containing *ballads, fairy-tales, old *romances, accounts of famous criminals, and other popular entertainments.

character, a personage in a *narrative or dramatic work (*see* characterization); also a kind of prose sketch briefly describing some recognizable type of person. As a minor literary *genre, the character originates with the *Characters* (late 3rd century BCE) of the Greek writer Theophrastus; it was revived in the 17th century, notably by Sir Thomas Overbury in his *Characters* (1614) and by La Bruyère in *Les Caractères* (1688). *See also* humours, stock character, type.

characterization, the representation of persons in *narrative and dramatic works. This may include direct methods like the attribution of qualities in description or commentary, and indirect (or 'dramatic') methods inviting readers to infer qualities from characters' actions, speech, or appearance. Since E. M. Forster's *Aspects of the Novel* (1927) a distinction has often been made between 'flat' and 'two-dimensional' characters, which are simple and unchanging, and 'round' characters, which are complex, 'dynamic' (i.e. subject to development), and less predictable. *See also* stock character, type.

Chaucerian stanza, *see* rhyme royal.

cheville, the French word for a plug, applied to any word or phrase of little semantic importance which is used by a poet to make up the required number of syllables in a metrical verse line (*see* metre). Chaucer used chevilles with shameless frequency, often plugging his lines with 'eek', 'for sothe', 'ywis', 'I gesse', 'I trowe', and similar interjections.

chiasmus [ky-az-mŭs] (plural **-mi**), a *figure of speech by which the order of the terms in the first of two parallel clauses is reversed in the second. This may involve a repetition of the same words ('Pleasure's a sin, and sometimes sin's a pleasure'—Byron), in which case the figure may be classified as *antimetabole, or just a reversed parallel between two corresponding pairs of ideas, as in this line from Mary Leapor's 'Essay on Woman' (1751):

> Despised, if ugly; if she's fair, betrayed.

The figure is especially common in 18th-century English poetry, but is also found in prose of all periods. It is named after the Greek letter *chi* (χ), indicating a 'criss-cross' arrangement of terms. *Adjective*: **chiastic**. *See also* anadiplosis, antithesis, parallelism.

Chicago critics, a group of critics associated with the University of Chicago, who contributed to the volume *Critics and Criticisms: Ancient and Modern* (1952) edited by the most prominent figure, R. S. Crane. Other members included W. R. Keast, Elder Olson, and Bernard Weinberg; Wayne C. Booth, the author of *The Rhetoric of Fiction* (1961), was also associated with the group. The Chicago critics were concerned with accounting for the variety of critical approaches to literature in terms of assumptions about the nature of literary works. They also emphasized the larger structures of literary works, following the example of Aristotle, whom they admired for basing his *Poetics* (4th century BCE) on actual examples rather than on preconceptions. Their interest in *plot and in the design of a work as a whole distinguishes them from the *New Critics, who concentrated on the study of *metaphor and *symbol in *lyric verse. *See also* Aristotelian.

chivalric romance [shi-**val**-rik], the principal kind of *romance found in medieval Europe from the 12th century onwards, describing (usually in verse) the adventures of legendary knights, and celebrating an idealized code of civilized behaviour that combines loyalty, honour, and *courtly love. The emphasis on heterosexual love and courtly manners distinguishes it from the *chanson de geste and other kinds of *epic, in which masculine military heroism predominates. The most famous examples are the Arthurian romances recounting the adventures of Lancelot, Galahad, Gawain, and the other Round Table knights. These include the *Lancelot* (late 12th century) of Chrétien de Troyes, the anonymous *Sir Gawain and the Green Knight* (late 14th century), and Malory's prose romance *Le Morte Darthur* (1485).

choral character, a term sometimes applied to a character in a play who, while participating in the action to some degree, also provides the audience with an ironic commentary upon it, thus performing a function similar to that of the *chorus in Greek *tragedy. Two examples are Thersites in Shakespeare's *Troilus and Cressida* and Wong in Brecht's *The Good Woman of Setzuan*.

choriamb [kor-i-am] or **choriambus,** a metrical unit combining one *trochee (or 'choree') and one *iamb into a single *foot of four syllables, with two stressed syllables enclosing two unstressed syllables, as in the word *hullabaloo* (or, in *quantitative verse, two long syllables enclosing two shorts). It was used frequently in Greek dramatic choruses and lyrics, and by the Roman poet Horace, and later in some German verse. Usually, as in the *Asclepiad, it is combined with other feet. A rare English example of choriambic verse is Swinburne's 'Choriambics' (1878), in which the line consists of one trochee, three choriambs, and one iamb:

> Ah, thy snow-coloured hands! once were they chains, mighty to bind fast;
> Now no blood in them burns, mindless of love, senseless of passions past.

chorus, a group of singers distinct from the principal performers in a dramatic or musical performance; also the song or *refrain that they sing. In classical Greek *tragedy a chorus of twelve or fifteen masked performers would sing, with dancing movements, a commentary on the action of the play, interpreting its events from the standpoint of traditional wisdom. This practice appears to have been derived from the **choral lyrics** of religious festivals. The Greek tradition of choral *lyric includes the *dithyramb, the *paean, and the choral *odes of Pindar. In some Elizabethan plays, like Shakespeare's *Henry V*, a single character called a chorus introduces the setting and action. Except in opera, the group chorus is used rarely in modern European drama: examples are T. S. Eliot's *Murder in the Cathedral* (1935) and Brecht's *The Caucasian Chalk Circle* (1948). The term has also been applied to certain groups of characters in novels, who view the main action from the standpoint of rural tradition, as in some works of George Eliot, Thomas Hardy, and William Faulkner. *See also* choral character.

chrestomathy [kres-tom-ă-thi], a collection or anthology of passages in prose or verse, often selected for purposes of literary or linguistic study.

chronicle, a written record of events presented in order of time, and updated regularly over a prolonged period. The chroniclers of the Middle Ages, from the compilers of King Alfred's *Anglo-Saxon Chronicle* (9th to 12th centuries) onward, tended to mix *legend and rumour with fact in their accounts. Significant chronicles in the later Middle Ages include those of Matthew Paris (St Albans, late 13th century) and the accounts of the wars against the English written by the French chronicler Jean Froissart (late 14th century). Raphael Holinshed and his collaborators published in 1577 the *Chronicles of England, Scotland, and Ireland* which (in an expurgated edition of 1587) were adapted by Shakespeare and other dramatists in their *chronicle plays.

chronicle play, a *history play, especially of the kind written in England in the 1590s and based upon the revised 1587 edition of Raphael Holinshed's *Chronicles*. This group of plays includes Marlowe's *Edward II* (1592) and the three parts of Shakespeare's *Henry VI* (*c.*1590–2).

chronotope, a term employed by the Russian literary theorist Mikhail Bakhtin (1895–1975) to refer to the co-ordinates of time and space invoked by a given *narrative; in other words to the 'setting', considered as a spatio-temporal whole.

circumlocution, the roundabout manner of referring to something at length rather than naming it briefly and directly, usually known in literary terminology as *periphrasis.

city comedy or **citizen comedy,** a kind of comic drama produced in the London theatres of the early 17th century, characterized by its contemporary urban subject-matter and its portrayal, often satirical, of middle-class life and manners. The principal examples are John Marston's *The Dutch Courtezan* (1605), Ben Jonson's *Bartholomew Fair* (1614), and Thomas Middleton's *A Chaste Maid in Cheapside* (1613).

claque [klahk], the French word for a handclap, applied to a group of people hired by a theatre manager to applaud a performance, thus encouraging the paying audience to do likewise. The French writer Villiers de l'Isle-Adam described this widespread corrupt practice in the theatres of 19th-century Paris as 'the avowed symbol of the Public's inability to distinguish by itself the worth of what it is listening to'.

classicism, an attitude to literature that is guided by admiration of the qualities of formal balance, proportion, *decorum, and restraint

attributed to the major works of ancient Greek and Roman literature
('the classics') in preference to the irregularities of later *vernacular
literatures, and especially (since about 1800) to the artistic liberties
proclaimed by *Romanticism. A **classic** is a work of the highest class,
and has also been taken to mean a work suitable for study in school
classes. During and since the *Renaissance, these overlapping
meanings came to be applied to (and to be virtually synonymous with)
the writings of major Greek and Roman authors from Homer to Juvenal,
which were regarded as unsurpassed models of excellence. The adjective
classical, usually applied to this body of writings, has since been
extended to outstandingly creative periods of other literatures: the 17th
century may be regarded as the classical age of French literature, and the
19th century the classical period of the Western novel, while the finest
fiction of the United States in the mid-19th century from Cooper to
Twain was referred to by D. H. Lawrence as Classic American Literature
(despite the opposition between 'classical' and 'romantic' views of art, a
romantic work can now still be a classic). A classical style or approach to
literary composition is usually one that imitates Greek or Roman models
in subject-matter (e.g. Greek legends) or in form (by the adoption of
*genres like *tragedy, *epic, *ode, or verse *satire), or both. As a
literary doctrine, classicism holds that the writer must be governed by
rules, models, or conventions, rather than by wayward inspiration: in its
most strictly codified form in the 17th and 18th centuries (*see* neoclassicism), it required the observance of rules derived from Aristotle's
Poetics (4th century BCE) and Horace's *Ars Poetica* (*c.*20 BCE), principally
those of decorum and the dramatic *unities. The dominant tendency of
French literature in the 17th and 18th centuries, classicism in a weaker
form also characterized the *Augustan Age in England; the later
German classicism of the late 18th and early 19th centuries was
distinguished by its exclusive interest in Greek models, as opposed to the
Roman bias of French and English classicisms. After the end of the 18th
century, 'classical' came to be contrasted with 'romantic' in an
opposition of increasingly generalized terms embracing moods and
attitudes as well as characteristics of actual works. While partisans of
Romanticism associated the classical with the rigidly artificial and the
romantic with the freely creative, the classicists condemned romantic
self-expression as eccentric self-indulgence, in the name of classical
sanity and order. The great German writer J. W. von Goethe summarized
his conversion to classical principles by defining the classical as healthy,
the romantic as sickly. Since then, literary classicism has often been less

a matter of imitating Greek and Roman models than of resisting the claims of Romanticism and all that it may be thought to stand for (Protestantism, liberalism, democracy, anarchy): the critical doctrines of Matthew Arnold and more especially of T. S. Eliot are classicist in this sense of reacting against the Romantic principle of unrestrained self-expression. For a fuller account, consult Dominique Secretan, *Classicism* (1973).

clausula (plural -**ulae**), the closing words of a prose sentence, especially when characterized by a distinct rhythm or *cadence, as in the Latin *oratory of Cicero (106–43 BCE) or his imitators.

clerihew, a form of comic verse named after its inventor, Edmund Clerihew Bentley (1875–1956). It consists of two metrically awkward *couplets, and usually presents a ludicrously uninformative 'biography' of some famous person whose name appears as one of the rhymed words in the first couplet:

> Geoffrey Chaucer
> Could hardly have been coarser,
> But this never harmed the sales
> Of his *Canterbury Tales*.

climax, any moment of great intensity in a literary work, especially in drama (*see also* anagnorisis, catastrophe, crisis, dénouement, peripeteia). Also in *rhetoric, a figure of speech in which a sequence of terms is linked by chain-like repetition through three or more clauses in ascending order of importance. A well-known example is Benjamin Franklin's cautionary maxim, 'For want of a nail, the shoe was lost; for want of a shoe the horse was lost; for want of a horse the rider was lost.' This figure uses a repetitive structure similar to that of *anadiplosis. *Adjective*: **climactic**. *See also* auxesis, scène à faire.

closed couplet, two lines of metrical verse in which the *syntax and sense come to a conclusion or a strong pause at the end of the second line, giving the couplet the quality of a self-contained *epigram. The term is applied almost always to rhyming couplets, especially to the *heroic couplet; but whereas the heroic couplets of Chaucer and Keats often allow the sense to run on over the end of the second line (*see* enjambment), those written by English poets in the late 17th century and in the 18th are usually *end-stopped, and are thus closed couplets, as in these lines about men from Sarah Fyge Egerton's 'The Emulation' (1703):

> They fear we should excel their sluggish parts,
> Should we attempt the sciences and arts;
> Pretend they were designed for them alone,
> So keep us fools to raise their own renown.

closet drama, a literary composition written in the form of a play (usually as a dramatic poem), but intended—or suited—only for reading in a closet (i.e. a private study) rather than for stage performance. *Senecan tragedy is thought to have been written for private recitation, and there are several important examples of closet drama in English, including Milton's *Samson Agonistes* (1671), Byron's *Manfred* (1817), Shelley's *Prometheus Unbound* (1820), and Arnold's *Empedocles on Etna* (1852).

closure, the sense of completion or resolution at the end of a literary work or part of a work (e.g. a *stanza or *closed couplet); or, in literary criticism, the reduction of a work's meanings to a single and complete sense that excludes the claims of other interpretations. The contrast between 'closed' texts and 'open' texts has been a common topic of modern criticism, as in Roland Barthes's theory of the *lisible.

coda, *see* tail-rhyme stanza.

code, a shared set of rules or *conventions by which *signs can be combined to permit a message to be communicated from one person to another; it may consist of a language in the normal sense (e.g. English, Urdu) or of a smaller-scale 'language' such as the set of hand-signals, horns, grimaces, and flashing lights used by motorists. The code is one of the six essential elements in Roman Jakobson's influential theory of communication (*see* function), and has an important place in *structuralist theories, which stress the extent to which messages (including literary works) call upon *already* coded meanings rather than fresh revelations of raw reality. An important work in this connection is Roland Barthes's *S/Z* (1970), in which a story by Balzac is broken down into five codes, ranging from the 'hermeneutic code' (which sets up a mystery and delays its solution) to the 'cultural code' (which refers to accepted prejudices, stereotypes, and values). *Verbs*: **codify, decode, encode.**

codex (plural **codices**), a book consisting of ancient manuscripts. The study of codices is called **codicology.**

cohesion, a term used in linguistic analyses of *texts such as those undertaken in *stylistics, in reference to the degrees and kinds of internal connection that link different parts of the same text. Cohesion between one sentence, stanza or other unit, and another may be established by sound-patterns such as *metre, *rhyme, and *alliteration, or by pronominal back-reference (*she, those*, etc.), or by the use of similar syntactical constructions (e.g. *parallelism), or by conjunctions and similar linking phrases (*nor, however, consequently*, etc.). *Adjective:* **cohesive.**

coinage, a newly invented word or expression. *See also* neologism, nonce word.

collage [kol-ah*zh*], a work assembled wholly or partly from fragments of other writings, incorporating *allusions, quotations, and foreign phrases. Originally applied to paintings with pasted-on elements, the term has been extended to an important kind of *modernist poetry, of which the most significant examples are the *Cantos* of Ezra Pound and T. S. Eliot's *The Waste Land*. The collage technique can also be found sometimes in prose works. *See also bricolage*, macaronic verse, pastiche.

collective unconscious, the term given by the Swiss psychologist C. G. Jung (1875–1961) to the inborn racial memory which he believed to be the primitive source of the *archetypes or 'universal' *symbols found in legends, poetry, and dreams. *See also* myth criticism.

colloquialism, the use of informal expressions appropriate to everyday speech rather than to the formality of writing, and differing in pronunciation, vocabulary, or grammar. An example is Kipling's *ballad beginning

> When 'Omer smote 'is bloomin' lyre
>   He'd 'eard men sing by land and sea;
> An' what he thought 'e might require,
>   'E went an' took—the same as me!

See also demotic, diction.

colophon, the publisher's imprint or emblem usually displayed on the title page of a book; or (in older books) an inscription placed at the end of a book, naming the printer and the date and place of publication.

colportage, cheap popular literature, originally sold by itinerant hawkers called colporteurs. The category includes religious tracts, sensational novels and *romances, *chapbooks, and *broadsides.

comedy, a play (or other literary composition) written chiefly to amuse
its audience by appealing to a sense of superiority over the characters
depicted. A comedy will normally be closer to the representation of
everyday life than a *tragedy, and will explore common human failings
rather than tragedy's disastrous crimes. Its ending will usually be happy
for the leading characters. In another sense, the term was applied in the
Middle Ages to narrative poems that end happily: the title of Dante's
Divine Comedy (*c.*1320) carries this meaning. As a dramatic form, comedy
in Europe dates back to the Greek playwright Aristophanes in the 5th
century BCE. His *Old Comedy combines several kinds of mischief,
including the satirical mockery of living politicians and writers. At the
end of the next century, Menander established the fictional form known
as *New Comedy, in which young lovers went through misadventures
among other *stock characters; this tradition was later developed in the
Roman comedy of Plautus and Terence, and eventually by Shakespeare
in England and Lope de Vega in Spain. The great period of European
comedy, partly influenced by the *commedia dell' arte, was the 17th
century, when Shakespeare, de Vega, and Jonson were succeeded by
Molière and by the *Restoration comedy of Congreve, Etheredge, and
Wycherley. There are several kinds of comedy, including the *romantic
comedy of Shakespeare's *A Midsummer Night's Dream* (*c.*1596), the *satire
in Jonson's *Volpone* (1606) or in Molière's *Le Tartuffe* (1669), the
sophisticated verbal wit of the *comedy of manners in Wilde's *The
Importance of Being Earnest* (1895), and the more topical 'comedy of ideas'
in the plays of George Bernard Shaw. Among its less sophisticated forms
are *burlesque and *farce. *See also* black comedy, comic relief, humours,
tragicomedy. For a fuller account, consult W. Moelwyn Merchant,
Comedy (1972).

comedy of humours, *see* humours.

comedy of manners, a kind of *comedy representing the complex
and sophisticated code of behaviour current in fashionable circles of
society, where appearances count for more than true moral character. Its
*plot usually revolves around intrigues of lust and greed, the self-
interested cynicism of the characters being masked by decorous
pretence. Unlike *satire, the comedy of manners tends to reward its
cleverly unscrupulous characters rather than punish their immorality.
Its humour relies chiefly upon elegant verbal wit and *repartee. In
England, the comedy of manners flourished as the dominant form of
*Restoration comedy in the works of Etheredge, Wycherley (notably

The Country Wife, 1675), and Congreve; it was revived in a more subdued form in the 1770s by Goldsmith and Sheridan, and later by Oscar Wilde. Modern examples of the comedy of manners include Noël Coward's *Design for Living* (1932) and Joe Orton's *Loot* (1965).

comic relief, the interruption of a serious work, especially a *tragedy, by a short humorous episode. The inclusion of such comic scenes, characters, or speeches can have various and complex effects, ranging from relaxation after moments of high tension to sinister ironic brooding. Famous instances are the drunken porter's speech in *Macbeth* (Act II, scene iii), and the dialogues between Hamlet and the gravediggers in *Hamlet* (Act V, scene i). Other playwrights of Shakespeare's time made frequent use of this technique, which can also be found in some prose works like Malcolm Lowry's tragic novel *Under the Volcano* (1947). *See also* satyr play, subplot, tragicomedy.

commedia dell' arte, the Italian term for 'professional comedy', a form of improvised comic performance popular between the 16th and 18th centuries in Italy, France, and elsewhere in Europe, acted in masks by travelling companies of professional actors each of whom specialized in a *stock character. The plots involved intrigues carried on by young lovers and their servants against the rich father ('Pantaloon') of the leading lady (the 'Inamorata'), and included stock characters like Harlequin, Pulcinella, and Scaramouche, who survive as part of theatrical folklore. This form of comedy had an important influence on later forms of *farce, *pantomime, and light opera, as well as on some major dramatists including Molière and Goldoni.

common measure or **common metre,** a form of verse *quatrain (also called the 'hymnal stanza') often used in hymns. Like the *ballad metre, its first and third lines have four *stresses, and its second and fourth have three; but it tends to be more regularly *iambic, and it more often rhymes not only the second and fourth lines (*abcb*) but the first and third too (*abab*). A variant form is **long measure** or **long metre**, in which all four lines have four stresses, and in which the rhyme scheme *aabb* is sometimes also used. *See also* short measure.

commonplace book, not a dull or trite book, as the usual sense of 'commonplace' would suggest, but a writer's notebook in which interesting ideas and quotations are collected for further reflection and possible future use. In this sense, a commonplace is a remark or written passage that is worth remembering or quoting. Notable examples of commonplace books that have been published include Ben Jonson's *Timber* (1640) and W. H. Auden's *A Certain World* (1971).

comparative literature, the combined study of similar literary works written in different languages, which stresses the points of connection between literary products of two or more cultures, as distinct from the sometimes narrow and exclusive perspective of *Eng. Lit. or similar approaches based on one national *canon. Advocates of comparative literature maintain that there is, despite the obvious disadvantages, much to be gained from studying literary works in translation.

competence, the term established by the American linguist Noam Chomsky to denote that unconscious store of linguistic knowledge which enables us to speak and understand our first language properly without having to think about it, permitting us to utter and comprehend sentences that we may never have heard before. Competence is what we know about the language we speak (without having to know that we know it), whereas performance is what we do with this knowledge in practice: that is, actual utterances. The distinction between competence and performance (similar to Saussure's distinction between *langue* and *parole*) is made in order to isolate the proper object of linguistics, which is to make the implicit rules of speakers' competence explicit in the form of grammar. The concept has been extended by theorists of communication, as 'communicative competence', and also adapted by some literary theorists who identify a 'literary competence' in experienced readers' implicit recognition of *narrative structures and other literary *conventions: a competent audience, for instance, will recognize the difference between the end of a scene and the end of the whole play, and so applaud at the right time.

complaint, a kind of *lyric poem common from the Middle Ages to the 17th century, in which the speaker bewails either the cruelty of a faithless lover or the advent of some misfortune like poverty or exile. This kind of *monologue became highly conventional in love poetry, as can be seen from 'The Complaint of Chaucer to His Purse', in which the poet wittily addresses his light purse as if it were a 'light' (i.e. promiscuous) mistress. Chaucer also wrote serious complaints, as did Villon, Surrey, and Spenser. *See also* lament.

conceit, an unusually far-fetched or elaborate *metaphor or *simile presenting a surprisingly apt parallel between two apparently dissimilar things or feelings: 'Griefe is a puddle, and reflects not cleare / Your beauties rayes' (T. Carew). Under *Petrarchan influence, European poetry of the *Renaissance cultivated fanciful comparisons and conceits to a high degree of ingenuity, either as the basis for whole poems (notably Donne's 'The Flea') or as an incidental decorative device. Poetic conceits are prominent in Elizabethan love *sonnets, in *metaphysical poetry, and in the French dramatic verse of Corneille and Racine. Conceits often employ the devices of *hyperbole, *paradox, and *oxymoron.

concordance, an alphabetical index of all the significant words used in a text or related group of texts, indicating all the places in which each word is used. Concordances to the Bible and to the complete works of Shakespeare have been followed, especially since the advent of computers, by similar reference books on other works.

concrete poetry, a kind of picture made out of printed type, and regarded in the 1950s and 1960s, when it enjoyed an international vogue, as an experimental form of poetry. It usually involves a punning kind of typography in which the visual pattern enacts or corresponds in some way to the sense of the word or phrase represented: a well-known early example is Guillaume Apollinaire's poem 'Il pleut' ('It rains', 1918), in which the words appear to be falling down the page like rain. The Scottish artist and poet Ian Hamilton Finlay is one of the few significant practitioners in English; his works come closer to sculpture than to two-dimensional art. Most concrete poems are apprehended instantaneously by the viewer as visual shapes, since they dispense with the linear sequence demanded by language; these therefore have little claim to the status of poetry. Others are closer to the traditional form of *pattern poetry, in which typographical presentation supports an already coherent poem.

confessional poetry, an autobiographical mode of verse that reveals the poet's personal problems with unusual frankness. The term is usually applied to certain poets of the United States from the late 1950s to the late 1960s, notably Robert Lowell, whose *Life Studies* (1959) and *For the Union Dead* (1964) deal with his divorce and mental breakdowns. Lowell's candour had been encouraged in part by that of the gay poet Allen Ginsberg in *Howl* (1956) and by the intensely personal poetry of Theodore Roethke. Other important examples of confessional poetry are Anne Sexton's *To Bedlam and Part Way Back* (1960) and *All My Pretty Ones*

(1962), including poems on abortion and life in mental hospitals; John Berryman's *Dream Songs* (1964) on alcoholism and insanity; Sylvia Plath's poems on suicide in *Ariel* (1965); and W. D. Snodgrass's *Heart's Needle* (1969) on his divorce. The term is sometimes used more loosely to refer to any personal or autobiographical poetry, but its distinctive sense depends on the candid examination of what were at the time of writing virtually unmentionable kinds of private distress. The genuine strengths of confessional poets, combined with the pity evoked by their high suicide rate (Berryman, Sexton, and Plath all killed themselves), encouraged in the reading public a romantic confusion between poetic excellence and inner torment.

confidant(e), a minor or secondary character in a play (or other literary work), in whom the *protagonist confides, revealing his or her state of mind in dialogue rather than in *soliloquies. Commonly the trusted servant of the leading lady in drama has the role of confidante: Charmian, for example, in Shakespeare's *Antony and Cleopatra*. See also *ficelle*, soubrette.

connotation, the range of further associations that a word or phrase suggests in addition to its straightforward dictionary meaning (the primary sense known as its **denotation**); or one of these secondary meanings. A word's connotations can usually be formulated as a series of qualities, contexts, and emotional responses commonly associated with its *referent (that to which it refers). Which of these will be activated by the word will depend on the context in which it is used, and to some degree on the reader or hearer. *Metaphors are made possible by the fact that the two terms they identify both have overlapping connotations. For example, the word *worm* denotes a small, slender invertebrate; but its connotation of slow burrowing activity also allows an ingratiating person to be described metaphorically as 'worming his way into favour', while other connotations based on emotional response (sliminess, insignificance) permit a person to be described simply as 'a worm'. *Adjective*: **connotative.** *Verb*: **connote.**

consonance, the repetition of identical or similar consonants in neighbouring words whose vowel sounds are different (e.g. *coming home*, *hot foot*). The term is most commonly used, though, for a special case of such repetition in which the words are identical except for the stressed vowel sound (*group/grope*, *middle/muddle*, *wonder/wander*); this device, combining *alliteration and terminal consonance, is sometimes known more precisely as 'rich consonance', and is frequently used in modern poetry at the ends of verse lines as an alternative to full rhyme (*see* half-rhyme). Consonance may be regarded as the counterpart to the vowel-sound repetition known as *assonance. The adjective **consonantal** is sometimes ambiguous in that it also means, more generally, 'pertaining to consonants'.

conte, the French word for a tale, applied since the 19th century to short stories, but previously used to denote a more fanciful kind of short prose fiction, usually both witty and morally instructive. Voltaire's *Zadig* (1747) and *Candide* (1759) belong to this category, along with some works by Perrault, La Fontaine, and others.

content, the term commonly used to refer to what is said in a literary work, as opposed to how it is said (that is, to the *form or *style). Distinctions between form and content are necessarily abstractions made for the sake of analysis, since in any actual work there can be no content that has not in some way been formed, and no purely empty form. The indivisibility of form and content, though, is something of a critical truism which often obscures the degree to which a work's matter can survive changes in its manner (in *revisions, translations, and *paraphrases); and it is only by positing some other manner in which this matter can be presented that one is able in analysis to isolate the specific form of a given work.

context, those parts of a *text preceding and following any particular passage, giving it a meaning fuller or more identifiable than if it were read in isolation. The context of any statement may be understood to comprise immediately neighbouring *signs (including punctuation such as quotation marks), or any part of—or the whole of—the remaining text, or the biographical, social, cultural, and historical circumstances in which it is made (including the intended audience or reader). The case of *irony shows clearly how the meaning of a statement can be completely reversed by a knowledge of its context. An interpretation of any passage or text that offers to explain it in terms of its context is sometimes said to **contextualize** it. *Adjective*: **contextual**.

convention, an established practice—whether in technique, style, structure, or subject-matter—commonly adopted in literary works by customary and implicit agreement or precedent rather than by natural necessity. The clearest cases of the 'unnatural' devices known as conventions appear in drama, where the audience implicitly agrees to suspend its disbelief and to regard the stage as a battlefield or kitchen, the actors as historical monarchs or fairy godmothers; likewise author and audience observe an unwritten agreement that a character speaking an *aside cannot be heard by other characters on stage. But conventions are, in less immediately striking ways, essential to poetry and to prose fiction as well: the use of *metre, *rhyme, and *stanzaic forms is conventional, as are the *narrative techniques of the *short story (e.g. the neat or surprising ending) and the *novel (including chronological presentation and *point of view), and the *stock characters of both fiction and drama. Some dramatic and literary forms are clearly composed of very elaborate or very recognizable conventions: opera, *melodrama, *kabuki, the pastoral *elegy, the *chivalric romance, the detective story, and the *Gothic novel are instances. In these and other cases an interrelated set of conventions in both *form and *content has constituted a *genre. Since the advent of *Romanticism and of *realism in the 19th century, however, it has become less apparent (although no less true) that literature is conventional, because realism—and later, *naturalism—attempted as far as possible to diminish or conceal those conventions considered unlifelike while Romanticism tried to discard those that were insincere, thus giving rise to that pejorative sense of 'conventional' which devalues traditionally predictable forms. As much modern criticism has to argue, such rebellions against conventions are fated to generate new conventions of their own, which may be less elaborate and less noticeable in their time. This does not render innovation futile, since the new conventions will often be appropriate to changed conditions, but it does mean that while some literary works may be 'unconventional', none can be conventionless. Literary theorists (notably those influenced by *structuralism) tend to confirm the inevitability of conventions by appealing to modern linguistics, which claims that languages can produce meanings only from '*arbitrary' or conventional *signs.

conversation poem, the term often applied to certain important *blank-verse poems written by Samuel Taylor Coleridge in the late 1790s. These are addressed to close friends, and are characterized by an informal but serious manner of deliberation that expands from a particular setting. Apart from 'The Nightingale' (1798)—which Coleridge subtitled 'A Conversation Poem'—the group of poems includes 'This Lime-Tree Bower My Prison', 'Frost at Midnight' (addressed to his infant son), and 'Fears in Solitude'. There are some equivalents among the poems of his friend William Wordsworth—most importantly 'Tintern Abbey' (1798). Sometimes the term 'conversation poem' or 'conversation piece' is applied more generally to informal verse *epistles by other poets.

copy-text, the specific *text used as the basis for a later *edition of a given work. The scholarly editor of a literary work by a deceased author will decide upon the copy-text and reproduce this, accompanied by lists of variant readings found in other editions (or manuscripts) of the same work. Standard editorial procedure is to adopt as the copy-text the last edition of the work that was published during the author's lifetime; but there may be strong reasons for preferring the first published edition, or a manuscript version, or a set of proofs corrected by the author.

corpus, a related 'body' of writings, usually sharing the same author or subject-matter. *See also* canon, oeuvre.

coterie [koh-tĕ-ri], a small group of writers (and others) bound together more by friendship and habitual association than by a common literary cause or style that might unite a school or movement. The term often has pejorative connotations of exclusive cliquishness. The *Bloomsbury group is one well-known example. See also *cénacle*, salon.

country house poem, a minor genre of poetry which has some importance in 17th-century English verse. It is defined by its subject-matter, which is the fruitfulness and stability of a patron's country estate, and the patron's own conservative virtues. Ben Jonson's 'To Penshurst' (1616) is the model in English, based partly on Latin poems by Martial and Horace. Later examples include Thomas Carew's 'To Saxham' (1640), and Andrew Marvell's 'Upon Appleton House' (written *c*.1652).

coup de théâtre [koo dĕ tay-**ahtr**], a sudden, surprising turn of events that gives a new twist to the plot of a play. Typical *coups de théâtre* involve the unveiling of a disguised character or the reappearance of one assumed by the audience to be dead. *See also* peripeteia.

couplet [kup-lit], a pair of rhyming verse lines, usually of the same length; one of the most widely used verse-forms in European poetry. Chaucer established the use of couplets in English, notably in the *Canterbury Tales*, using rhymed iambic *pentameters later known as *heroic couplets: a form revived in the 17th century by Ben Jonson, Dryden and others, partly as the equivalent in *heroic drama of the *alexandrine couplets which were the standard verse-form of French drama in that century. Alexander Pope followed Dryden's use of heroic couplets in non-dramatic verse to become the master of the form, notably in his use of *closed couplets. The octosyllablic couplet (of 8-syllable or 4-stress lines) is also commonly found in English verse. A couplet may also stand alone as an *epigram, or form part of a larger *stanza, or (as in Shakespeare) round off a *sonnet or a dramatic *scene. *See also* distich.

courtesy book, a book that gives advice to aspiring young courtiers in etiquette and other aspects of behaviour expected at royal or noble courts. This kind of work—sometimes written in verse—first became popular in various parts of Europe in the late Middle Ages. In the *Renaissance, some important courtesy books expanded more philosophically on the nature of the ideal gentleman and his varied accomplishments. The most influential of these was Baldessare Castiglione's *Il Libro del Cortegiano* (1528), a sequence of dialogues on court life and platonic love. English examples include Henry Peacham's *The Compleat Gentleman* (1622).

courtly love, a modern term (coined by the French scholar Gaston Paris in 1883, as *amour courtois*) for the literary cult of heterosexual love that emerged among the French aristocracy from the late 11th century onwards, with a profound effect on subsequent Western attitudes to love. Probably influenced by Arabic love poetry, the *troubadours of southern France were followed by northern French *trouvères, by German *Minnesänger, and by Dante, Petrarch, and other Italian poets in converting sexual desire from a degrading necessity of physical life into a spiritually ennobling emotion, almost a religious vocation. An elaborate code of behaviour evolved around the tormented male lover's abject obedience to a disdainful, idealized lady, who was usually his social superior. Some of these conventions may derive from misreadings of the Roman poet Ovid, but this form of adoration also imitated both feudal servitude and Christian worship, despite celebrating the excitements of clandestine adultery (as in stories of Lancelot and Guinevere) rather than the then merely economic relation of marriage. The most important literary treatments of courtly love appear in Chrétien de Troyes's *romance *Lancelot* (late 12th century), and in the first part of the 13th-century allegorical poem, the *Roman de la Rose* by

Guillaume de Lorris, later translated by Chaucer. Middle English
literature shows less enthusiasm for, or understanding of, courtly love:
Chaucer treated the cult sceptically, if sympathetically, but its later
influence, established and modified through the *Petrarchan tradition,
is strong in 16th-century English *lyrics. For a fuller account, consult
David Burnley, *Courtliness and Literature in Medieval England* (1998).

Cowleyan ode, *see* ode.

cretic, *see* amphimacer.

crisis, a decisive point in the plot of a play or story, upon which the
outcome of the remaining action depends, and which ultimately
precipitates the *catastrophe or *dénouement. *See also* anagnorisis,
climax, peripeteia.

criterion [kry-teer-iŏn] (plural **-eria**), a standard or principle by which
literary works can be judged or compared.

criticism, the reasoned discussion of literary works, an activity which
may include some or all of the following procedures, in varying
proportions: the defence of *literature against moralists and censors,
classification of a work according to its *genre, interpretation of its
meaning, analysis of its structure and style, judgement of its worth by
comparison with other works, estimation of its likely effect on readers,
and the establishment of general principles by which literary works
(individually, in categories, or as a whole) can be evaluated and
understood. Contrary to the everyday sense of criticism as 'fault-finding',
much modern criticism (particularly of the academic kind) assumes that
the works it discusses are valuable; the functions of judgement and
analysis having to some extent become divided between the market
(where reviewers ask 'Is this worth buying?') and the educational world
(where academics ask 'Why is this so good?'). The various kinds of
criticism fall into several overlapping categories: theoretical, practical,
*impressionistic, *affective, *prescriptive, or descriptive. Criticism
concerned with revealing the author's true motive or intention
(sometimes called 'expressive' criticism) emerged from *Romanticism
to dominate much 19th- and 20th-century critical writing, but has
tended to give way to 'objective' criticism, focusing on the work itself (as
in *New Criticism and *structuralism), and to a shift of attention to
the reader in *reader-response criticism. Particular schools of
criticism also seek to understand literature in terms of its relations to

history, politics, gender, social class, mythology, linguistic theory, or psychology. *See also* exegesis, hermeneutics, metacriticism, poetics.

critique, a considered assessment of a literary work, usually in the form of an essay or review. Also, in philosophy, politics, and the social sciences, a systematic inquiry into the nature of some principle, idea, institution, or ideology, usually devoted to revealing its limits or self-contradictions.

crossed rhyme, the rhyming of one word in the middle of a long verse line with a word in a similar position in the next line. Sometimes found in rhyming *couplets, crossed rhyme has the effect of making the couplet sound like a *quatrain rhyming *abab*, as in Swinburne's 'Hymn to Proserpine' (1866):

Will ye bridle the deep sea with reins, will ye chasten the high sea with rods?
Will ye take her to chain her with chains, who is older than all ye Gods?

crown, a linked sequence of *lyric poems (usually *sonnets), in which the last line of each poem is repeated as the first line of the next, until the final line of the last (usually the seventh) poem repeats the opening line of the first. An Italian form of poetic tribute to the person addressed, the crown of sonnets was used in English by John Donne in the introductory sequence of his *Holy Sonnets* (1633). Sir Philip Sidney had earlier written a crown of *dizains* in his *Arcadia* (1590).

crux (plural **cruces**), a difficult or ambiguous passage in a literary work, upon which interpretation of the rest of the work depends.

cultural materialism, an approach to the analysis of literature, drama, and other cultural forms, adopted by some critics, mainly in Britain, since the early 1980s. Its principles, derived from western Marxist traditions, were outlined most influentially by Raymond Williams in his later writings, notably *Problems in Materialism and Culture* (1980) and *Culture* (1981). Here the orthodox Marxist model of an economic 'base' determining a cultural (and political, religious etc.) 'superstructure' is challenged and replaced by a more flexible model in which cultural activities themselves are regarded as 'material' and productive processes. Cultural materialist approaches to literature emphasize the social and economic contexts (publishing, theatre, education) in which it is produced and consumed. They are also interested in the ways in which the meanings of literary and dramatic works are remade in new social and institutional contexts, especially in re-stagings of Shakespeare. Critics who have identified their work as cultural materialist include Alan Sinfield, Catherine Belsey, and Jonathan Dollimore. Their approach has been distinguished from the somewhat similar school of *new historicism in that they hold a less pessimistic view of the prospects of cultural dissidence and resistance to established powers. For a fuller account, consult Scott Wilson, *Cultural Materialism* (1995).

curtain-raiser, a brief dramatic entertainment, usually a light one-act play, preceding the full-length drama that formed the main part of a theatre's programme. A common form in the late 19th-century theatre, although now obsolete.

curtal sonnet, the name given by the English poet Gerard Manley Hopkins (1844–89) to a curtailed form of the *sonnet which he invented. The curtal sonnet has ten lines with an additional half-line at the end. Hopkins wrote two of these: 'Peace' and 'Pied Beauty'.

cut-up, a technique used by the novelist William S. Burroughs in some passages of his works, notably *The Ticket That Exploded* (1962), whereby a pre-existing written text is cut into segments which are reshuffled at random before being printed in the resulting accidental order. *See also* aleatory, collage.

cyberpunk, a phase of American *science fiction in the 1980s and 1990s most often associated with William Gibson's novel *Neuromancer* (1984) and its sequels, and with the work of Bruce Sterling, who edited *Mirrorshades: The Cyberpunk Anthology* (1986). By contrast with earlier mainstream science fiction, which commonly implied a utopian confidence in technological progress, cyberpunk fiction is influenced by the gloomier world of hard-boiled detective fiction and by *film noir* thrillers; it foresees a near future in which sinister multinational corporations dominate the 'cyberspace' (that is, the world computerized information network) upon which an impoverished metropolitan populace depends. In a broader sense, the term refers to a larger body of work in the 1980s and after—including such films as Ridley Scott's *Blade Runner* (1982)—in which the interpenetration of human and technological or electronic realms, in androids or in 'virtual' reality, is taken as the basis of fictional speculation, usually *dystopian. For fuller accounts, consult Larry McCaffery (ed.), *Storming the Reality Studio* (1992).

cycle, a group of works, usually narrative poems, that either share a common theme or subject (e.g. the Trojan war, Charlemagne, the Knights of the Round Table), or are linked together as a sequence. In addition to *epics, *sagas, *romances, and *chansons de geste*, which scholars have categorized into different cycles, the *mystery plays of the Middle Ages that were performed as a sequence during the same festival at a particular place are referred to as the York Cycle, the Chester Cycle etc. The term is also applied to sequences of sonnets by the same author, and sometimes to sequences of novels or stories (see *roman-fleuve*). *Adjective*: **cyclic**.

dactyl, a metrical unit (*foot) of verse, having one stressed syllable followed by two unstressed syllables, as in the word *carefully* (or, in *quantitative verse, one long syllable and two short ones). Dactylic *hexameters were used in Greek and Latin *epic poetry, and in the elegiac *distich, but **dactylic verse** is rare in English: Tennyson's 'The Charge of the Light Brigade' uses it, as does Thomas Hardy's 'The Voice', which begins

> Woman much missed, how you call to me, call to me

See also falling rhythm, metre, triple metre.

Dada or **Dadaism,** an *avant-garde* movement of anarchic protest against bourgeois society, religion, and art, founded in 1916 in Switzerland by Tristan Tzara, a Rumanian-born French poet. From 1919 the Dadaist group assembled in Paris, issuing nihilistic manifestos against the culture which had been discredited by the 1914–18 war, and experimenting with anti-logical poetry and *collage pictures and sculptures. The group included the artists Marcel Duchamp and Man Ray, the poet-sculptor Hans Arp, and the young poets André Breton, Paul Éluard, and Louis Aragon. Dada was short-lived, but it ushered in the *Surrealism which superseded it from 1922.

débat [day-bah], a poem in the form of a debate between two characters, who are usually *personifications of opposed principles or qualities: body and soul, water and wine, winter and summer, etc. The *débat* was much practised in Europe during the 12th and 13th centuries, both in Latin and in the *vernacular languages. The outstanding English example is the early 13th-century poem *The Owl and the Nightingale*, in which the two birds—probably representing religious and secular poetry respectively—dispute over the benefits they bring to mankind. In French, François Villon later wrote a *débat* between the heart and the body. The *débat* commonly ends with an inconclusive reference of the issue to a judge. The form has some classical precedents in the *agon of Aristophanes' comedies and the *eclogues of Theocritus; and it may in turn have influenced the structures of later medieval drama. *See also* amoebean verses, dialogue.

decadence, a state of decay shown in either the inferior literary quality or the looser moral standards of any period's works compared with a preceding period, as with *Hellenistic Greek or post-*Augustan Latin literatures; or the 19th-century literary movement in Paris, London, and Vienna that cultivated the exhausted refinement and artificiality it admired in the 'decadent' ages of Greek and Latin literature. Although the term has various unfavourable connotations ranging from simple inferiority to moral 'degeneracy', several writers in the late 19th century accepted the description proudly, thus implying a shocking parallel between their imperial societies and the decline of the Roman empire. The Decadent movement, closely associated with the doctrines of *Aestheticism, can be traced back to the writings of Théophile Gautier and Edgar Allan Poe in the 1830s, but became a significant presence only after the publication of Charles Baudelaire's influential collection of poems, *Les Fleurs du mal* (1857), and culminated in the *fin-de-siècle* culture of the 1880s and 1890s. The basic principle of this decadence, expounded in the 1860s by Gautier and Baudelaire, was complete opposition to Nature: hence its systematic cultivation of drugs, cosmetics, Catholic ritual, supposedly 'unnatural' sexual practices, and sterility and artificiality in all things. A complete decadent way of life is portrayed in Joris-Karl Huysmans' novel *A Rebours* (*Against the Grain* or *Against Nature*, 1884), upon which Oscar Wilde's *The Picture of Dorian Gray* (1891) is partly based. In France, decadence became almost synonymous with the work of the *Symbolists, some of whom were associated in the 1880s with the journal *Le Décadent*. In England, it emerged from the *Pre-Raphaelite circle, in the poetry of D. G. Rossetti and in Swinburne's scandalous *Poems and Ballads* (1866), leading to the work of Wilde, Ernest Dowson, and Arthur Symons in the 1890s, until Wilde's imprisonment in 1895 suddenly ended the decadent episode. Symons, in his essay 'The Decadent Movement in Literature' (1893), described the phenomenon as 'an interesting disease' typical of an over-luxurious civilization, characterized by 'an intense self-consciousness, a restless curiosity in research, an over-subtilizing refinement upon refinement, a spiritual and moral perversity'. For a fuller account, consult R. K. R. Thornton, *The Decadent Dilemma* (1983).

deconstruction, a philosophically sceptical approach to the possibility of coherent meaning in language, initiated by the French philosopher Jacques Derrida in a series of works published in 1967 (later translated as *Speech and Phenomena*, *Of Grammatology*, and *Writing and Difference*), and adopted by several leading literary critics in the United States—notably at Yale University—from the early 1970s onwards. Derrida's claim is that the dominant Western tradition of thought has attempted to establish grounds of certainty and truth by repressing the limitless instability of language. This '*logocentric' tradition sought some absolute source or guarantee of meaning (a 'transcendental signified') which could centre or stabilize the uncertainties of signification, through a set of 'violent hierarchies' privileging a central term over a marginal one: nature over culture, male over female, and most importantly speech over writing. The '*phonocentric' suspicion of writing as a parasite upon the authenticity of speech is a crucial target of Derrida's subversive approach to Western philosophy, in which he inverts and dissolves conceptual hierarchies to show that the repressed or marginalized term has always already contaminated the privileged or central term. Thus, drawing on Saussure's theory of the *sign, Derrida argues that the stable self-identity which we attribute to speech as the authentic source of meaning is illusory, since language operates as a self-contained system of internal differences rather than of positive terms or presences: writing, distrusted in the Western 'metaphysics of presence' because it displays the absence of any authenticating voice, is in this sense logically prior to speech.

Derrida's central concept (although in principle it ought not to occupy such a 'hierarchical' position) is presented in his coining of the term **différance*, a French *portmanteau word combining 'difference' with 'deferral' to suggest that the differential nature of meanings in language ceaselessly defers or postpones any determinate meaning: language is an endless chain or 'play of *différance*' which logocentric discourses try vainly to fix to some original or final term that can never be reached. Deconstructive readings track down within a *text the *aporia or internal contradiction that undermines its claims to coherent meaning; or they reveal how texts can be seen to deconstruct themselves. Derrida's difficult and paradoxical attitude to the metaphysical tradition seeks to subvert it while also claiming that there is no privileged vantage-point from which to do this from outside the instabilities of language. Deconstruction thus undermines its own radical scepticism by admitting that it leaves everything exactly as it was; it is an unashamedly self-contradictory effort to think the 'unthinkable', often by recourse to strange *neologisms, *puns, and other word-play. Although initially

directed against the scientific pretensions of *structuralism in the
human sciences, it was welcomed enthusiastically into literary studies at
Yale University and elsewhere in the English-speaking world, partly
because it seemed to place literary problems of *figurative language and
interpretation above philosophers' and historians' claims to truth, and
partly because it opened up limitless possibilities of interpretation.
The writings of Paul de Man, Barbara Johnson, J. Hillis Miller, and
Geoffrey Hartman in the 1970s and 1980s applied and extended
Derrida's concepts to critical questions of interpretation, tending to
challenge the status of the author's intention or of the external world as a
source of meaning in texts, and questioning the boundary between
criticism and literature. These and other deconstructionists came under
fierce attack for dogmatic nihilism and wilful obscurity. For an extended
introduction to this sometimes bewildering school of thought, consult
Christopher Norris, *Deconstruction: Theory and Practice* (1982). *See also*
dissemination, indeterminacy, post-structuralism.

decorum [di-kor-ŭm], a standard of appropriateness by which certain
styles, characters, forms, and actions in literary works are deemed
suitable to one another within a hierarchical model of culture bound by
class distinctions. Derived from Horace's *Ars Poetica* (*c*.20 BCE) and other
works of classical criticism, decorum was a major principle of late
*Renaissance taste and of *neoclassicism. It ranked and fixed the
various literary *genres in 'high', 'middle', and 'low' stations, and
expected the style, characters, and actions in each to conform to its
assigned level: thus a *tragedy or *epic should be written in a high or
'grand' style about high-ranking characters performing grand deeds,
whereas a *comedy should treat humble characters and events in a 'low'
or colloquial style. The mixture of high and low levels, as in Shakespeare,
was seen as indecorous, although it could be exploited for humorous
effect in *burlesques and *mock-heroic works. The strict application
of these principles of decorum was overturned by the advent of
*Romanticism; although in a general sense writers always suit style to
subject-matter according to their purposes. *See also* convention, diction,
style.

deep structure, the underlying structure of meaning in any utterance,
as opposed to the observable arrangement (the **surface structure**) in
which it is presented. The distinction between deep structure and
surface structure is a major principle of the revolution in grammatical
theory led by the American linguist Noam Chomsky in the 1960s, and

has been adopted by some theorists of *narratology. According to
Chomsky, the deep structure of a sentence is its underlying semantic
content, an abstraction decoded from the actual syntactic sequence of its
surface structure (*see* semantics, syntax). Thus the sentence *The mariner
shot the albatross* differs in surface structure from *The albatross was shot by
the mariner*, but shares the same deep structure. The distinction is broadly
similar to that between *content and *form. Some narratologists have
attempted to define the deep structures of narratives on the model of
linguistic analyses of sentences: thus A. J. Greimas distinguishes the
underlying *binary oppositions between basic roles (or *actants) from
their surface realization as contrasts between characters in a sequential
*plot.

defamiliarization, the distinctive effect achieved by literary works in
disrupting our habitual perception of the world, enabling us to 'see'
things afresh, according to the theories of some English Romantic poets
and of *Russian Formalism. Samuel Taylor Coleridge in *Biographia
Literaria* (1817) wrote of the 'film of familiarity' that blinds us to the
wonders of the world, and that Wordworth's poetry aimed to remove.
P. B. Shelley in his essay 'The Defence of Poetry' (written 1821) also
claims that poetry 'makes familiar objects be as if they were not familiar'
by stripping 'the veil of familiarity from the world'. In modern usage, the
term corresponds to Viktor Shklovsky's use of the Russian word
ostranenie ('making strange') in his influential essay 'Poetry as Technique'
(1917). Shklovsky argued that art exists in order to recover for us the
sensation of life which is diminished in the 'automatized' routine of
everyday experience. He and the other Formalists set out to define the
devices by which literary works achieve this effect, usually in terms of
the '*foregrounding' of the linguistic medium. Brecht's theory of the
*alienation effect in drama starts from similar grounds. *See also*
literariness.

defective foot, an incomplete *foot in a line of metrical verse. The
term, sometimes applied to *catalectic lines, is misleadingly pejorative,
since the deficiency is usually not in the verse itself but rather in the
metrical analysis that attempts to make the *metre conform to an
abstract scheme of feet. *See also* acephalous, truncation.

deixis, a term used in linguistics to denote those aspects of an utterance
that refer to and depend upon the situation in which the utterance is
made. **Deictic** words indicate the situational 'co-ordinates' of person

(*I/you*, *us/them*), place (*here/there*, *this/that*), and time (*now/then*, *yesterday/ today*).

demotic [di-mot-ik], derived from or using the language of the common people rather than the more formal style of a priesthood or other educated élite. *See also* colloquialism, vernacular.

demotion, the use of a stressed syllable in an 'offbeat' position in a metrical verse line that would normally be occupied by an unstressed syllable. An important means of variation in English verse, demotion usually has the effect of slowing the rhythm of the line, as in the *iambic verse of Tennyson's 'Ulysses':

> The long day wanes, the slow moon climbs; the deep
> Moans round with many voices

where 'day', 'moon', and 'Moans' are all demoted to offbeat positions. This does not mean that they should be read as unstressed: in fact the effect depends upon their retaining at least some of their normal *stress. The demotion rules formulated by Derek Attridge in *The Rhythms of English Verse* (1982) permit a stressed syllable to realize an offbeat between two other stressed syllables or at the beginning of a line before a stressed syllable. In similar positions in *triple metre, a stressed syllable may realize an offbeat, either on its own, or with an unstressed syllable, or (more rarely) with another stressed syllable. The concepts of demotion and *promotion account more successfully for those metrical variations that traditional *prosody described in terms of *substitution. *See also* metre.

denotation, *see* connotation.

dénouement [day-noo-mah^n], the clearing up or 'untying' of the complications of the *plot in a play or story; usually a final scene or chapter in which mysteries, confusions, and doubtful destinies are clarified. *See also* catastrophe.

deus ex machina [day-uus eks mak- ină], the 'god from a machine' who was lowered on to the stage by mechanical contrivance in some ancient Greek plays (notably those of Euripides) to solve the problems of the *plot at a stroke. A later example is Shakespeare's introduction of Hymen into the last scene of *As You Like It* to marry off the main characters. The term is now used pejoratively for any improbable or unexpected contrivance by which an author resolves the complications of the plot in a play or novel, and which has not been convincingly prepared for in the preceding action: the discovery of a lost will was a favourite resort of Victorian novelists. See also *coup de théâtre*, dénouement, machinery.

device, an all-purpose term used to describe any literary technique deliberately employed to achieve a specific effect. In the theories of *Russian Formalism and *Brechtian theatre, the phrase 'baring the device' refers to the way that some works expose or highlight the means (linguistic or theatrical) by which they operate on us, rather than conceal them. *See also* foregrounding, metadrama.

diachronic [dy-ă-**kron**-ik], relating to historical change over a span of time. The revolution in linguistics begun by Ferdinand de Saussure in the *Cours de linguistique générale* (1915) is founded partly on the distinction between the diachronic study of linguistic features evolving in time and the *synchronic study of a language as a complete system operating at a given moment. Saussure argued, against the historical bias of 19th-century *philology, that the synchronic dimension or 'axis' must be given precedence. *Noun:* **diachrony**.

diacritic, a mark placed above or below a letter or syllable to specify its distinctive sound value. Diacritics commonly found are the acute accent (é), grave accent (è), circumflex (ô), umlaut (ö), and cedilla (ç). Diacritical markings commonly used in *scansion include the macron (–) for long syllables, the breve (⌣) for short syllables, the acute accent or the virgule (′) for stressed syllables, and the ˣ symbol for unstressed syllables.

diaeresis or **dieresis** [dy-**err**-ĕsis] (plural **-eses**), a Greek word for 'division', used in three different senses: (i) in classical *prosody, the coincidence of a word ending with the end of a *foot; (ii) the separation of two adjacent vowels into distinct sounds (e.g. Zoë, coöperate), also the umlaut mark which indicates this; (iii) in *rhetoric, a *figure by which the parts or attributes of anything are enumerated.

dialect, a distinctive variety of a language, spoken by members of an identifiable regional group, nation, or social class. Dialects differ from one another in pronunciation, vocabulary, and (often) in grammar. Traditionally they have been regarded as variations from a 'standard' educated form of the language, but modern linguists point out that standard forms are themselves dialects which have come to predominate for social and political reasons. The study of variations between different dialects is known as **dialectology**. *Adjective:* **dialectal**.

dialectic, (1) the art of formal reasoning, especially the procedure of seeking truth through debate or discussion; (2) the reasoning or logical structure that holds together a continuous argument or exposition; (3) the interplay of contradictory principles or opposed forces, as understood in the European tradition of philosophy influenced by G. W. F. Hegel and including Marx and Engels. Some schematic versions of **dialectical** philosophy speak of a unification of opposites in which the *thesis* is opposed by the *antithesis* but united with it in a higher *synthesis*.

dialogic or **dialogical,** characterized or constituted by the interactive, responsive nature of *dialogue rather than by the single-mindedness of *monologue. The term is important in the writings of the Russian theorist Mikhail Bakhtin, whose book *Problems of Dostoevsky's Poetics* (1929) contrasts the dialogic or *polyphonic interplay of various characters' voices in Dostoevsky's novels with the 'monological' subordination of characters to the single viewpoint of the author in Tolstoy's. In the same year, *Marxism and the Philosophy of Language* (probably by Bakhtin, although published under the name of V. N. Voloshinov) argued, against Saussure's theory of la *langue*, that actual utterances are 'dialogic' in that they are embedded in a context of dialogue and thus respond to an interlocutor's previous utterances and/or try to draw a particular response from a specific auditor. *See also* carnivalization, multi-accentuality. *Noun:* **dialogism.**

dialogue, spoken exchanges between or among characters in a dramatic or narrative work; or a literary form in prose or verse based on a debate or discussion, usually between two speakers. Dialogue is clearly a major aspect of drama, and is usually a significant component of prose fictions and of some narrative poetry, as in the *ballad. As a literary form, the dialogue was much favoured in ancient Greek and Latin literature for *didactic and *satirical purposes as well as in *pastoral poetry. The *Socratic dialogues of Plato (4th century BC) are the most influential ancient works in dialogue form; a modern counterpart is Wilde's *The Critic as Artist* (1891). The *débat* and the *flyting are special varieties of verse dialogue. In modern poetry, W. B. Yeats often used the dialogue form, as in 'Michael Robartes and the Dancer' (1921). *See also* amoebean verses.

diction, the choice of words used in a literary work. A writer's diction may be characterized, for example, by *archaism, or by *Latinate or Anglo-Saxon derivations; and it may be described according to the oppositions formal/colloquial, abstract/concrete, and literal/figurative. For the specific *conventions of diction in poetry, *see* poetic diction.

didactic [dy-**dak**-tik], instructive; designed to impart information, advice, or some doctrine of morality or philosophy. Much of the most ancient surviving literature is didactic, containing genealogies, proverbial wisdom, and religious instruction. Most European literary works of the Middle Ages have a strong didactic element, usually expounding doctrines of the Church. Practical advice has often been presented in verse, as in the *Georgics* (37–30 BCE) of Virgil, which give advice on farming, and in the imitative *georgics of the 18th century. Since the ascendancy of *Romanticism and *Aestheticism in the 19th century, didactic writing has been viewed unfavourably as foreign to true art, so that the term **didacticism** refers (usually pejoratively) to the use of literary means to a doctrinal end. Some imaginative works still contain practical information, however: B. S. Johnson's novel *Christie Malry's Own Double Entry* (1973) contains precise instructions for the manufacture of petrol bombs. The boundaries of didactic literature are open to dispute, since both the presence and the prominence of doctrinal content are subject to differing interpretations. In the broadest sense, most *allegories and *satires implying a moral or political view may be regarded as didactic, along with many other kinds of work in which the *theme embodies some philosophical or other belief of the author. A stricter definition would confine the term to those works that explicitly tell readers what they should do. *See also* propagandism.

diegesis [dy-ĕ-**jee**-sis], an analytic term used in modern *narratology to designate the narrated events or *story (French, *histoire*) as a 'level' distinct from that of the *narration. The **diegetic** level of a narrative is that of the main story, whereas the 'higher' level at which the story is told is **extradiegetic** (i.e. standing outside the sphere of the main story). An *embedded tale-within-the-tale constitutes a lower level known as **hypodiegetic**. In an older sense outlined in Aristotle's *Poetics*, diegesis is the reporting or narration of events, contrasted with *mimesis, which is the imitative representation of them: so a character in a play who performs a certain action is engaged in mimesis, but if she recounts some earlier action, she is practising diegesis. The distinct is often cast as that between 'showing' and 'telling'.

dieresis, *see* diaeresis.

différance [dif-air-ah^n s], a term coined by the philosopher Jacques

Derrida to combine two senses of the French verb *différer* (to differ, and to defer or postpone) in a noun which is spelt differently from *différence* but pronounced in the same way. The point of this *neologism is to indicate simultaneously two senses in which language denies us the full presence of any meaning: first, that no linguistic element (according to Saussure's theory of the *sign) has a positive meaning, only an effect of meaning arising from its differences from other elements; second, that presence or fullness of meaning is always deferred from one sign to another in an endless sequence. Thus if you look up a word in a dictionary, all it can give you is other words to explain it; so—in theory, at least—you will then have to look these up, and so on without end. *Différance*, then, may be conceived as an underlying principle of non-identity which makes signification possible only by 'spacing out' both *signifiers and concepts (*signifieds) so that meaning appears merely as a 'trace' of other terms within or across any given term. Derrida has tried to avoid placing *différance* as a fixed concept, preferring to use it as an unstable term, although it is fundamental to his philosophy of *deconstruction. *See also* dissemination.

digression, a temporary departure from one subject to another more or less distantly related topic before the discussion of the first subject is resumed. A valuable technique in the art of storytelling, digression is also employed in many kinds of non-fictional writing and *oratory. *Adjective*: **digressive**. *See also* excursus.

dimeter [dim-it-er], a line of verse consisting of two metrical feet (*see* foot). In English verse, this means a line with two main *stresses. The term originally referred, in classical *prosody, to a line of two *dipodies, i.e. four feet.

Dionysian, *see* Apollonian.

diphthong, a vowel sound that changes noticeably in quality during the pronunciation of a syllable, as in the English words *wide*, *late*, *beer*, or *round*. Diphthongs are thus distinguished from simple vowels (*cat*, *feed* etc.), which are referred to by phoneticians as **monophthongs**. *Adjective*: **diphthongal**.

dipody [dip-ŏdi], a pair of metrical feet (*see* foot) considered as a single unit. Dipodic verse, commonly found in *ballads and nursery rhymes, is characterized by the pairing together of feet, in which one usually has a stronger *stress.

dirge, a song of lamentation in mourning for someone's death; or a poem in the form of such a song, and usually less elaborate than an *elegy. An ancient *genre employed by Pindar in Greek and notably by Propertius in Latin, the dirge also occurs in English, most famously in Ariel's song 'Full fathom five thy father lies' in Shakespeare's *The Tempest*.

dirty realism, a critical label attached since the early 1980s to a group of American short-story writers, of whom the best-known are Raymond Carver, Jayne Anne Phillips, and Tobias Wolff. The term refers to a tendency for their stories to recount incidents of impoverished life among blue-collar workers in small-town America, in a bare, unsensational style.

discours [dis-koor], the French word for *discourse or conversation. When it appears in this form in modern theoretical writings in English, it usually carries a special sense given to it by the linguist Émile Benveniste in his *Problèmes de linguistique générale* (1966), in which he distinguishes *discours* as a 'subjective' mode of speech (or writing) from *histoire*, which is apparently 'objective'. In *discours*, the present situation of speech or writing is indicated by signs of *deixis (e.g. the pronouns *I* and *you*, the adverbs *here*, *now*, *there* etc.) and by the use of tense (*she has gone* rather than *she went*). While *discours* thus displays its nature as an enunciation involving a relationship between a speaker/writer and a listener/reader, *histoire* conceals this by its concentration on the enounced (*see énoncé*). Confusingly, another distinction is made between these two terms in *narratology, where *histoire* is *story, and *discours* is language or *narration.

discourse, any extended use of speech or writing; or a formal exposition or dissertation. In linguistics, discourse is the name given to units of language longer than a single sentence; **discourse analysis** is the study of *cohesion and other relationships between sentences in written or spoken discourse. In modern cultural theory, especially in the *post-structuralism associated with the French historian Michel Foucault, the term has been used to denote any coherent body of statements that produces a self-confirming account of reality by defining an object of attention and generating concepts with which to analyse it (e.g. medical discourse, legal discourse, aesthetic discourse). The specific discourse in which a statement is made will govern the kinds of connections that can be made between ideas, and will involve certain assumptions about the kind of person(s) addressed. By extension, as a free-standing noun ('discourse' as such), the term denotes language in actual use within its social and ideological context and in institutionalized representations of the world called **discursive** practices. In general, the increased use of this term in modern cultural theory arises from dissatisfaction with the rather fixed and abstract term 'language' (see *langue*); by contrast, 'discourse' better indicates the specific contexts and relationships involved in historically produced uses of language. See *discours* for a further sense. *See also* episteme, rhetoric. For a fuller account, consult Sara Mills, *Discourse* (1997).

discovery, a term sometimes used as an English equivalent for *anagnorisis, that is, a point in a play or story at which a character recognizes the true state of affairs. *See also* dénouement.

discussion play, a kind of drama in which debate and discussion are more important than plot, action, or character. Some of Bernard Shaw's plays are of this kind, notably *Misalliance* (1910) and *Heartbreak House* (1919). *See also* problem play.

dissemination, in the terminology of *deconstruction, the dispersal of meanings among infinite possibilities; the effect of *différance* in the 'free play' of signification beyond the control of concepts or stable interpretation. Whereas *ambiguity usually involves a limited number of possible meanings, dissemination is an endless proliferation of possibilities. *See also* indeterminacy.

dissociation of sensibility, the separation of thought from feeling, which T. S. Eliot diagnosed as the weakness of English poetry from the Revolution of the 1640s until his own time. In his influential essay 'The Metaphysical Poets' (1921), Eliot argued that whereas in Donne and other pre-Revolutionary poets 'there is a direct sensuous apprehension of thought, or a recreation of thought into feeling', from the time of Milton and Dryden 'a dissociation of sensibility set in, from which we have never recovered'. This view had some influence in British and American criticism in the mid-20th century, notably in the *Cambridge school and among the *New Critics, but it has frequently been challenged as a misleading simplification of literary history.

dissonance, harshness of sound and/or rhythm, either inadvertent or deliberate. The term is nearly equivalent to *cacophony, but tends to denote a lack of harmony between sounds rather than the harshness of a particular sound in isolation. Browning, Hopkins, and many other poets have made deliberate use of dissonance. *Adjective*: **dissonant**.

distich [**dis**-tik], a pair of verse lines, usually making complete sense, as in the *closed couplet. The term is most often applied to the Greek verse form in which a dactylic *hexameter is followed by a 'pentameter' (actually composed of two dactylic half-lines of two-and-a-half feet each). This form, known as the **elegiac distich** or **elegiac couplet**, was used in Greek and Latin verse for *elegies and *epigrams, and later by some German poets including Goethe.

dithyramb [**dith**-i-ram], a form of *hymn or choral *lyric in which the god Dionysus was honoured in Greek religious festivities from about the 7th century BCE onwards. Later in Athenian competitions, dithyrambs were composed—by Pindar among others—on episodes from myths of other gods, and the arrangement in matched *strophes came to be relaxed. Dithyrambs seem to have been performed by a large *chorus of singers, possibly dressed as satyrs, to flute accompaniment. A rare English imitation is Dryden's *Alexander's Feast* (1697). The adjective **dithyrambic** is sometimes applied to *rhapsodies, or wildly impassioned chants.

dizain [dee-ze^{n}], a French verse *stanza of ten lines, of which each normally has ten syllables, or more rarely eight. The *dizain* was employed by French poets of the 15th and 16th centuries either as an independent poem rhyming *ababbccded* or as a stanza of the *ballade or *chant royal*. In English, Sir Philip Sidney wrote a *crown of *dizains* rhyming *ababbcacdd*.

doggerel, clumsy verse, usually monotonously rhymed, rhythmically awkward, and often shallow in sentiment, as in greetings cards. The notoriously irregular verses of William McGonagall (?1830–1902) are doggerel. Some poets, like Skelton and Stevie Smith, have deliberately imitated doggerel for comic effect. *See also* clerihew, Hudibrastic, light verse, Skeltonics.

domestic tragedy, a kind of *tragedy in which the leading characters belong to the middle class rather than to the royal or noble ranks usually represented in tragic drama, and in which the action concerns family affairs rather than public matters of state. A few English verse plays from Shakespeare's time belong to this category: the chief examples are the anonymous *Tragedy of Mr Arden of Feversham* (1592),

Thomas Heywood's *A Woman Killed with Kindness* (1603) and *A Yorkshire Tragedy* (1608, of uncertain authorship). Domestic tragedy was revived in prose by George Lillo with *The London Merchant* (1732) and his new version of *Arden of Feversham* (1759). Lillo's influence led to the appearance of 'domestic' prose dramas in Germany with G. E. Lessing's tragedy *Miss Sara Sampson* (1755), and in France with Diderot's *drames. A later revival is seen in the American tragedies of Tennessee Williams and Arthur Miller. Domestic tragedy is sometimes known as 'bourgeois tragedy'.

donnée, a French word for something 'given', sometimes used to refer to the original idea or starting-point from which a writer elaborates a complete work. This initial choice of subject-matter may be a very simple situation or a basic relationship between two characters which is then complicated as the work takes shape.

double entendre [doo-blah^n-tah^{n}dr], a French phrase for 'double meaning', adopted in English to denote a *pun in which a word or phrase has a second, usually sexual, meaning, as in Elizabethan uses of the verb 'die' referring both to death and to orgasm. *See also* ambiguity, equivoque.

double rhyme, a *rhyme on two syllables, the first stressed and the second unstressed (e.g. *tarry/marry, adore us/chorus*), also known as *feminine rhyme, and opposed to *masculine rhyme, which matches single stressed syllables.

drama, the general term for performances in which actors impersonate the actions and speech of fictional or historical characters (or non-human entities) for the entertainment of an audience, either on a stage or by means of a broadcast; or a particular example of this art, i.e. a play. Drama is usually expected to represent stories showing situations of conflict between characters, although the *monodrama is a special case in which only one performer speaks. Drama is a major *genre of literature, but includes non-literary forms (in *mime), and has several dimensions that lie beyond the domain of the literary **dramatist** or playwright (*see mise en scène*). The major dramatic genres in the West are *comedy and *tragedy, but several other kinds of dramatic work fall outside these categories (*see drame*, history play, masque, melodrama, morality play, mystery play, tragicomedy). **Dramatic poetry** is a category of verse composition for theatrical performance; the term is now commonly extended, however, to non-theatrical poems that involve a similar kind of impersonation, as in the *closet drama and the *dramatic monologue.

dramatic irony, *see* irony.

dramatic monologue, a kind of poem in which a single fictional or historical character other than the poet speaks to a silent 'audience' of one or more persons. Such poems reveal not the poet's own thoughts but the mind of the impersonated character, whose personality is revealed unwittingly; this distinguishes a dramatic monologue from a *lyric, while the implied presence of an auditor distinguishes it from a *soliloquy. Major examples of this form in English are Tennyson's 'Ulysses' (1842), Browning's 'Fra Lippo Lippi' (1855), and T. S. Eliot's 'The Love Song of J. Alfred Prufrock' (1917). Some plays in which only one character speaks, in the form of a *monologue or soliloquy, have also been called dramatic monologues; but to avoid confusion it is preferable to refer to these simply as monologues or as *monodramas. For a fuller account, consult Alan Sinfield, *Dramatic Monologue* (1977).

dramatis personae [dram-ă-tis per-**soh**-ny], the Latin phrase for 'persons of the play', used to refer collectively to the characters represented in a dramatic work (or, by extension, a *narrative work). This phrase is the conventional heading for a list of characters published in the text of a play or in a theatrical programme.

dramaturgy [dram-ă-ter-ji], the theory and practice of *drama, now usually called dramatics. A **dramaturge** or **dramaturgist** is a playwright, or in some contexts (especially German) a literary advisor or theatrical director. *Adjective:* **dramaturgic** or **dramaturgical**.

drame [dramm], the French word for drama, applied more specifically by Denis Diderot and later writers to plays that are intermediate between *comedy and *tragedy. Diderot outlined his theory of the *drame* in the prefaces to his plays *Le Fils naturel* (1757) and *Le Père de famille* (1758), which both exemplify this moralizing blend of *sentimental comedy with *domestic tragedy, being serious in content but still ending happily. The category of *drames* came to include both the *drame bourgeois* of contemporary domestic problems in the middle classes, and, closer to tragedy and *melodrama, the *drame romantique* of the 19th century, of which Victor Hugo's *Hernani* (1830) was an influential example. *See also* tragicomedy.

dream vision or **dream allegory,** a kind of *narrative (usually but not always in verse) in which the narrator falls asleep and dreams the events of the tale. The story is often a kind of *allegory, and commonly consists of a tour of some marvellous realm, in which the dreamer is conducted and instructed by a guide, as Dante is led through hell by Virgil in his *Divine Comedy* (*c.*1320)—the foremost example of the form. The dream vision was much favoured by medieval poets, most of them influenced by the 13th-century *Roman de la rose* by the French poets Guillaume de Lorris and Jean de Meung. In English, Chaucer devoted much of his early work to dream visions, including *The Parlement of Foules*, while Langland wrote the more substantial *Piers Plowman*; another fine 14th-century example is the anonymous poem *Pearl*. Some later poets have adopted the *conventions of the dream vision, as in Shelley's *The Triumph of Life* (1824). Significant examples in prose include Bunyan's *The Pilgrim's Progress* (1678) and William Morris's vision of socialism in *News from Nowhere* (1890).

dub poetry, a kind of poetry that emerged in Jamaica and England during the early 1970s, influenced by the rhythms of reggae music. The term was at first applied to the improvised 'rapping' of the Jamaican disc-jockeys known as 'toasters', who sang or recited their own words over the dub versions of reggae records (i.e. the purely instrumental re-mixed versions on the B-sides); but it has come to be adopted as a collective label for a tradition of popular poetry in the Jamaican (and black British) *vernacular or 'Patwah', inaugurated by Mutabaruka and Oku Onuora in Jamaica and by Linton Kwesi Johnson in England. Dub poetry includes *lyrics and *narrative poems on various subjects including protest against racism and police brutality, the celebration of sex, music, and ganja, and Rastafarian religious themes. Although primarily an oral poetry for public performance, it has increasingly appeared in print, notably in Johnson's *Dread Beat and Blood* (1975) and Benjamin Zephaniah's *The Dread Affair* (1985). Other leading dub poets include Michael Smith, Jean Binta Breeze, and Levi Tafari.

dumb show, a short piece of silent action or *mime included in a play. A common device in Elizabethan and *Jacobean drama, it was sometimes used to summarize the succeeding spoken scene, as in the dumb show preceding the players' main performance in *Hamlet* (Act III, scene ii).

duodecimo [dew-oh-**des**-i-moh], a small size of book in which the page size results from folding a standard printer's sheet of paper into twelve leaves (i.e. 24 pages). Abbreviated as 12mo, it is thus sometimes called 'twelvemo'. *See also* folio, octavo, quarto.

duple metre, a term covering poetic *metres based upon a *foot of two syllables (a **duple foot**), as opposed to *triple metre, in which the predominant foot has three syllables. Most English metrical verse is in duple metre, either *iambic or *trochaic, and thus displays an alternation of stressed syllables with single unstressed syllables (*see* stress). In the context of classical Greek and Latin poetry, however, the term often refers to verse composed of *dipodies.

dystopia [dis-toh-piă], a modern term invented as the opposite of *utopia, and applied to any alarmingly unpleasant imaginary world, usually of the projected future. The term is also applied to fictional works depicting such worlds. A significant form of *science fiction and of modern *satire, dystopian writing is exemplified in H. G. Wells's *The Time Machine* (1895), George Orwell's *Nineteen Eighty-Four* (1949), and Russell Hoban's *Riddley Walker* (1980).

eclogue [ek-log], a short *pastoral poem, often in the form of a shepherds' *dialogue or a *soliloquy. The term was first applied to the 'bucolic' poems of Virgil, written in imitation of the *idylls of Theocritus; Virgil's work became known as the *Eclogues* (42–37 BCE). The form was revived in the Italian *Renaissance by Dante, Petrarch, and Boccaccio, and appears in English in Spenser's *The Shephearde's Calender* (1579). Some later poets have extended the term to include non-pastoral poems in dialogue form.

écriture [ay-kri-tewr], the French word for 'writing'. Where it appears in this form in English texts, it refers to one or more specific senses used by modern French theorists: (i) writing as style, in Roland Barthes's book *Le Degré Zéro de l'Écriture* (*Writing Degree Zero*, 1953), which attacks the illusion of a blank or neutral writing on the grounds that all writing has some style or *discourse that shapes our view of the world; (ii) writing as an intransitive activity, as proposed in Barthes's later essay 'Écrivains et écrivants' ('Writers and Authors', 1960) which contrasts *écrivants* writing 'about' something for an ulterior purpose with *écrivains* for whom writing is self-directed, about itself as language; (iii) writing as *différance* as opposed to the illusory authenticity of speech (*see* logocentrism) according to Jacques Derrida's philosophy of *deconstruction; (iv) *écriture féminine*, or specifically gendered women's writing, as conceived by Hélène Cixous, whose works of the 1970s discuss the sense in which women's writing overflows the *binary oppositions of patriarchal logic.

Edda, the Old Norse name given to two important collections of early Icelandic writing. The Elder or Poetic Edda is a collection of poems written down in the late 13th century but including works from an oral tradition going back to the 9th century; it contains heroic *narrative poems about Sigurd and other heroes, along with mythological tales of the Norse gods. The Younger or Prose Edda is a handbook of *poetics by Snorri Sturluson, written in the early 13th century; it also contains mythological lore. *Adjective*: **Eddaic.**

edition, a printed version of a given work that may be distinguished from other versions either by its published format (e.g. paperback edition, popular edition, abridged edition), or by its membership of a complete batch of copies printed from the same setting of type, usually at the same time and place. These batches come to be numbered as first, second, third, etc. editions, each time a new version is set again from fresh type; where the same type is used to run off further copies, the batches are known as second, third, fourth, etc. 'printings' or 'impressions' of the relevant edition. The term is also applied rather differently to the works of an author as edited by a particular scholar or by a team of scholars sharing the same procedures, e.g. Christopher Ricks's edition of Tennyson, or the Arden editions of Shakespeare. *See also* variorum edition.

egotistical sublime, the phrase by which John Keats criticized what he felt to be the excessively self-centred quality of Wordsworth's poetry, in contrast with his own ideal of *negative capability, which he found in the more anonymous imagination of Shakespeare. *See also* sublime.

eiron [I-ron], a *stock character in Greek *comedy, who pretends to be less intelligent than he really is, and whose modesty of speech contrasts with the boasting of the stock braggart or *alazon.* Our word *irony derives from the pretence adopted by the *eiron.*

elegy, an elaborately formal *lyric poem lamenting the death of a friend or public figure, or reflecting seriously on a solemn subject. In Greek and Latin verse, the term referred to the *metre of a poem (alternating dactylic *hexameters and *pentameters in couplets known as **elegiac** *distichs), not to its mood or content: love poems were often included. Likewise, John Donne applied the term to his amorous and satirical poems in *heroic couplets. But since Milton's 'Lycidas' (1637), the term in English has usually denoted a *lament (although Milton called his poem a 'monody'), while the adjective 'elegiac' has come to refer to the mournful mood of such poems. Two important English elegies that follow Milton in using *pastoral conventions are Shelley's 'Adonais' (1821) on the death of Keats, and Arnold's 'Thyrsis' (1867). This tradition of the **pastoral elegy,** derived from Greek poems by Theocritus and other Sicilian poets in the 3rd and 2nd centuries BCE, evolved a very elaborate series of *conventions by which the dead friend is represented as a shepherd mourned by the natural world; pastoral elegies usually include many mythological figures such as the nymphs who are supposed to have guarded the dead shepherd, and the *muses invoked by the **elegist**. Tennyson's *In Memoriam A. H. H.* (1850) is a long series of elegiac verses (in the modern sense) on his friend Arthur Hallam, while Whitman's 'When Lilacs Last in the Dooryard Bloom'd' (1865) commemorates a public figure— Abraham Lincoln—rather than a friend; Auden's 'In Memory of W. B. Yeats' (1939) does the same. In a broader sense, an elegy may be a poem of melancholy reflection upon life's transience or its sorrows, as in Gray's 'Elegy Written in a Country Churchyard' (1751), or in Rilke's *Duino Elegies* (1912–22). The **elegiac stanza** is a *quatrain of iambic pentameters rhyming *abab*, named after its use in Gray's Elegy. In an extended sense, a prose work dealing with a vanished way of life or with the passing of youth may sometimes be called an elegy. *See also* dirge, graveyard poetry, monody, threnody.

elision, the slurring or suppression of a vowel sound or syllable, usually by fusing a final unstressed vowel with a following word beginning with a vowel or mute *h*, as in French *l'homme* or in Shakespeare's 'Th'expense of spirit'. In poetry, elision is used in order to fit the words to the *metre of a verse line (*see* synaeresis). Another form of contraction sometimes distinguished from elision is *syncope, in which a letter or syllable within a word is omitted (e.g. *o'er* for over, *heav'n* for heaven). *Verb*: **elide**. *See also* hiatus.

ellipsis or **ellipse** (plurals **-pses**), the omission from a sentence of a word or words that would be required for complete clarity but which can usually be understood from the context. A common form of compression both in everyday speech and in poetry (e.g. Shakespeare, 'I will [go] to Ireland'), it is used with notable frequency by T. S. Eliot and other poets of *modernism. The sequence of three dots (…) employed to indicate the omission of some matter in a text is also known as an ellipsis. *Adjective*: **elliptical** or **elliptic**. *See also* asyndeton, lacuna, paratactic.

embedded, enclosed within a *frame narrative as a tale-within-the-tale, like the pilgrims' stories in the *Canterbury Tales*, which are embedded within Chaucer's account of the journey to Canterbury.

emblem, a picture with a symbolic meaning, as in heraldry or visual *allegory; or a simple kind of literary *symbol with a fixed and relatively clear significance. In the 16th and 17th centuries the term was applied to a popular kind of woodcut or engraving accompanied by a motto and a short verse explanation of its meaning. The vogue for the **emblem books** in which these were found began with Andrea Alciato's *Emblemata* (1531) and culminated in England with the *Emblems* (1635) of Francis Quarles. Poets of this period often drew upon such works for their *imagery. The term **emblem poem** is sometimes applied to *pattern poems. *Adjective*: **emblematic.**

emendation, a correction made to a *text in the belief that the author's original wording has been wrongly altered, e.g. by scribal error, printer's misreading, or the intervention of censorship. Unlike an amendment, which creates a fresh wording, an emendation aims to restore a lost original.

empiricism [im-**pi**-ri-sizm], the belief in observation and experience as the basis of knowledge, rather than logical deduction. As used in modern literary theory, the term usually has an unfavourable sense, referring to those critical approaches that dismiss theoretical abstraction in the belief that *texts (or facts of history or biography) can 'speak for themselves' without the intervention of analysis and interpretation. The more neutral adjective **empirical** refers to research based upon observation. One who pursues any inquiry within the limits of empiricism, or who regards theory as a distraction, is an **empiricist.**

encomium [in-**koh**-mi-ŭm] (plural **-mia**) a composition in prose or verse written in praise of some person, event, or idea; a eulogy. Originally denoting a Greek choral song in praise of a victorious athlete, the term was later extended to include prose compositions devoted to praise, usually involving elaborate *rhetoric. Many *odes and *elegies are wholly or partly **encomiastic.** An author of encomia is an **encomiast.** *See also* panegyric.

Encyclopédistes, the group of writers and philosophers led by Denis Diderot and Jean d'Alembert who contributed to the *Encyclopédie ou Dictionnaire raisonnée des sciences, des arts et des métiers* which began to appear in 1751 under Diderot's editorship, eventually running to 35 volumes including indexes. Other leading contributors were Condillac, Helvétius, Voltaire, and the Baron d'Holbach, who played host to the meetings of this loose association. The *Encyclopédistes* were the leading spirits of the *Enlightenment, hoping through this ambitious project to sweep away the superstitions of Church and State by offering a rational account of the universe. See also *philosophes.*

end-rhyme, rhyme occurring at the ends of verse lines, as opposed to *internal rhyme and 'head-rhyme' (*alliteration); the most familiar kind of rhyming.

end-stopped, brought to a pause at which the end of a verse line coincides with the completion of a sentence, clause, or other independent unit of *syntax. End-stopping, the opposite of *enjambment, gives verse lines an appearance of self-contained sense; it was favoured especially by Pope and other 18th-century poets in English in their *heroic couplets, and by the classical French poets in their *alexandrines. *See also* closed couplet.

Eng. Lit., a common abbreviation for English Literature as an academic subject or as a *canon of 'set texts' for study. This abbreviated usage often implies a disrespectful attitude to the traditional limits of the canon or to the routine examination cramming that has beset the subject.

enjambment or **enjambement,** the running over of the sense and grammatical structure from one verse line or couplet to the next without a punctuated pause. In an **enjambed** line (also called a 'run-on line'), the completion of a phrase, clause, or sentence is held over to the following line so that the line ending is not emphasized as it is in an *end-stopped line. Enjambment is one of the resources available to poets in English *blank verse, but it appears in other verse-forms too, even in *heroic couplets: Keats rejected the 18th-century *closed couplet by using frequent enjambment in *Endymion* (1818), of which the first and fifth lines are end-stopped while the lines in between are enjambed.

> A thing of beauty is a joy for ever:
> Its loveliness increases; it will never
> Pass into nothingness; but still will keep
> A bower quiet for us, and a sleep
> Full of sweet dreams, and health, and quiet breathing.

Enlightenment, the, a general term applied to the movement of intellectual liberation that developed in Western Europe from the late 17th century to the late 18th (the period often called the 'Age of Reason'), especially in France and Switzerland. The Enlightenment culminated with the writings of Jean-Jacques Rousseau and the *Encyclopédistes, the philosophy of Immanuel Kant, and the political ideals of the American and French Revolutions, while its forerunners in science and philosophy included Bacon, Descartes, Newton, and Locke. Its central idea was the need for (and the capacity of) human reason to clear away ancient superstition, prejudice, dogma, and injustice. Kant defined enlightenment (*die Aufklärung*) as man's emancipation from his self-incurred immaturity. Enlightenment thinking encouraged rational scientific inquiry, humanitarian tolerance, and the idea of universal human rights. In religion, it usually involved the sceptical rejection of superstition, dogma, and revelation in favour of 'Deism'—a belief confined to those universal doctrines supposed to be common to all religions, such as the existence of a venerable Supreme Being as creator. The advocates of enlightenment tended to place their faith in human progress brought about by the gradual propagation of rational principles, although their great champion Voltaire, more militant and less optimistic, waged a bitter campaign against the abuses of the *ancien régime* under the virtually untranslatable slogan *écrasez l'infâme!* (for which a rough equivalent would be 'smash the system!'). In English, the attitudes of the Enlightenment are found in the late 18th century, in the historian Edward Gibbon and the political writers Thomas Paine and William Godwin, as well as in the feminist Mary Wollstonecraft. The flourishing of philosophy and science in Edinburgh and Glasgow in the 18th century is known as the **Scottish Enlightenment;** its leading figures included David Hume and Adam Smith. See also *philosophes*. For more extended accounts, consult Norman Hampson, *The Enlightenment* (1968) and, on the British dimension, Roy Porter, *Enlightenment* (2000).

énoncé and **énonciation,** terms of a distinction observed in *structuralist theory, between what is said (the *énoncé*) and the act or process of saying it (the *énonciation*). The linguist Émile Benveniste has defined *énonciation* as a process by which a speaker (or writer) adopts a position within language as an 'I' addressing a 'you' and perhaps referring to a 'they'. Whenever I say 'I', however, the I who speaks can be distinguished (as the 'subject of the *énonciation*') from the 'I' that is thus spoken of (the 'subject of the *énoncé*'). This splitting of the subject by language has been of great interest to theorists of *post-structuralism, notably the psychoanalyst Jacques Lacan. In literary analysis, the distinction leads to a further differentiation between *discours*, in which first- and second-person pronouns and other markers of the situation of the *énonciation* are evident (*see* deixis), and the more 'objective' mode of *histoire* in which the *énonciation* seems to have disappeared into or behind the *énoncé*. So while a *first-person narrative will show a split between the narrating I of the *énonciation* and the younger 'I' spoken of (*énoncé*) in the narrative, a *third-person narrative will often be able to disguise the distinction between the process of narration and its result.

entremés (plural *-meses*), the Spanish term for a short comical performance presented between the acts of a more serious drama. This form flourished on the Spanish stage in the first half of the 17th century. Numerous *entremeses* are attributed to Lope de Vega (1562–1635) and his associates, and a few to Cervantes.

envelope, a structural device in poetry, by which a line or *stanza is repeated either identically or with little variation so as to enclose between its two appearances the rest (or part) of the poem: a stanza may begin and end with the same line, or a poem may begin and end with the same line or stanza. A well-known example is Blake's poem 'The Tiger', in which the opening stanza is repeated as the last with only one change of wording. The effect of an envelope pattern is subtly different from that of a *refrain. The term **envelope stanza** has also been applied to stanzas not involving repeated lines but having a symmetrical *rhyme scheme (almost always *abba*) which encloses one set of rhymes within another, as in the *In Memoriam stanza*.

envoi or **envoy,** the additional half-stanza that concludes certain kinds of French poetic form, principally the *ballade but also the *chant royal* and the *sestina. Its length is usually four lines in a ballade, five or seven in a *chant royal*, and three in a sestina. In the ballade and *chant royal* it repeats the *metre and *rhyme scheme of the previous half-stanza, along with the poem's *refrain, and is conventionally addressed to a prince or other noble personage.

epanalepsis, a *figure of speech in which the initial word of a sentence or verse line reappears at the end. *See also* ploce.

épater les bourgeois [ay-pat-ay lay boor-*zh*wah], a French phrase that can be translated only rather clumsily, as 'to shock the (respectable) middle-class citizens'. This has often been the conscious aim of the literary and artistic *avant-garde* in Europe since the late 19th century, especially in the movements of *decadence, *Dada, and *Surrealism.

epic, a long *narrative poem celebrating the great deeds of one or more legendary heroes, in a grand ceremonious style. The hero, usually protected by or even descended from gods, performs superhuman exploits in battle or in marvellous voyages, often saving or founding a

nation—as in Virgil's *Aeneid* (30–20 BCE)—or the human race itself, in
Milton's *Paradise Lost* (1667). Virgil and Milton wrote what are called
'secondary' or literary epics in imitation of the earlier 'primary' or
traditional epics of Homer, whose *Iliad* and *Odyssey* (*c*.8th century BCE)
are derived from an oral tradition of recitation. They adopted many of
the *conventions of Homer's work, including the *invocation of a muse,
the use of *epithets, the listing of heroes and combatants, and the
beginning *in medias res* (for other epic conventions, *see* epic simile,
formulaic, machinery). The Anglo-Saxon poem *Beowulf* (8th century CE) is
a primary epic, as is the oldest surviving epic poem, the Babylonian
Gilgamesh (*c*.3000 BCE). In the *Renaissance, epic poetry (also known as
'heroic poetry') was regarded as the highest form of literature, and was
attempted in Italian by Tasso in *Gerusalemme Liberata* (1575), and in
Portuguese by Camoëns in *Os Lusiadas* (1572). Other important national
epics are the Indian *Mahābhārata* (3rd or 4th century CE) and the German
Nibelungenlied (*c*.1200). The action of epics takes place on a grand scale,
and in this sense the term has sometimes been extendeded to long
*romances, to ambitious *historical novels like Tolstoy's *War and
Peace* (1863–9), and to some large-scale film productions on heroic or
historical subjects. For a fuller account, consult Paul Merchant, *The Epic*
(1971).

epic simile, an extended *simile elaborated in such detail or at such
length as to eclipse temporarily the main action of a *narrative work,
forming a decorative *digression. Usually it compares one complex
action (rather than a simple quality or thing) with another: for example,
the approach of an army with the onset of storm-clouds. Sometimes
called a **Homeric simile** after its frequent use in Homer's epic poems, it
was also used by Virgil, Milton, and others in their literary epics.

epic theatre, a revolutionary form of drama developed by the German
playwright Bertolt Brecht from the late 1920s under the influence of
Erwin Piscator. It involved rejecting the *Aristotelian models of
dramatic unity in favour of a detached *narrative (hence 'epic')
presentation in a succession of loosely related episodes interspersed with
songs and commentary by a *chorus or narrator. As a Marxist, Brecht
turned against the bourgeois tradition of theatre in which the audience
identifies emotionally with psychologically rounded characters in a
*well-made play; he aimed instead for an *alienation effect which
would keep the audience coolly reflective and critical, partly by setting
his plays in remote times and places, and also by stressing the contrived

nature of the drama. The best examples of this drama are Brecht's plays *The Threepenny Opera* (1928), *Mother Courage* (1941), and *The Good Woman of Setzuan* (1943).

epideictic, intended for display at public occasions. Epideictic *oratory was one of the three branches of classical *rhetoric, differing from legal argument or political persuasion in being devoted to public praise (or blame), as in funeral orations, *panegyrics, etc. Epideictic poetry is verse for special occasions, such as *epithalamia, many *odes, and other kinds of poem now usually referred to as *occasional verses. *See also* encomium.

epigone [ep-ig-ohn] (plural -**oni** or -**ones**), an inferior or derivative follower of some more distinguished writer.

epigram, a short poem with a witty turn of thought; or a wittily condensed expression in prose. Originally a form of monumental inscription in ancient Greece, the epigram was developed into a literary form by the poets of the *Hellenistic age and by the Roman poet Martial, whose *Epigrams* (86–102 CE) were often obscenely insulting. This epigram by Herrick is adapted from Martial:

> Lulls swears he is all heart, but you'll suppose
> By his proboscis that he is all nose.

The art of the epigram was cultivated in the 17th and 18th centuries in France and Germany by Voltaire, Schiller, and others. In English, epigrams have been written by several poets since Ben Jonson's *Epigrams* (1616), and are found in the prose of Oscar Wilde and other authors, who are thus known as **epigrammatists.** Some of the more pointed *closed couplets of Pope are called epigrams although they are not independent poems. *Adjective*: **epigrammatic.** *See also* aphorism.

epigraph, a quotation or motto placed at the beginning of a book, chapter, or poem as an indication of its theme. The term can also refer to an inscription on a monument or coin. **Epigraphy** is the collective term for any body of epigraphs in either sense, and for the study of epigraphs. *Adjective*: **epigraphic.**

epilogue [ep-i-log], a concluding section of any written work. At the end of some plays in the age of Shakespeare and Jonson, a single character would address the audience directly, begging indulgence and applause; both the speech and the speaker were known as the epilogue, as in Rosalind's closing address in *As You Like It*. Some novels have epilogues in which the characters' subsequent fates are briefly outlined. *Verb*: **epilogize**. *Adjective*: **epilogistic**.

epiphany [i-**pif**-ăni], the term used in Christian theology for a manifestation of God's presence in the world. It was taken over by James Joyce to denote secular revelation in the everyday world, in an early version of his novel *A Portrait of the Artist as a Young Man* (1916) later published as *Stephen Hero* (1944). Here Joyce defined an epiphany as 'a sudden spiritual manifestation' in which the 'whatness' of a common object or gesture appears radiant to the observer. Much of Joyce's fiction is built around such special moments of sudden insight, just as Wordsworth's long autobiographical poem *The Prelude* (1850) is constructed around certain revelatory 'spots of time'. *Adjective*: **epiphanic**.

episodic, constructed as a narrative by a succession of loosely connected incidents rather than by an integrated *plot. *Picaresque novels and many medieval *romances have an episodic structure in which the only link between one episode and the next is the presence of the same central character.

episteme [ep-is-teem] or *épistème* [ay-pi-stem], the accepted mode of acquiring and arranging knowledge in a given period. An episteme unites the various *discourses (legal, scientific, etc.) and guarantees their coherence within an underlying structure of implicit assumptions about the status of knowledge. The term has gained currency from the work of the French historian Michel Foucault, especially his *Les Mots et les choses* (*The Order of Things*, 1966). Foucault attempted to show how an episteme based on the detection of resemblances was replaced in the 17th century by a new episteme of differences and distinctions, while the 19th century introduced a further episteme of historical evolution. *Adjective*; **epistemic**.

epistle [ip-**iss**-ŭl], a letter. As a literary form, the **verse epistle** is a poem in the form of a letter to a friend or patron in a familiar, conversational style. The theme of the most common kind (the *Horatian, moral, or familiar epistle) is usually some moral, philosophical, or literary subject. The chief classical model is Horace's *Epistulae* (*c*.15 BCE), written in *hexameters and treating various matters from the pleasures of his rural retreat to the state of Roman literature. The Horatian epistle was a favoured form among poets from the *Renaissance to the 18th century: Jonson's 'Epistle to Elizabeth, Countess of Rutland' (1616) and Pope's

Epistle to Dr Arbuthnot (1735) are fine examples; more recent epistles in English include Auden's *New Year Letter* (1940) and Derek Mahon's 'Beyond Howth Head' (1975). A distinct tradition of 'sentimental' epistles derives from Ovid's *Heroides* (*c*.20 BCE); these are in the form of letters imagined as being addressed by heroines of legend to their husbands or lovers, and were imitated in English by Drayton in *England's Heroical Epistles* (1597). Pope's 'Eloisa to Abelard' is a later Ovidian epistle. *Adjective*: **epistolary.**

epistolary novel, a novel written in the form of a series of letters exchanged among the characters of the story, with extracts from their journals sometimes included. A form of narrative often used in English and French novels of the 18th century, it has been revived only rarely since then, as in John Barth's *Letters* (1979). Important examples include Richardson's *Pamela* (1740–1) and *Clarissa* (1747–8), Rousseau's *La Nouvelle Héloïse* (1761), and Laclos's *Les Liaisons dangereuses* (1782).

epistrophe [i-**pis**-trŏfi], a rhetorical *figure by which the same word or phrase is repeated at the end of successive clauses, sentences, or lines, as in Whitman's *Song of Myself* (1855):

> The moth and the fish-eggs are in their place,
> The bright suns I see and the dark suns I cannot see are in their place,
> The palpable is in its place and the impalpable is in its place.

Adjective: **epistrophic.** *See also* anaphora, antistrophe.

epitaph, a form of words in prose or verse suited for inscription on a tomb—although many facetious verses composed as epitaphs have not actually been inflicted on their victims' graves. Epitaphs may take the form of appeals from the dead to passers-by, or of descriptions of the dead person's merits. Many ancient Greek epitaphs survive in the *Greek Anthology* (*c*.920 CE), and both Johnson and Wordsworth wrote essays on the epitaph as an art. *Adjective*: **epitaphic.** *See also* lapidary.

epithalamion [epi-thă-**lay**-mion] or **epithalamium** (plural **-amia**), a song or poem celebrating a wedding, and traditionally intended to be sung outside the bridal chamber on the wedding night. Some epithalamia survive from ancient literature, notably by Catullus, but the form flourished in the Renaissance: Edmund Spenser's 'Epithalamion' (1595) is the most admired English model, but others were written by Sidney, Donne, Jonson, Marvell and Dryden. Later examples are those by Shelley and Auden. *Adjective*: **epithalamic.**

epithet, an adjective or adjectival phrase used to define a characteristic quality or attribute of some person or thing. Common in historical titles (Catherine the Great, Ethelred the Unready), 'stock' epithets have been used in poetry since Homer. The **Homeric epithet** is an adjective (usually a compound adjective) repeatedly used for the same thing or person: 'the wine-dark sea' and 'rosy-fingered Dawn' are famous examples. In the **transferred epithet** (or *hypallage), an adjective appropriate to one noun is attached to another by association: thus in the phrase *sick room* it is not strictly the room that is sick but the person in it. *Adjective*: **epithetic.** *See also* antonomasia.

epizeuxis, a rhetorical *figure by which a word is repeated for emphasis, with no other words intervening: *sick, sick, sick!*

epode [ep-ohd], the third part of the triadic structure used in the Pindaric *ode and in Greek dramatic *choruses, following the *strophe and *antistrophe and differing from them in length and metrical form. The term was also used for a Greek *metre invented by Archilochus (7th century BCE), in which a longer line was followed by a shorter one (e.g. a *trimeter followed by a *dimeter); in this metre, adopted in Latin by Horace, the shorter line can also be called the epode. *Adjective*: **epodic.**

eponymous [ip-on-imŭs], name-giving: a term applied to a real or fictitious person after whom a place, thing, institution, meal, or book is named. Thus Anna Karenina is called the eponymous heroine of Tolstoy's novel *Anna Karenina*. The term is often extended beyond its strict sense to describe a character who is referred to indirectly (i.e. not by name) in the title of a work: thus Michael Henchard is called the eponymous character of Hardy's *The Mayor of Casterbridge*. An **eponym** is a name transferred from a person to a place or thing, either in its original form or as adapted (e.g. Bolivar or Bolivia). *See also* antonomasia.

epos, the *epic poetry of an early oral tradition.

epyllion (plural -llia), a miniature *epic poem, resembling an epic in *metre and/or style but not in length. The term dates from the 19th century, when it was applied to certain shorter *narrative poems in Greek and Latin, usually dealing with a mythological love story in an elaborately digressive and allusive manner, as in Catullus' poem on Peleus and Thetis. The nearest equivalents in English poetry are the Elizabethan erotic narratives such as Marlowe's *Hero and Leander* (1598) and Shakespeare's *Venus and Adonis* (1593), although the term has also been applied to later non-erotic works including Arnold's *Sohrab and Rustum* (1853).

equivoque [ek-wi-vohk], a *pun or deliberately ambiguous expression. *Adjective*: **equivocal.** *Verb*: **equivocate.** *See also* ambiguity, *double entendre*, paronomasia.

erasure, the placing of a concept under suspicion by marking the word for it as crossed (e.g. ~~philosophy~~), in order to signal to readers that it is both unreliable and at the same time indispensable. The device of placing words *sous rature* ('under erasure') has sometimes been adopted in modern philosophy and criticism, notably in *deconstruction.

erlebte Rede, the German term for *free indirect style.

ermetismo, see hermeticism.

Erziehungsroman, another term for *Bildungsroman.

eschatology [esk-ă-**tol**-ŏji], the theological study or artistic representation of the end of the world. Eschatological writing is found chiefly in religious *allegories, but also in some *science fiction. The term should not be confused with *scatology, which is the scientific or humorous consideration of excrement. *See also* anagogical, apocalyptic.

essay, a short written composition in prose that discusses a subject or proposes an argument without claiming to be a complete or thorough exposition. A minor literary form, the essay is more relaxed than the formal academic dissertation. The term ('trying out') was coined by the French writer Michel de Montaigne in the title of his *Essais* (1580), the first modern example of the form. Francis Bacon's *Essays* (1597) began the tradition of essays in English, of which important examples are those of Addison, Steele, Hazlitt, Emerson, D. H. Lawrence, and Virginia Woolf. The verse essays of Pope are rare exceptions to the prose norm.

esthetics, *see* aesthetics.

estrangement, *see* defamiliarization.

euphony [yoo-**fō**ni], a pleasing smoothness of sound, perceived by the ease with which the words can be spoken in combination. The use of long vowels, liquid consonants (*l*, *r*), and semi-vowels (*w*, *y*), contributes to euphony, along with the avoidance of adjacent stresses; the meaning of the words, however, has an important effect too. Euphony is the opposite of *cacophony. *Adjective*: **euphonious.**

euphuism [yoo-few-izm], an elaborately ornate prose style richly decorated with rhetorical *figures. The term comes from the popularity of two prose romances by John Lyly: *Euphues: The Anatomy of Wit* (1578), and its sequel *Euphues and His England* (1580). Lyly's style, later parodied by Shakespeare among others, is marked by the repeated use of *antitheses reinforced by *alliteration, along with *rhetorical questions and various figures of repetition. It is also notable for its frequent use of *sententiae* and elaborate *similes drawn from real and fabulous birds and beasts. This example comes from a *soliloquy spoken by the character Euphues:

> Ah Euphues, into what misfortune art thou brought! In what sudden misery art thou wrapped! It is like to fare with thee as with the eagle, which dieth neither for age nor with sickness but with famine, for although thy stomach hunger, thy heart will not suffer thee to eat. And why shouldst thou torment thyself for one in whom is neither faith not fervency? Oh the counterfeit love of women! Oh inconstant sex! I have lost Philautus. I have lost Lucilla. I have lost that which I shall hardly find again: a faithful friend. Ah, foolish Euphues! Why didst thou leave Athens, the nurse of wisdom, to inhabit Naples, the nourisher of wantonness? Had it not been better for thee to have eaten salt with the philosophers in Greece than sugar with the courtiers in Italy?

Adjective: **euphuistic.**

exclamatio, a rhetorical *figure in which high emotion is expressed in the form of a sudden exclamation, which is often an *apostrophe: 'O Richard! York is too far gone with grief' (Shakespeare, *Richard II*).

excursus (plural **-suses**), a *digression in which some point is discussed at length; or an appendix devoted to detailed examination of some topic held over from the main body of the text. *Adjective*: **excursive.**

exegesis [eks-ĕ-jee-sis] (plural **-geses**), the interpretation or explanation of a *text. The term was first applied to the interpretation of religious scriptures (or oracles and visions), but has been borrowed by literary *criticism for the analysis of any poetry or prose. Literary scholars have likewise inherited some of the procedures of biblical exegesis, for instance the decoding of *allegories (*see* typology). A person who practises exegesis is an **exegete.** *Adjective*: **exegetic** or **exegetical.**

exemplum (plural **-pla**), a short tale used as an example to illustrate a moral point, usually in a sermon or other *didactic work. The form was cultivated in the late Middle Ages, for instance in Robert Mannyng of Brunne's *Handlyng Synne* (early 14th century) and in Chaucer's *Pardoner's Tale* and *Nun's Priest's Tale*, as well as in many prose collections for the use of preachers. *See also* allegory, fable, parable.

existentialism [eksi-**stench**-ăl-izm], a current in European philosophy distinguished by its emphasis on lived human existence. Although it had an important precursor in the Danish theologian Søren Kierkegaard in the 1840s, its impact was fully felt only in the mid-20th century in France and Germany: the German philosophers Martin Heidegger and Karl Jaspers prepared some of the ground in the 1920s and 1930s for the more influential work of Jean-Paul Sartre and the other French existentialists including Simone de Beauvoir, Albert Camus, and Maurice Merleau-Ponty. In terms of its literary impact, the thought of Sartre has been the most significant, presented in novels (notably *La Nausée* (*Nausea*), 1938) and plays (including *Les Mouches* (*The Flies*), 1943) as well as in the major philosophical work *L'Être et le néant* (*Being and Nothingness*), 1943). Sartrean existentialism, as distinct from the Christian existentialism derived from Kierkegaard, is an atheist philosophy of human freedom conceived in terms of individual responsibility and authenticity. Its fundamental premise, that 'existence precedes essence', implies that we as human beings have no given essence or nature but must forge our own values and meanings in an inherently meaningless or *absurd world of existence. Obliged to make our own choices, we can either confront the anguish (or *Angst) of this responsibility, or evade it by claiming obedience to some determining convention or duty, thus acting in 'bad faith'. Paradoxically, we are 'condemned to be free'. Similar themes can be found in the novels and essays of Camus; both authors felt that the absurdity of existence could be redeemed through the individual's decision to become *engagé* ('committed') within social and political causes opposing fascism and imperialism. Some of the concerns of French existentialism are echoed in English in Thom Gunn's early collection of poems. *The Sense of Movement* (1957), and in the fiction of Iris Murdoch and John Fowles. *See also* phenomenology.

exordium, the first part of a speech, according to the structure recommended in classical *rhetoric; or the introductory section of a written work of argument or exposition. *Adjective:* **exordial.**

experimentalism, the commitment to exploring new concepts and representations of the world through methods that go beyond the established *conventions of literary tradition. Experimentalism was an important characteristic of 20th-century literature and art, in which successive *avant-garde* movements arose in continual reaction against what they regarded as decayed or ossified forms of expression. For examples, *see* Dada, expressionism, Futurism, modernism, *nouveau roman*, Surrealism, Vorticism.

explication, the attempt to analyse a literary work thoroughly, giving full attention to its complexities of form and meaning. The term has usually been associated with the kind of analysis practised in the USA by *New Criticism and in Britain under the name of *practical criticism. Explication in this sense is normally a detailed explanation of the manner in which the language and formal structure of a short poem work to achieve a unity of *form and *content; such analysis tends to emphasize ambiguities and complexities of the text while putting aside questions of historical or biographical context. A less thorough form of analysis is the French school exercise known as *explication de texte*, in which students give an account of a work's meaning and its stylistic features. *Adjective:* **explicatory** or **explicative.** *See also* criticism, exegesis, hermeneutics.

exposition, the setting forth of a systematic explanation of or argument about any subject; or the opening part of a play or story, in which we are introduced to the characters and their situation, often by reference to preceding events. *Adjective:* **expository.** *Verb:* **expound.**

expressionism, a general term for a mode of literary or visual art which, in extreme reaction against *realism or *naturalism, presents a world violently distorted under the pressure of intense personal moods, ideas, and emotions: image and language thus express feeling and imagination rather than represent external reality. Although not an organized movement, expressionism was an important factor in the painting, drama, poetry, and cinema of German-speaking Europe between 1910 and 1924. The term did not come into use until 1911, but has since been applied retrospectively to some important forerunners of expressionist technique, going as far back as Georg Büchner's plays of the 1830s and Vincent Van Gogh's paintings of the 1880s; other significant precursors include the Norwegian painter Edvard Munch, the Swedish playwright August Strindberg (in his *Dream Play*, 1902), and the German playwright Frank Wedekind. Within the period 1910–24, consciously expressionist techniques of abstraction were promoted by Wassily Kandinsky and the 'Blue Rider' group of painters, while in drama various anti-naturalist principles of abstract characterization and structural discontinuity were employed in the plays of Ernst Toller, Georg Kaiser, and Walter Hasenclever; these had some influence on the early plays of Bertolt Brecht, notably *Baal* (1922). The poetry of Georg Trakl, Gottfried Benn, August Stramm, and Franz Werfel displayed comparable distortions of accepted structures and syntax in favour of symbolized mood. The nightmarish labyrinths of Franz Kafka's novels are the nearest equivalent in prose fiction. German expressionism is best known today through the wide influence of its cinematic masterpieces: Robert Wiene's *The Cabinet of Dr Caligari* (1920), F. W. Murnau's *Nosferatu* (1922), and Fritz Lang's *Metropolis* (1926). Along with their much-imitated visual patterns of sinister shadows, these films reveal a shared obsession with automatized, trance-like states, which appears in expressionist literature too: a common concern of expressionism is with the eruption of irrational and chaotic forces from beneath the surface of a mechanized modern world. Some of its explosive energies issued into *Dada, *Vorticism, and other *avant-garde* movements of the 1920s. In the English-speaking world, expressionist dramatic techniques were adopted in some of the plays of Eugene O'Neill and Sean O'Casey, and in the 'Circe' episode of James Joyce's novel *Ulysses* (1922); in poetry, T. S. Eliot's *The Waste Land* (1922) may be considered expressionist in its fragmentary rendering of post-war desolation. In a further sense, the term is sometimes applied to the belief that literary works are essentially expressions of their authors' moods and thoughts; this has been the dominant assumption about literature since the rise of *Romanticism. For a fuller account, consult R. S. Furness, *Expressionism* (1973).

expurgate, to remove objectionable (especially sexual or politically sensitive) passages from a text. *Noun*: **expurgation.** *See also* bowdlerize.

extempore [iks-**tem**-pŏ-ri], composed on the spur of the moment, without preparation. Some kinds of oral poetry involve a degree of extemporization. *Verb*: **extemporize.**

extravaganza, a theatrical entertainment consisting of a mild *burlesque of some *myth or fairy tale enlivened by *puns, music, dance, and elaborate spectacle. The form was made popular in the mid-19th century by J. R. Planché, and influenced the development both of *pantomime and of the light operas of Gilbert and Sullivan. The term is now applied to any lavishly staged musical *revue.

eye rhyme, a kind of *rhyme in which the spellings of paired words appear to match but without true correspondence in pronunciation: *dive/give*, *said/maid*. Some examples, like *love/prove*, were originally true rhymes but have become eye rhymes through changes in pronunciation: these are known as 'historical rhymes'. *See also* consonance, half-rhyme, poetic licence.

fable, a brief tale in verse or prose that conveys a moral lesson, usually by giving human speech and manners to animals and inanimate things (*see* beast fable). Fables often conclude with a moral, delivered in the form of an *epigram. A very old form of story related to *folklore and *proverbs, the fable in Europe descends from tales attributed to Aesop, a Greek slave in the 6th century BCE: his fable of the fox and the grapes has given us the phrase 'sour grapes'. An Indian collection, the *Bidpai*, dates back to about 300 CE. The French **fabulist** La Fontaine revived the form in the 17th century with his witty verse adaptations of Greek fables. More recent examples are Kipling's *Just So Stories* (1902), Thurber's *Fables of Our Time* (1940), and Orwell's *Animal Farm* (1945). *Adjectives*: **fabular, fabulous.** *See also* allegory, exemplum.

fabliau [fab-li-oh] (plural **-liaux**), a coarsely humorous short story in verse, dealing in a bluntly realistic manner with *stock characters of the middle class involved in sexual intrigue or obscene pranks. Fabliaux flourished in France in the 12th and 13th centuries, and were usually written in *octosyllabic couplets; some 150 French examples survive, most of them anonymous. They were imitated in English by Chaucer (in rhyming *pentameters), notably in his *Miller's Tale* and *Reeve's Tale*. Many fabliaux involve *satire against the clergy. A standard plot is the cuckolding of a slow-witted husband by a crafty and lustful student.

fabula, the term used in *Russian Formalism for the 'raw material' of *story events as opposed to the finished arrangement of the *plot (or *sjuzet*); the distinction reappears in later French *narratology as that between *histoire* (story) and *récit* (account). In Latin literature, *fabula* (plural *-lae*) is also the general name for various kinds of play, of which the most significant *genres are *fabula Atellana* or Atellan *farce, and *fabula palliata* or Roman *New Comedy.

fabulation, a term used by some modern critics for a mode of modern fiction that openly delights in its self-conscious verbal artifice, thus departing from the conventions of *realism. Robert Scholes in his book

The Fabulators (1967) describes fabulation in the works of John Barth, Kurt Vonnegut, and others as an essentially comic and *allegorical mode of fiction that often adopts the forms of *romance or of the *picaresque novel. *See also* magic realism, metafiction, postmodernism, surfiction.

faction, a short-lived *portmanteau word denoting works that present verifiably factual contents in the form of a fictional novel, as in Norman Mailer's *The Armies of the Night* (1968). Although still sometimes used by journalists, the term suffers from the disadvantage of already meaning something else (i.e. a conspiratorial group within a divided organization).

falling rhythm (also called 'descending rhythm'), a rhythmical effect often found in metrical verse in which the unstressed syllables are perceived as being attached to the preceding stressed syllables rather than to those following. In the terms of classical *prosody, lines composed of *dactyls or *trochees may be marked by falling rhythm, although this is not inevitable. Falling rhythm is less common in English verse than its opposite, *rising rhythm.

fancy, the mind's ability to produce new combinations of images or ideas, usually in a more limited, superficial, or whimsical manner than that achieved by the *imagination proper. Before S. T. Coleridge's distinction between the faculties of fancy and imagination, the terms were often synonymous, 'fancy' being an abbreviation of 'fantasy'. Coleridge, in *Biographia Literaria* (1817), argued that the fancy was merely 'a mode of memory emancipated from the order of time and space' and was thus able to combine and reassemble ready-made images in new spatial and temporal arrangements, but not able to dissolve and unite them in new creations as the imagination could.

fantastic, the, a mode of fiction in which the possible and the impossible are confounded so as to leave the reader (and often the narrator and/or central character) with no consistent explanation for the story's strange events. Tzvetan Todorov, in his *Introduction à la littérature fantastique* (1970; translated as *The Fantastic*, 1973), argues that fantastic narratives involve an unresolved hesitation between the supernatural explanation available in *marvellous tales and the natural or psychological explanation offered by tales of the *uncanny. The literature of the fantastic flourished in 19th-century ghost stories and related fiction: Henry James's mysterious tale *The Turn of the Screw* (1898) is a classic example.

fantasy, a general term for any kind of fictional work that is not primarily devoted to realistic representation of the known world. The category includes several literary *genres (e.g. *dream vision, *fable, fairy tale, *romance, *science fiction) describing imagined worlds in which magical powers and other impossibilities are accepted. Recent theorists of fantasy have attempted to distinguish more precisely between the self-contained magical realms of the *marvellous, the psychologically explicable delusions of the *uncanny, and the inexplicable meeting of both in the *fantastic.

farce, a kind of *comedy that inspires hilarity mixed with panic and cruelty in its audience through an increasingly rapid and improbable series of ludicrous confusions, physical disasters, and sexual innuendos among its *stock characters. Farcical episodes of buffoonery can be found in European drama of all periods since Aristophanes, notably in medieval France, where the term originated to describe short comic *interludes; but as a distinct form of full-length comedy farce dates from the 19th century, in the works of Eugène Labiche in the 1850s, and of A. W. Pinero and Georges Feydeau in the 1880s and 1890s. Brandon Thomas's *Charley's Aunt* (1892) is recognized as a classic of the *genre. The bedroom farce, involving bungled adultery in rooms with too many doors, has had prolonged commercial success in London's *West End since the 1920s, when Ben Travers perfected the genre at the Aldwych Theatre. Joe Orton used its *conventions to create a disturbing kind of *satire in *What the Butler Saw* (1969). For a fuller account, consult Jessica Milner Davis, *Farce* (1978).

Fastnachtspiel (plural *-spiele*), a kind of short popular drama performed by townsfolk in Germany during the Shrove Tuesday (*Fastnacht*) festivals in the 16th century. Most surviving examples are from Nuremburg, where Hans Sachs (1494–1576) was the foremost author of such plays.

feminine ending, the ending of a metrical verse line on an unstressed syllable, as in the regular *trochaic line. In English iambic *pentameters, a feminine ending involves the addition of an eleventh syllable, as in Shakespeare's famous line

> To be, or not to be; that is the question

In French, a feminine line is one ending with a mute *e*, *es*, or *ent*. A feminine *caesura is a pause following an unstressed syllable, usually in the middle of a line. *See also* metre, stress.

feminine rhyme (also called double rhyme), a rhyme on two syllables, the first stressed and the second unstressed (e.g. *mother/another*), commonly found in many kinds of poetry but especially in humorous verse, as in Byron's *Don Juan*:

> Christians have burned each other, quite persuaded
> That all the Apostles would have done as they did.

*Masculine rhyme, on the other hand, does not employ unstressed syllables. Where more than one word is used in one of the rhyming units, as in the example above, the rhyme is sometimes called a 'mosaic rhyme'. In French verse, the alternation of masculine and feminine rhymes become the norm during the 16th century.

Festschrift (plural -**iften**), a volume of essays written by the disciples of an eminent scholar or writer, to whom it is presented as a tribute on a special occasion such as a birthday or retirement. The custom and the term ('celebration-writing') originated in German universities in the 19th century.

feuilleton [fer-yĕ-to^n], a French term for the literary section of a daily newspaper: originally the lower part of the front page, devoted to drama criticism, but later a separate page or pages. The *roman-feuilleton* is a novel serialized in a newspaper; this form flourished in France in the 1840s, bringing great financial rewards to Balzac, George Sand, Dumas *père* and other authors.

ficelle [fi-sell], the term used by Henry James in the prefaces to some of his novels to denote a fictional character whose role as *confidant or confidante is exploited as a means of providing the reader with information while avoiding direct address from the *narrator: in James's novel *The Ambassadors* (1903), Maria Gostrey is the *ficelle* to whom the *protagonist Lambert Strether discloses confidentially his opinions about the complex state of affairs in which he is involved. In French, the word denotes a string used to manipulate a puppet, or more broadly, any underhand trick.

fiction, the general term for invented stories, now usually applied to novels, short stories, novellas, romances, fables, and other *narrative works in prose, even though most plays and narrative poems are also fictional. The adjective **fictitious** tends to carry the unfavourable sense of falsehood, whereas 'fictional' is more neutral, and the archaic adjective **fictive,** revived by the poet Wallace Stevens and others, has a

more positive sense closer to 'imaginative' or 'inventive'. *Verb*:
fictionalize. *See also* metafiction.

figure (or **figure of speech**), an expression that departs from the
accepted literal sense or from the normal order of words, or in which an
emphasis is produced by patterns of sound. Such **figurative language**
is an especially important resource of poetry, although not every poem
will use it; it is also constantly present in all other kinds of speech and
writing, even though it usually passes unnoticed. The ancient theory of
*rhetoric named and categorized dozens of figures, drawing a rough
and often disputed distinction between those (known as *tropes or
figures of thought) that extend the meaning of words, and those that
merely affect their order or their impact upon an audience (known as
figures of speech, schemes, or rhetorical figures). The most important
tropes are *metaphor, *simile, *metonymy, *synecdoche,
*personification, and *irony; others include *hyperbole
(overstatement), *litotes (understatement), and *periphrasis
(circumlocution). The minor rhetorical figures can emphasize or
enliven a point in several different ways: by placing words in contrast
with one another (*antithesis), by repeating words in various patterns
(*anadiplosis, *anaphora, *antistrophe, *chiasmus), by changing the
order of words (*hyperbaton), by missing out conjunctions
(*asyndeton), by changing course or breaking off in mid-sentence
(*anacoluthon, *aposiopesis), or by assuming special modes of address
(*apostrophe) or inquiry (*rhetorical question). A further category of
figures, sometimes known as 'figures of sound', achieves emphasis by
the repetition of sounds, as in *alliteration, *assonance, and
*consonance.

fin de siècle [fa^n dě si-airkl], the French phrase ('end of century') often
used to refer to the characteristic world-weary mood of European culture
in the 1880s and 1890s, when writers and artists like Oscar Wilde,
Aubrey Beardsley, and the French *symbolists, under the slogan '*art
for art's sake', adopted a 'decadent' rejection of any moral or social
function for art. Reacting against *realism and *naturalism, they
sought a pure beauty entirely removed from the imperfections of nature
and from the drabness of contemporary society. *See also* Aestheticism,
decadence.

first-person narrative, a narrative or mode of storytelling in which
the *narrator appears as the 'I' recollecting his or her own part in the

events related, either as a witness of the action or as an important participant in it. The term is most often used of novels such as Charlotte Brontë's *Jane Eyre* (1847), in which the narrator is also the central character. The term does not mean that the narrator speaks only in the first person, of course: in discussions of other characters, the third person will be used.

fit, an obsolete term for a *canto or division of a long poem. The 14th-century English poem *Sir Gawain and the Green Knight* is composed of four fits.

fixed forms, the general term covering the various kinds of poem in which the *metre and *rhyme scheme are governed by a prescribed pattern. The term usually refers to a class of medieval French verse-forms including the *ballade, *chant royal, *rondeau, *sestina, *triolet, and *villanelle; but there are some other fixed poetic forms, the most significant being the *sonnet, the *haiku, and the *limerick. Various established *stanza forms such as *ottava rima and *rhyme royal may also be considered as 'fixed'.

flashback, *see* analepsis.

flyting, a slanging match in verse, usually between two poets who insult each other alternately in profanely abusive verses. The finest example from the strong Scottish tradition is the early 16th-century *Flyting of Dunbar and Kennedie*. The term has also been applied to the boasting matches between warriors in some *epic poems. *See also* amoebean verses, *débat*, invective.

focalization, the term used in modern *narratology for *'point of view'; that is, for the kind of perspective from which the events of a story are witnessed. Events observed by a traditional *omniscient narrator are said to be non-focalized, whereas events witnessed within the story's world from the constrained perspective of a single character are 'internally focalized'. The nature of a given narrative's focalization is to be distinguished from its narrative 'voice', as seeing is from speaking.

foil, a character whose qualities or actions serve to emphasize those of the *protagonist (or of some other character) by providing a strong contrast with them. Thus in Charlotte Brontë's *Jane Eyre*, the passive obedience of Jane's school-friend Helen Burns makes her a foil to the rebellious heroine.

folio, a large size of book in which the page size results from folding a standard printer's sheet of paper in half, forming two leaves (i.e. four pages). The collected editions of Shakespeare's plays published after his death, as distinct from the earlier unauthorized *quarto editions, are often referred to as the Folios: the First Folio was published by his colleagues Heming and Condell in 1623, and three others followed in 1632, 1663, and 1685.

folk song, a song of unknown authorship that has been passed on, preserved, and adapted (often in several versions) in an *oral tradition before later being written down or recorded. Folk songs usually have an easily remembered melody and a simple poetic form such as the *quatrain. The most prominent categories are the narrative *ballad and the *lyric love-song, but the term also covers lullabies, *carols, and various songs to accompany working (e.g. the sea shanty), dancing, and drinking.

folklore, a modern term for the body of traditional customs, superstitions, stories, dances, and songs that have been adopted and maintained within a given community by processes of repetition not reliant on the written word. Along with *folk songs and *folktales, this broad category of cultural forms embraces all kinds of *legends, *riddles, jokes, *proverbs, games, charms, omens, spells, and rituals, especially those of pre-literate societies or social classes. Those forms of verbal expression that are handed on from one generation or locality to the next by word of mouth are said to constitute an *oral tradition. *Adjective*: **folkloric**.

folktale, a story passed on by word of mouth rather than by writing, and thus partly modified by successive re-tellings before being written down or recorded. The category includes *legends, *fables, jokes, *tall stories, and fairy tales or *Märchen*. Many folktales involve mythical creatures and magical transformations.

foot (plural **feet**), a group of syllables taken as a unit of poetic *metre in traditional *prosody, regardless of word-boundaries. As applied to English verse, the foot is a certain fixed combination of syllables, each of which is counted as being either stressed (●) or unstressed (○); but in Greek and Latin *quantitative verse, from which the various names of feet are derived, it is a combination of long (–) and short (◡) syllables. While the concept of the foot is clearly applicable to the quantitative principles of Greek and Latin verse, its widespread use in the analysis of the very different stress-based patterns of English verse is often very unhelpful and misleading, especially in *accentual verse. It is worth remembering that the foot is only an abstract unit of analysis in *scansion, not a substantial rhythmic entity. The most common feet in English prosody are the *iamb (○● : *to be*) and the *trochee (●○: *beat it*); these disyllabic or 'duple' feet are the units of metrical lines described as iambic and trochaic respectively, according to the perceived predominance of one or other foot in the line. Less common in English are the trisyllabic or 'triple' feet known as the *dactyl (●○○: *heavenly*) and the *anapaest (○○●: *to the wall*); again, these feet when predominant in a line give their names to dactylic and anapaestic metres. Two other feet are sometimes referred to in English prosody, although they do not form the basis for whole lines: these are the *spondee (●●: *home-made*) and the *pyrrhic (○○: *in a*), which are both regarded as devices of metrical *substitution. There are several other Greek quantitative feet, for which equivalents are occasionally found or fabricated in English: these include the *amphibrach (‿ − ‿), the *amphimacer or cretic (− ‿ −), the *choriamb (− ‿ ‿ −), the *ionic (‿ ‿ − − or − − ‿ ‿), the *paeon (− ‿ ‿ ‿ or ‿ ‿ ‿ −), and the epitrite (− ‿ − − or − − ‿ −). In traditional prosody, it is the number of feet in a line that determines the description of its length: thus a line of four feet is called a *tetrameter, while a line of five feet is a *pentameter.

foregrounding, giving unusual prominence to one element or property of a *text, relative to other less noticeable aspects. According to the theories of *Russian Formalism, literary works are special by virtue of the fact that they foreground their own linguistic status, thus drawing attention to how they say something rather than to what they say: poetry 'deviates' from everyday speech and from prose by using *metre, surprising *metaphors, *alliteration, and other devices by which its language draws attention to itself. *See also* defamiliarization, literariness.

form, a critical term with a confusing variety of meanings. It can refer to a *genre (e.g. 'the short story form'), or to an established pattern of poetic devices (as in the various *fixed forms of European poetry), or, more abstractly, to the structure or unifying principle of design in a given work. Since the rise of *Romanticism, critics have often contrasted the principle of *organic form, which is said to evolve from within the developing work, with 'mechanic form', which is imposed as a predetermined design. When speaking of a work's **formal** properties, critics usually refer to its structural design and patterning, or sometimes to its style and manner in a wider sense, as distinct from its *content.

formalism, in the most general sense, the cultivation of artistic technique at the expense of subject-matter, either in literary practice or in criticism. The term has been applied, often in a derogatory sense, to several kinds of approach to literature in which *form is emphasized in isolation from a work's meanings or is taken as the chief criterion of aesthetic value. In modern critical discussion, however, the term frequently refers more specifically to the principles of certain Russian and Czech theorists: for this sense, *see* Russian Formalism.

formulaic, characterized by the repetition of certain stock phrases, known as **formulae.** Many orally composed poems, especially *epics, are formulaic in that they repeatedly use the same *epithets and the same forms of introduction to episodes and speeches. In another sense, a work may be called formulaic if it conforms in a predictable way to the established patterns of a *genre.

four-hander, a play written for only four speaking parts, such as Harold Pinter's *No Man's Land* (1975).

fourteener, a line of verse containing fourteen syllables. It usually has seven stresses in an *iambic metre, in which case it can also be called an iambic *heptameter. Fourteeners, usually in rhyming *couplets or *poulter's measure, were often used by English poets in the 15th and 16th centuries, but rarely after George Chapman's famous translation of the *Iliad* (1611), from which this fourteener comes:

> So Agamemnon did sustain the torment of his wound.

In couplets, fourteeners strongly resemble the *ballad metre.

frame narrative or **frame story,** a story in which another story is enclosed or *embedded as a 'tale within the tale', or which contains several such tales. Prominent examples of frame narratives enclosing several tales are Boccaccio's *Decameron* (1353) and Chaucer's *Canterbury Tales* (c.1390), while some novels such as Mary Shelley's *Frankenstein* (1818) and Emily Brontë's *Wuthering Heights* (1847) employ a narrative structure in which the main action is relayed at second hand through an enclosing frame story. *See also* diegesis.

free indirect style or **free indirect discourse,** a manner of presenting the thoughts or utterances of a fictional character as if from that character's point of view by combining grammatical and other features of the character's 'direct speech' with features of the narrator's 'indirect' report. Direct discourse is used in the sentence *She thought, 'I will stay here tomorrow'*, while the equivalent in indirect discourse would be *She thought that she would stay there the next day*. Free indirect style, however, combines the person and tense of indirect discourse ('she would stay') with the indications of time and place appropriate to direct discourse ('here tomorrow'), to form a different kind of sentence: *She would stay here tomorrow*. This form of statement allows a *third-person narrative to exploit a first-person *point of view, often with a subtle effect of *irony, as in the novels of Jane Austen. Since Flaubert's celebrated use of this technique (known in French as *le style indirect libre*) in his novel *Madame Bovary* (1857), it has been widely adopted in modern fiction.

free verse (or, in French, *vers libre*), a kind of poetry that does not conform to any regular *metre: the length of its lines is irregular, as is its use of rhyme—if any. Instead of a regular metrical pattern it uses more flexible *cadences or rhythmic groupings, sometimes supported by *anaphora and other devices of repetition. Now the most widely practised verse form in English, it has precedents in translations of the biblical Psalms and in some poems of Blake and Goethe, but established itself only in the late 19th and early 20th centuries with Walt Whitman, the French *Symbolists, and the poets of *modernism. Free verse should not be confused with *blank verse, which does observe a regular metre in its unrhymed lines.

function, a concept employed in *structuralist literary theory in two senses: either as a kind of use to which language can be directed, or as an action contributing towards the development of a *narrative. The first sense is employed in the influential model of communication outlined in Roman Jakobson's 'Closing statement: linguistics and poetics' (1960). Here Jakobson defines six linguistic functions according to the element of the communicative act that each function makes predominant. Thus the *emotive* function orients the communication towards the 'addresser' (i.e. speaker or writer), expressing an attitude or mood; the *conative* (or connotative) function orients a communication towards its 'addressee' or recipient, as in commands; the most commonly used function, the *referential*, orients a message towards a context beyond itself, conveying some information; the *phatic* function is oriented to the 'contact' between addresser and addressee, maintaining or confirming their link (e.g., in conversation, 'well, here we are, then'; or by radio, 'receiving you loud and clear'); the *metalingual* function is oriented towards the *code, usually to establish that it is shared by both parties (e.g. 'understood?' or 'it depends what you mean by …'); finally, the *poetic* function is oriented towards the 'message' itself, that is, to the communication's linguistic features of sound, *syntax, and *diction (*see also* foregrounding). The second sense of 'function' is used in *narratology, denoting a fundamental component of a tale: an action performed by a character that is significant in the unfolding of the story. Vladimir Propp, in his *Morphology of the Folktale* (1928), described 31 such narrative functions in Russian fairy tales, claiming that their order of appearance is invariable, although not every function will appear in one tale. Thus the 11th function ('the hero leaves home') necessarily precedes the 18th ('the villain is defeated') and the 20th ('the hero returns').

fustian, pretentiously inflated or pompous language. *See also* bombast, rodomontade.

Futurism, a short-lived *avant-garde* movement in European art and literature launched in 1909 by the Italian poet Filippo Marinetti in the first of many Futurist manifestos. Futurism violently rejected all previous artistic traditions and conventions along with accepted grammatical rules, in an attempt to express the dynamism and speed of the 20th-century machine age. Its new poetic techniques included typographic experiments and the composition of poems made up of meaningless sounds. Marinetti's aggressive masculine cult of machinery and warfare was eventually exploited by Mussolini as part of official Fascist culture in Italy, although a distinct revolutionary socialist group of Futurists also appeared in Russia in 1912, led by the poet and play-wright Vladimir Mayakovsky. Elsewhere in Europe, Futurism influenced the French poet Guillaume Apollinaire and the *Dada movement, and provoked the emergence of *Vorticism. The adjective **futuristic** usually has no reference to this movement, but is applied to fictional works (usually of *science fiction or *utopian fantasy) that describe some imagined future society.

gaff, a 19th-century term for a rudimentary kind of theatre offering cheap entertainment, usually in the form of *melodrama; such theatres were often referred to as 'penny gaffs', on the basis of the admission price.

galliambics, verses written in a Greek *metre associated with the Galli, who were the eunuch priests of the goddess Cybele. Used in Greek by Callimachus, and more famously in Latin by Catullus, the galliambic line is a variant of the *ionic tetrameter. A rare adaptation of this metre into English stress-patterns is Tennyson's poem 'Boadicea', written in awkwardly long lines of between 16 and 18 syllables:

> Lash the maiden into swooning, me they lash'd and humiliated.

gazal, *see* ghazal.

Geneva school, a group of critics associated with the University of Geneva at various times since the 1940s. Its most prominent figure has been the Belgian critic Georges Poulet, while in the USA J. Hillis Miller was a significant practitioner of the school's methods before he adopted those of *deconstruction; others include Jean Rousset, Jean Starobinski, and Jean-Pierre Richard. Drawing on the philosophical tradition of *phenomenology, these 'critics of consciousness' (as they have sometimes been called) saw the critic's task as one of identifying, and fully identifying *with*, the unique mode of consciousness pervading a given author's works. Thus an author's particular sense of time and space would be seen as the unifying source of his or her entire *oeuvre*, regardless of the differences between individual works. Although related to some of the assumptions of biographical criticism, the 'phenomenological' approach of the Geneva critics differs in that it works back from the texts to the mind behind them, not from the life to the texts. An impressive example of this approach at work in English is J. Hillis Miller's *Charles Dickens: The World of his Novels* (1959).

genre [zhah^{n}r], the French term for a type, species, or class of composition. A literary genre is a recognizable and established category of written work employing such common *conventions as will prevent readers or audiences from mistaking it for another kind. Much of the confusion surrounding the term arises from the fact that it is used simultaneously for the most basic modes of literary art (*lyric, *narrative, dramatic); for the broadest categories of composition (poetry, prose fiction), and for more specialized sub-categories, which are defined according to several different criteria including formal structure (*sonnet, *picaresque novel), length (*novella, *epigram), intention (*satire), effect (*comedy), origin (*folktale), and subject-matter (*pastoral, *science fiction). While some genres, such as the pastoral *elegy or the *melodrama, have numerous conventions governing subject, style, and form, others—like the *novel—have no agreed rules, although they may include several more limited *subgenres. *Adjective*: **generic.** *See also* decorum, form, mode, type.

Georgian poetry, a body of English verse published in the first half of George V's reign (1910–36) in five anthologies edited by Edward Marsh as *Georgian Poetry* (1912–22). The group of poets represented here included Rupert Brooke, Walter de la Mare, John Drinkwater, James Elroy Flecker, John Masefield, and J. C. Squire. They are now usually regarded as minor poets, quietly traditional in form and devoted to what Robert Graves called 'uncontroversial subjects' of rural and domestic life. The term **Georgianism** is sometimes used in a slightly extended sense to embrace this group along with other more or less traditional poets of the time (e.g. Edward Thomas) in contrast with the contemporary movement of *modernism in English verse. The term Georgian is only rarely applied to the literature of the period of the first four Georges (1714–1830).

georgic [jor-jik], a *didactic poem giving instruction on farming, husbandry, or some comparable pursuit, often involving praise of rural life. The earliest Greek example is Hesiod's *Works and Days* (8th century BCE), but the most influential work was the *Georgics* (37–30 BCE) of the Roman poet Virgil, which includes advice on bee-keeping and vines. Several English poets in the 18th century produced banal georgics in imitation of Virgil, including John Dyer in *The Fleece* (1757) and James Grainger in *The Sugar-Cane* (1759). Apart from its didactic intention, the georgic is distinguished from the *pastoral in that it regards nature in terms of necessary labour, not of harmonious idleness.

ghazal or **ghasel** (also spelt gazal, ghazel), a short *lyric poem written in *couplets using a single rhyme (*aa*, *ba*, *ca*, *da* etc.), sometimes mentioning the poet's name in the last couplet. The ghazal is an important lyric form in Arabic, Persian, Turkish, and Urdu poetry, often providing the basis for popular love songs. Its usual subject-matter is amatory, although it has been adapted for religious, political, and other uses. Goethe and other German poets of the early 19th century wrote some imitations of the Persian ghazal.

gloss, an explanation or translation of a difficult word or phrase, usually added to a text by a later copyist or editor, as in many modern editions of Chaucer. When placed between the lines of a text, it is known as an 'interlinear gloss', but it may appear in the margin, or as a footnote, or in an appendix, and may form an extended commentary. A rare example of a poem that includes the author's own marginal glosses is Coleridge's 'The Rime of the Ancient Mariner' (1798; glosses added 1817). A **glossary** is a list of difficult words and phrases with accompanying explanations. *Verb*: **gloss**.

gnomic [noh-mik], characterized by the expression of popular wisdom in the condensed form of *proverbs or *aphorisms, also known as **gnomes**. The term was first used of the 'Gnomic Poets' of 6th-century Greece, although there are older traditions of gnomic writing in Chinese, Egyptian, and other cultures; the Hebrew book of Proverbs is a well-known collection. The term is often extended to later writings in which moral truths are presented in maxims or aphorisms. See also *sententia*.

goliardic verse [gohli-ard-ik], a kind of medieval lyric poetry typically celebrating love and drink, attributed to the **goliards,** who were supposedly wandering scholars in France, Germany, and England in the 12th and 13th centuries. Some of the goliardic lyrics also contain *satire against the clergy. The most famous examples of goliardic verse appear in the *Carmina Burana*, a 13th-century collection of Latin and German poems discovered in a Bavarian monastery in the 19th century.

Gothic novel or **Gothic romance,** a story of terror and suspense, usually set in a gloomy old castle or monastery (hence 'Gothic', a term applied to medieval architecture and thus associated in the 18th century with superstition). Following the appearance of Horace Walpole's *The Castle of Otranto* (1764), the Gothic novel flourished in Britain from the 1790s to the 1820s, dominated by Ann Radcliffe, whose *Mysteries of Udolpho* (1794) had many imitators. She was careful to explain away the apparently supernatural occurrences in her stories, but other writers, like M. G. Lewis in *The Monk* (1796), made free use of ghosts and demons along with scenes of cruelty and horror. The fashion for such works, ridiculed by Jane Austen in *Northanger Abbey* (1818), gave way to a vogue for *historical novels, but it contributed to the new emotional climate of *Romanticism. In an extended sense, many novels that do not have a medievalized setting, but which share a comparably sinister, *grotesque, or claustrophobic atmosphere have been classed as Gothic: Mary Shelley's *Frankenstein* (1818) is a well-known example; and there are several important American tales and novels with strong Gothic elements in this sense, from Poe to Faulkner and beyond. A popular modern variety of women's *romance dealing with endangered heroines in the manner of Charlotte Brontë's *Jane Eyre* (1847) and Daphne du Maurier's *Rebecca* (1938) is also referred to as Gothic. *See also* fantastic, preromanticism. For a fuller account, consult Fred Botting, *Gothic* (1996).

grammatology, the title adopted by the French philosopher Jacques Derrida, in his book *De la grammatologie* (1967), for the general theory of writing; this is a mode of inquiry involving the critique of *phonocentrism, rather than a science with a known object. *See* deconstruction.

Grand Guignol [grah^n gween-yol], a popular French form of *melodrama featuring bloody murders, rapes, and other sensational outrages, presented in lurid and gruesome detail. It is named after Guignol, a French puppet-character similar to Mr Punch. The term is now often applied to horror movies; while in contemporary fiction, several of Angela Carter's stories are studies in *Grand Guignol*.

grapheme, the smallest meaningful unit of a written language. As with the concept of the *phoneme, a grapheme is defined negatively by its differences from other units of writing. Thus the letter *b* makes a difference in meaning because it differs from the letter *d*, so *big* and *dig* mean different things. The study of graphic signs in a given language is known as **graphemics** or **graphology**.

graveyard poetry, the term applied to a minor but influential 18th-century tradition of meditative poems on mortality and immortality, often set in graveyards. The so-called 'graveyard school' of poets in England and Scotland was not in fact an organized group. The best-known examples of this melancholic kind of verse are 'A Night-Piece on

Death' (1721) by the Irish poet Thomas Parnell, Edward Young's *Night Thoughts* (1742–6), the Scottish clergyman Robert Blair's *The Grave* (1743), and the culmination of this tradition in English, Thomas Gray's 'Elegy written in a Country Churchyard' (1751; usually called 'Gray's Elegy'). These works had many imitators in Europe, and constitute a significant current of *preromanticism.

griot [gree-oh], a kind of *bard or itinerant minstrel found in western African societies, who usually sings of local legends, histories, genealogies, or heroic deeds.

grotesque, characterized by bizarre distortions, especially in the exaggerated or abnormal depiction of human features. The literature of the grotesque involves freakish caricatures of people's appearance and behaviour, as in the novels of Dickens. A disturbingly odd fictional character may also be called a grotesque.

Grub Street, a street in London (now renamed Milton Street) off Chiswell Street by Finsbury Square, which was occupied in the 18th century by impoverished writers reduced to turning out third-rate poems, reference books, and histories to make a living. The term now covers any such underworld of literary penury and its products, as in George Gissing's novel *New Grub Street* (1891). Its writers are known as 'hacks'; an abbreviation of 'hackney', a hired horse.

gynocritics, the branch of modern feminist literary studies that focuses on women as writers, as distinct from the feminist critique of male authors. The term was coined by Elaine Showalter in her article 'Toward a Feminist Poetics' (1979), in which she explains that gynocritics is concerned 'with woman as the producer of textual meaning, with the history, themes, genres, and structures of literature by women'. It thus includes critical works like Showalter's *A Literature of Their Own* (1977), Sandra Gilbert and Susan Gubar's *The Madwoman in the Attic* (1979), and several other such studies published since the mid-1970s. Some writers have amended the term to 'gynocriticism', using 'gynocritics' to denote instead the practitioners of this kind of feminist study. *Adjective*: **gynocritical**.

hagiography [hag-i-og-răfi], writing devoted to recording and glorifying the lives of saints and martyrs. This form of Christian propaganda was much practised in the Middle Ages but has few equivalents in modern literary equivalents apart from G. B. Shaw's play *Saint Joan* (1923). By extension, the term is now often applied to modern biographies that treat their subjects reverentially as if they were saints. A writer of such works is a **hagiographer**. *Adjective*: **hagiographic.**

haiku [hy-koo], a form of Japanese *lyric verse that encapsulates a single impression of a natural object or scene, within a particular season, in seventeen syllables arranged in three unrhymed lines of five, seven, and five syllables. Arising in the 16th century, it flourished in the hands of Bashō (1644–94) and Buson (1715–83). At first an opening *stanza of a longer sequence (*haikai*), it became a separate form in the modern period under the influence of Masaoka Shiki (1867–1902). The haiku *convention whereby feelings are suggested by natural images rather than directly stated has appealed to many Western imitators since *c*.1905, notably the *Imagists. *See also* tanka.

half-rhyme, an imperfect *rhyme (also known by several other names including near rhyme, pararhyme and slant rhyme) in which the final consonants of stressed syllables agree but the vowel sounds do not match; thus a form of *consonance (*cape/deep*), sometimes taking the form of 'rich' consonance, in which the preceding consonants also correspond (*cape/keep*). Employed regularly in early Icelandic, Irish, and Welsh poetry, it appeared only as an occasional *poetic licence in English verse until the late 19th century, when Emily Dickinson and G. M. Hopkins made frequent use of it. The example provided by W. B. Yeats and Wilfred Owen has encouraged its increasingly widespread use in English since the early 20th century. *See also* eye rhyme.

hamartia, the Greek word for error or failure, used by Aristotle in his *Poetics* (4th century BCE) to designate the false step that leads the *protagonist in a *tragedy to his or her downfall. The term has often been translated as 'tragic flaw', but this misleadingly confines the cause of the reversal of fortunes to some personal defect of character, whereas Aristotle's emphasis was rather upon the protagonist's *action*, which could be brought about by misjudgement, ignorance, or some other cause. *See also* hubris, peripeteia.

Harlem Renaissance, a notable phase of black American writing centred in Harlem (a predominantly black area of New York City) in the 1920s. Announced by Alain Locke's anthology *The New Negro* (1925), the movement included the poets Langston Hughes, Jean Toomer, Countee Cullen, and Claude McKay, continuing into the 1930s with the novels of Zora Neale Hurston and Arna Bontemps. It brought a new self-awareness and critical respect to black literature in the United States.

Hellenistic, the term designating a period of Greek literature and learning from the death of Alexander the Great (323 BCE) to that of Cleopatra (31 BCE), when the centre of Greek culture had shifted to the settlements of the eastern Mediterranean, notably the great library of Alexandria. This period includes the poetry of Callimachus and Theocritus, the philosophy of Epicurus and the Stoics, and the scientific achievements of Aristarchus, Archimedes, and Euclid (*see also* Alexandrianism). A **Hellenist** is a student or admirer of Greek civilization, or, in a special sense promoted by Matthew Arnold in *Culture and Anarchy* (1869), a devotee of **Hellenism** (the life of intellect and beauty), which Arnold contrasted with Hebraism (the life of moral obedience) in his sketch of the two contending ideals within Western culture. Phrases or constructions derived from the Greek language (e.g. *hoi polloi*) are also called Hellenisms.

hemistich [hem-i-stik], a half-line of verse, either standing as an unfinished line for dramatic or other emphasis, or forming half of a complete line divided by a *caesura. In the second sense, the hemistich is an important structural unit of the early Germanic *alliterative metre. In verse drama, *dialogue in which characters exchange short utterances of half a line is known as **hemistichomythia** (*see* stichomythia). *Adjective*: **hemistichic.**

hendecasyllabics, verses written in lines of eleven syllables. Hendecasyllabic verse is found in some ancient Greek works, and was used frequently by the Roman poet Catullus. The **hendecasyllable** later became the standard line of Italian verse, both in *sonnets and in *epic poetry, and was also used by some Spanish poets. It is very rare in English, although Tennyson and Swinburne attempted imitations of Catullus's *metre, as in this line from Swinburne's 'Hendecasyllabics' (1866):

> Sweet sad straits in a soft subsiding channel.

hendiadys [hen-**dy**-ă-dis], a *figure of speech described in traditional *rhetoric as the expression of a single idea by means of two nouns joined by the conjunction 'and' (e.g. *house and home* or *law and order*), rather than by a noun qualified by an adjective. The commonest English examples, though, combine two adjectives (*nice and juicy*) or verbs (*come and get it*). Shakespeare uses this figure quite often in his later works, as in the first part of this line from *Hamlet*:

> The flash and outbreak of a fiery mind.

heptameter [hep-**tamm**-it-er], a metrical verse line composed of seven feet (*see* foot). In the context of English verse, in which a heptameter is a seven-stress line, it is often referred to as a *fourteener. It is sometimes known as a septenary.

hermeneutic circle, a model of the process of interpretation, which begins from the problem of relating a work's parts to the work as a whole: since the parts cannot be understood without some preliminary understanding of the whole, and the whole cannot be understood without comprehending its parts, our understanding of a work must involve an anticipation of the whole that informs our view of the parts while simultaneously being modified by them. This problem, variously formulated, has been a recurrent concern of German philosophy since the work of the theologian Friedrich Schleiermacher in the early 19th century. The writings of Hans-Georg Gadamer in the 1960s tackled a similar hermeneutic circle in which we can understand the present only in the context of the past, and vice versa; his solutions to this puzzle have influenced the emergence of *reception theory.

hermeneutics, the theory of interpretation, concerned with general problems of understanding the meanings of texts. Originally applied to the principles of *exegesis in theology, the term has been extended since the 19th century to cover broader questions in philosophy and *criticism, and is associated in particular with a tradition of German thought running from Friedrich Schleiermacher and Wilhelm Dilthey in the 19th century to Martin Heidegger and Hans-Georg Gadamer in the

20th. In this tradition, the question of interpretation is posed in terms of the *hermeneutic circle, and involves basic problems such as the possibility of establishing a determinate meaning in a text, the role of the author's intention, the historical relativity of meanings, and the status of the reader's contribution to a text's meaning. A significant modern branch of this hermeneutic tradition is *reception theory. *See also* phenomenology. For an extended account, consult Richard E. Palmer, *Hermeneutics* (1969).

hermeticism [her-**met**-iss-izm], a tendency towards obscurity in modern poetry, involving the use of private or occult *symbols and the rejection of logical expression in favour of musical suggestion. Hermetic poetry is associated primarily with the French *Symbolists and the poets influenced by them, notably the Italians Giuseppe Ungaretti, Eugenio Montale, and Salvatore Quasimodo, who are sometimes grouped together as exponents of *ermetismo*.

hero or **heroine,** the main character in a narrative or dramatic work. The more neutral term *protagonist is often preferable, to avoid confusion with the usual sense of heroism as admirable courage or nobility, since in many works (other than *epic poems, where such admirable qualities are required in the hero), the leading character may not be morally or otherwise superior. When our expectations of heroic qualities are strikingly disappointed, the central character may be known as an *anti-hero or anti-heroine.

heroic couplet, a rhymed pair of iambic *pentameter lines:

> Let Observation with extensive View
> Survey Mankind, from China to Peru   (Johnson)

Named from its use by Dryden and others in the *heroic drama of the late 17th century, the heroic couplet had been established much earlier by Chaucer as a major English verse-form for narrative and other kinds of non-dramatic poetry; it dominated English poetry of the 18th century, notably in the *closed couplets of Pope, before declining in importance in the early 19th century.

heroic drama, a kind of *tragedy or *tragicomedy that came into vogue with the Restoration of the English monarchy in 1660. Influenced by French classical tragedy and its dramatic *unities, it aimed at *epic (thus 'heroic') grandeur, usually by means of *bombast, exotic settings, and lavish scenery. The noble hero would typically be caught in a conflict between love and patriotic duty, leading to emotional scenes presented in a manner close to opera. The leading English exponent of heroic drama was John Dryden: his *The Conquest of Granada* (1670–1) and *Aureng-Zebe* (1675) were both written in *heroic couplets.

heroic poetry, another name for *epic poetry. The kind of verse line used for epic poetry in a given language is known as the **heroic line**: the dactylic *hexameter in Greek and Latin, the iambic *pentameter in English, the *alexandrine in French, the *hendecasyllabic line in Italian. The **heroic quatrian** or **heroic stanza** is not used for epics, but is so named because it employs the English heroic line: it consists of four pentameters rhyming *abab*, as in Gray's 'Elegy written in a Country Churchyard' (1751), or *aabb*.

heteroglossia, the existence of conflicting *discourses within any field of linguistic activity, such as a national language, a novel, or a specific conversation. The term appears in translations of the writings of the Russian linguistic and literary theorist Mikhail Bakhtin (1895–1975), as an equivalent for his Russian term *raznorechie* ('differentspeechness'). In Bakhtin's works, this term addresses linguistic variety as an aspect of social conflict, as in tensions between central and marginal uses of the same national language; these may be echoed in, for example, the differences between the narrative voice and the voices of the characters in a novel. *Adjectives:* **heteroglot, heteroglossic.**

hexameter [hek-**samm**-it-er], a metrical verse line of six feet (*see* foot). Its most important form is the *dactylic hexameter used in Greek and Latin *epic poetry and in the elegiac *distich: this *quantitative metre permitted the substitution of any of the first four dactyls (and more rarely of the fifth) by a *spondee, and was *catalectic in that the final foot was either a spondee or a *trochee. Although successfully adapted to the stress-based metres of German, Russian, and Swedish verse (by, among others, Goethe and Pushkin), the dactylic hexameter has not found an established place in English or French verse, except in some rather awkward experiments such as A. H. Clough's *The Bothie of Tober-na-Vuolich* (1848), from which this hexameter comes:

This was the final retort from the eager, impetuous Philip.

The *iambic hexameter in English is more usually known as an *alexandrine.

hiatus [hy-**ay**-tŭs], (i) a break in pronunciation between two adjacent vowels, either within a word (forming two distinct syllables, as in *doing*, rather than a *diphthong as in *joint*) or between the end of one word and the beginning of the next (e.g. *the expense* rather than the *elision of *th'expense*); (ii) any gap or omission in a sentence, verse, or logical argument. *See also* diaeresis, ellipsis, lacuna.

higher criticism, the name given in the 19th century to a branch of biblical scholarship concerned with establishing the dates, authorship, sources, and interrelations of the various books of the Bible, often with disturbing results for orthodox Christian dogma. It was 'higher' not in status but in the sense that it required a preliminary basis of 'lower' *textual criticism, which reconstructed the original wording of biblical texts from faulty copies.

histoire [ees-twah], the French word for story or history, used in modern *narratology to denote the *story, that is, the narrated events as distinct from the form of *narration in which they are presented: thus the *histoire* is the sequence of narrated events as reconstructed by readers in a chronological order that may differ from the order in which the *plot arranges them (see also *fabula*). In another sense, linguists have used the term to designate an apparently 'objective' way of relating events without *deixis, that is, without reference to the speaker or writer, to the auditor or reader, or to their situation, as in most kinds of historical writing and *third-person narrative; in this sense, *histoire* is contrasted with *discours*. See also *énoncé*.

historical novel, a *novel in which the action takes place during a specific historical period well before the time of writing (often one or two generations before, sometimes several centuries), and in which some attempt is made to depict accurately the customs and mentality of the period. The central character—real or imagined—is usually subject to divided loyalties within a larger historic conflict of which readers know the outcome. The pioneers of this *genre were Walter Scott and James Fenimore Cooper; Scott's historical novels, starting with *Waverley* (1814), set the pattern for hundreds of others: outstanding 19th-century examples include Victor Hugo's *Notre Dame de Paris* (1831), Dumas *père's* *Les Trois Mousquetaires* (1844), Flaubert's *Salammbô* (1862), and Tolstoy's *War and Peace* (1863–9). While the historical novel attempts a serious study of the relationship between personal fortunes and social conflicts, the popular form known as the historical or 'costume' *romance tends to employ the period setting only as a decorative background to the leading characters.

history play, a play representing events drawn wholly or partly from recorded history. The term usually refers to *chronicle plays, especially those of Shakespeare, but it also covers some later works such as Schiller's *Maria Stuart* (1800) and John Osborne's *Luther* (1961). In a somewhat looser sense, it has been applied also to some plays that take as their subject the impact of historical change on the lives of fictional characters: David Hare's *Licking Hitler* (1978) has been reprinted with two other works under the title *The History Plays* (1984).

hokku, another name for a *haiku, originally applied to the first *stanza in a longer poem known as a *haikai*, before the haiku became an independent form.

holograph, a document written entirely in the author's own handwriting.

Homeric [hoh-**merr**-ik], characteristic of or resembling the Greek *epic poems the *Iliad* and the *Odyssey* (*c*.8th century BCE), which are by custom attributed to 'Homer', a figure about whom nothing is known. For **Homeric simile,** *see* epic simile; for **Homeric epithet,** *see* epithet. The **Homeric Hymns** are a group of 33 ancient Greek poems of various dates from the 8th century BCE onwards and of unknown authorship (although some were formerly attributed to Homer); they celebrate the qualities of various Greek deities, sometimes in the form of prolonged *invocations.

homily, a sermon or morally instructive lecture. An author of homilies is a **homilist,** while the art of composing homilies is known as **homiletics.** *Adjective*: **homiletic.**

homology, a correspondence between two or more structures. The Marxist critic Lucien Goldmann developed a theory of the relations between literary works and social classes in terms of homologies. In his *Le Dieu Caché* (1959), he observed a homology between the underlying structure of Racine's tragedies and that of the world-view held by a particular group in the French nobility. This method was extended to the modern novel in Goldmann's *Pour une sociologie du roman* (1964). An example of something that bears a resemblance to something else is called a **homologue,** and is said to be **homologous** with it.

homonym, a word that is identical in form with another word, either in sound (as a *homophone) or in spelling (as a **homograph**), or in both, but differs from it in meaning: *days/daze*, or *lead* (guide)/*lead* (metal), or *pitch* (throw)/*pitch* (tar). Identity of form between two or more words is known as **homonymy**. *Adjective*: **homonymic**.

homophone, a word that is pronounced in the same way as another word but differs in meaning and/or in spelling; thus a kind of *homonym. Examples of this identity of sound, known as **homophony**, include *maid/made* and *left* (opposite of right)/*left* (abandoned). Homophony is often exploited in *puns. *Adjective*: **homophonic**.

homostrophic, composed of *stanzas that all share the same form, with identical numbers of lines of corresponding lengths, and with identical *rhyme schemes. Nearly all stanzaic verse is homostrophic. The term is used chiefly to distinguish the *Horatian ode, which is homostrophic, from the *Pindaric and irregular ode forms, which are not.

Horatian, characteristic of or derived from the work of the Roman poet Quintus Horatius Flaccus (65–8 BCE), usually known as Horace. The **Horatian ode**, as distinct from the *Pindaric ode, is *homostrophic and usually private and reflective in mood: Keats's odes (1820) are English examples of this form. **Horatian satire**, often contrasted with the bitterness of *Juvenalian satire, is a more indulgent, tolerant treatment of human inconsistencies and follies, ironically amused rather than outraged. Pope's verse satires, some of them directly modelled upon Horace's work, are generally Horatian in tone. For Horatian epistle, *see* epistle. *See also* ode, satire.

horizon of expectations, a term used in the *reception theory of Hans Robert Jauss to designate the set of cultural norms, assumptions, and criteria shaping the way in which readers understand and judge a literary work at a given time. It may be formed by such factors as the prevailing *conventions and definitions of art (e.g. *decorum), or current moral codes. Such 'horizons' are subject to historical change, so that a later generation of readers may see a very different range of meanings in the same work, and revalue it accordingly.

hubris [hew-bris] or **hybris,** the Greek word for 'insolence' or 'affront', applied to the arrogance or pride of the *protagonist in a *tragedy in which he or she defies moral laws or the prohibitions of the gods. The

protagonist's transgression or *hamartia* leads eventually to his or her
downfall, which may be understood as divine retribution or *nemesis.
Hubris is commonly translated as 'overweening (i.e. excessively
presumptuous) pride'. In proverbial terms, hubris is thus the pride that
comes before a fall. *Adjective*: **hubristic**.

Hudibrastic verse (or **Hudibrastics**) [hew-di-**bras**-tik], a kind of
comic verse written in *octosyllabic couplets with many ridiculously
forced *feminine rhymes. It is named after the long *mock-heroic
poem *Hudibras* (1663–78), a *satire on Puritanism by the English poet
Samuel Butler. These lines from Canto III give some impression of the
style:

> He would an elegy compose
> On maggots squeez'd out of his nose;
> In lyric numbers write an ode on
> His mistress, eating a black-pudden;
> And, when imprison'd air escap'd her,
> It puft him with poetic rapture.

Several poets, including Jonathan Swift, wrote Hudibrastic verse in
imitation, and the form became popular in poetic *burlesques. *See also*
doggerel, light verse.

huitain [wee-te^n], a French *stanza form consisting of eight lines of
either 8 or 10 syllables each, usually rhyming *ababbcbc* or *abbaacac*. It may
form an independent poem or part of a longer work such as a *ballade.
The *huitain* was used by François Villon in his *Lais* (1456) and in his famous
Testament (1461). In English, the stanza used earlier by Chaucer in his
Monk's Tale has the same form.

humanism, a 19th-century term for the values and ideals of the
European *Renaissance, which placed a new emphasis on the
expansion of human capacities. Reviving the study of Greek and Roman
history, philosophy, and arts, the Renaissance **humanists** developed an
image of 'Man' more positive and hopeful than that of medieval ascetic
Christianity: rather than being a miserable sinner awaiting redemption
from a pit of fleshly corruption, 'Man' was a source of infinite
possibilities, ideally developing towards a balance of physical, spiritual,
moral, and intellectual faculties. Most early humanists like Erasmus and
Milton in the 16th and 17th centuries combined elements of Christian
and classical cultures in what has become known as **Christian
humanism**, but the 18th-century *Enlightenment began to detach the

ideal of human perfection from religious supernaturalism, so that by the 20th century humanism came to denote those moral philosophies that abandon theological dogma in favour of purely human concerns. While being defined against theology on the one side, humanism came also to be contrasted with scientific materialism on the other: from the mid-19th century onwards, Matthew Arnold and others (including the **New Humanists** in the United States, led by Paul More and Irving Babbitt in the 1920s) opposed the claims of science with the ideal of balanced human perfection, self-cultivation, and ethical self-restraint. This Arnoldian humanism, which has enjoyed wide influence in Anglo-American literary culture, is one variety of the prevalent **liberal humanism**, which centres its view of the world upon the notion of the freely self-determining individual. In modern literary theory, liberal humanism (and sometimes all humanism) has come under challenge from *post-structuralism, which replaces the unitary concept of 'Man' with that of the 'subject', which is gendered, 'de-centred', and no longer self-determining. For a fuller account, consult Tony Davies, *Humanism* (1996).

humours, the bodily fluids to which medieval medicine attributed the various types of human temperament, according to the predominance of each within the body. Thus a preponderance of blood would make a person 'sanguine', while excess of phlegm would make him or her 'phlegmatic'; too much choler (or yellow bile) would give rise to a 'choleric' disposition, while an excess of black bile would produce a 'melancholic' one. The **comedy of humours**, best exemplified by Ben Jonson's play *Every Man in His Humour* (1598), and practised by some other playwrights in the 17th century, is based on the eccentricities of characters whose temperaments are distorted in ways similar to an imbalance among the bodily humours.

hybris, *see* hubris.

hymn, a song (or *lyric poem set to music) in praise of a divine or venerated being. The title is sometimes given to a poem on an elevated subject, like Shelley's 'Hymn to Intellectual Beauty' (1816), or praising a historical hero, like MacDiarmid's 'First Hymn to Lenin' (1931). The term **hymnody** is used to refer either to a particular body of hymns or to the art of hymn-writing, while a composer of hymns is called a **hymnodist** or **hymnist**. *See also* antiphon, ode, psalm.

hypallage [hy-**pal**-ăji], a *figure of speech by which an *epithet is transferred from the more appropriate to the less appropriate of two nouns: in Milton's line 'If Jonson's learnèd sock be on', *learnèd* should qualify Jonson, not his sock. Similarly in everyday speech, a person with a *blind dog* is more likely to be blind than the dog is. The term has sometimes also been applied to other constructions in which the elements of an utterance exchange their normal positions (*see* hyperbaton). *Adjective*: **hypallactic**.

hyperbaton [hy-**per**-bă-ton], a *figure of speech by which the normal order of words in a sentence is significantly altered. A very common form of *poetic licence, of which Milton's *Paradise Lost* affords many spectacular examples. *See also* inversion.

hyperbole [hy-**per**-bŏli], exaggeration for the sake of emphasis in a *figure of speech not meant literally. An everyday example is the complaint 'I've been waiting here for ages.' Hyperbolic expressions are common in the inflated style of dramatic speech known as *bombast, as in Shakespeare's *Antony and Cleopatra* when Cleopatra praises the dead Antony:

> His legs bestrid the ocean: his reared arm
> Crested the world.

hypermetrical or **hypercatalectic,** having an extra syllable or syllables in excess of the normal length of a specified metrical verse line. *See also* anacrusis, feminine ending.

hypertext, a term used in the discussion of computerized text, referring to the realm of electronically interlinked texts and multimedia resources now commonly found on the World Wide Web (from 1990) and on CD-ROM reference sources. Hypertext is sometimes distinguished from 'linear' printed text in terms of the reader's changed experience of moving around and among texts. In a different sense, the term is also applied, in discussions of *intertextuality, to a text that in some way derives from an earlier text (the 'hypotext') as a *parody of it, a sequel to it, etc.

hypotactic, marked by the use of connecting words between clauses or sentences, explicitly showing the logical or other relationships between them: 'I am tired *because* it is hot.' Such use of syntactic subordination of one clause to another is known as **hypotaxis**. The opposite kind of construction, referred to as *paratactic, simply juxtaposes clauses or sentences: 'I am tired; it is hot'. *See also* syntax.

iamb [I-am *or* I-amb] (also called **iambus**), a metrical unit (*foot) of verse, having one unstressed syllable followed by one stressed syllable, as in the word 'beyond' (or, in Greek and Latin *quantitative verse, one short syllable followed by one long syllable). Lines of poetry made up predominantly of iambs are referred to as **iambics** or as **iambic verse**, which is by far the most common kind of metrical verse in English. Its most important form is the 10-syllable iambic *pentameter, either rhymed (as in *heroic couplets, *sonnets etc.) or unrhymed in *blank verse:

> Beyond the utmost bound of human thought.   (Tennyson)

The iambic pentameter permits some variation in the placing of its five *stresses; thus it may often begin with a stressed syllable followed by an unstressed syllable (a reversal called trochaic *inversion or *substitution) before resuming the regular iambic pattern:

> Oft she rejects, but never once offends   (Pope)

The 8-syllable iambic *tetrameter is another common English line:

> Come live with me, and be my love   (Marlowe)

Iambic tetrameters were also used in ancient Greek dramatic dialogue. The English iambic *hexameter or six-stress line is usually referred to as the *alexandrine. *See also* metre.

icon [I-kon] or **iconic sign**, in the *semiotics of the American philosopher C. S. Peirce, a sign that stands for its object mainly by resembling or sharing some features (e.g. shape) with it; such resemblance having a status called **iconicity**. A photograph or diagram of an object is iconic, but the signs of language (apart from a few *onomatopoeic words) have a merely conventional or *arbitrary relation to their objects: in Peirce's terminology, they are not icons but *symbols. *See also* index.

ictus (plural -**uses**), the *stress or *accent that is placed on a syllable in a line of verse, as distinct from the stressed syllable itself. *Adjective*: **ictal**.

idiolect [id-i-oh-lekt], the particular variety of a language used by an individual speaker or writer, which may be marked by peculiarities of vocabulary, grammar, and pronunciation. *Adjective*: **idiolectal** or **idiolectic**. *See also* dialect.

idiom, a phrase or grammatical construction that cannot be translated literally into another language because its meaning is not equivalent to that of its component words. Common examples, of which there are thousands in English, include *follow suit*, *hell for leather*, *flat broke*, *on the wagon*, *well hung*, etc. By extension, the term is sometimes applied more loosely to any style or manner of writing that is characteristic of a particular group or movement. *Adjective*: **idiomatic**.

idyll or **idyl** [id-il], a short poem describing an incident of country life in terms of idealized innocence and contentment; or any such episode in a poem or prose work. The term is virtually synonymous with *pastoral poem, as in Theocritus' *Idylls* (3rd century BCE). The title of Tennyson's *Idylls of the King* (1842–85), a sequence of Arthurian *romances, bears little relation to the usual meaning. Browning in *Dramatic Idyls* (1879–80) uses the term in another sense, as a short self-contained poem. *Adjective*: **idyllic**. *See also* bucolic poetry, eclogue.

illocutionary act, an utterance that accomplishes something in the act of speaking. In the *speech act theory proposed by J. L. Austin in *How to Do Things with Words* (1962), an utterance involves not only the simple 'locutionary' act of producing a grammatical sentence, but also an 'illocutionary force' of effectiveness either as an affirmation or as a promise, a threat, a warning, a command, etc. The most explicit illocutionary acts are the *performatives, which accomplish the very deed to which they refer, when uttered by authorized speakers in certain conditions: 'I arrest you in the name of the law'; 'I hereby renounce the Devil and all his works'; 'I promise to defend and uphold the constitution.' *See also* perlocutionary.

imagery, a rather vague critical term covering those uses of language in a literary work that evoke sense-impressions by literal or *figurative reference to perceptible or 'concrete' objects, scenes, actions, or states, as distinct from the language of abstract argument or exposition. The imagery of a literary work thus comprises the set of **images** that it uses; these need not be mental 'pictures', but may appeal to senses other than sight. The term has often been applied particularly to the figurative language used in a work, especially to its *metaphors and *similes. Images suggesting further meanings and associations in ways that go beyond the fairly simple identifications of metaphor and simile are often called *symbols. The critical emphasis on imagery in the mid-20th century, both in *New Criticism and in some influential studies of Shakespeare, tended to glorify the supposed concreteness of literary works by ignoring matters of structure, convention, and abstract argument: thus Shakespeare's plays were read as clusters or patterns of 'thematic imagery' according to the predominance of particular kinds of image (of animals, of disease, etc.), without reference to the action or to the dramatic meaning of characters' speeches. *See also* motif.

imagination, the mind's capacity to generate images of objects, states, or actions that have not been felt or experienced by the senses. In the discussion of psychology and art prior to *Romanticism, imagination was usually synonymous with *fancy, and commonly opposed to the faculty of reason, either as complementary to it or as contrary to it. S. T. Coleridge's famous distinction between fancy and imagination in his *Biographia Literaria* (1817) emphasized the imagination's vitally creative power of dissolving and uniting images into new forms, and of reconciling opposed qualities into a new unity. This freely creative and transforming power of the imagination was a central principle of Romanticism.

Imagism, the doctrine and poetic practice of a small but influential group of American and British poets calling themselves Imagists or Imagistes between 1912 and 1917. Led at first by Ezra Pound, and then— after his defection to *Vorticism—by Amy Lowell, the group rejected most 19th-century poetry as cloudy verbiage, and aimed instead at a new clarity and exactness in the short *lyric poem. Influenced by the Japanese *haiku and partly by ancient Greek lyrics, the Imagists cultivated concision and directness, building their short poems around single images; they also preferred looser *cadences to traditional regular rhythms. Apart from Pound and Lowell, the group also included Richard Aldington, 'H.D.' (Hilda Doolittle), F. S. Flint, D. H. Lawrence, Ford Madox Ford, and William Carlos Williams. Imagist poems and manifestos appeared in the American magazine *Poetry* and the London journal *The Egoist*. Pound edited *Des Imagistes: An Anthology* (1914), while the three further anthologies (1915–17), all entitled *Some Imagist Poets*, were edited by Lowell. *See also* modernism.

imperfect rhyme, *see* half-rhyme.

implied author, a term coined by Wayne C. Booth in *The Rhetoric of Fiction* (1961) to designate that source of a work's design and meaning which is inferred by readers from the text, and imagined as a personality standing behind the work. As an imaginary entity, it is to be distinguished clearly from the real author, who may well have written other works implying a different kind of *persona or implied author behind them. The implied author is also to be distinguished from the *narrator, since the implied author stands at a remove from the narrative voice, as the personage assumed to be responsible for deciding what kind of narrator will be presented to the reader; in many works this distinction produces an effect of *irony at the narrator's expense.

implied reader, a term used by Wolfgang Iser and some other theorists of *reader-response criticism to denote the hypothetical figure of the reader to whom a given work is designed to address itself. Any *text may be said to presuppose an 'ideal' reader who has the particular attitudes (moral, cultural, etc.) appropriate to that text in order for it to achieve its full effect. This implied reader is to be distinguished from *actual* readers, who may be unable or unwilling to occupy the position of the implied reader: thus, most religious poetry presupposes a god-fearing implied reader, but many actual readers today are atheists. The implied reader is also not the same thing as the *narratee, who is a figure imagined within the text as listening to—or receiving a written narration from—the narrator (e.g. the wedding guest in Coleridge's 'The Rime of the Ancient Mariner').

impressionism, in the literary sense borrowed from French painting, a rather vague term applied to works or passages that concentrate on the description of transitory mental impressions as felt by an observer, rather than on the explanation of their external causes. Impressionism in literature is thus neither a school nor a movement but a kind of subjective tendency manifested in descriptive techniques. It is found in *Symbolist and *Imagist poetry, and in much modern verse, but also in many works of prose fiction since the late 19th century, as in the novels of Joseph Conrad and Virginia Woolf. **Impressionistic criticism** is the kind of *criticism that restricts itself to describing the critic's own subjective response to a literary work, rather than ascribing intrinsic qualities to it in the light of general principles. Walter Pater's defence of such criticism, in the Preface to his *Studies in the History of the Renaissance* (1873), was that 'in aesthetic criticism the first step towards seeing one's object as it really is, is to know one's own impression as it really is, to discriminate it, to realise it distinctly'. The most common kind of impressionistic criticism is found in theatre and book reviews: 'I laughed all night'; 'I couldn't put it down'.

in medias res [in med-i-ahs rayss], the Latin phrase meaning 'into the middle of things', applied to the common technique of storytelling by which the *narrator begins the story at some exciting point in the middle of the action, thereby gaining the reader's interest before explaining preceding events by *analepses ('flashbacks') at some later stage. It was conventional to begin *epic poems *in medias res*, as Milton does in *Paradise Lost*. The technique is also common in plays and in prose fiction: for example, Katherine Mansfield's short story 'A Dill Pickle' (1920) begins *in medias res* with the sentence 'And then, after six years, she saw him again.' *See also* anachrony.

In Memoriam stanza, a *stanza of four iambic *tetrameter lines rhyming *abba*, used by Tennyson in the sequence of lyrics making up his *In Memoriam A. H. H.* (1850). This was the most notable English use of this *envelope stanza, although not the first. *See also* quatrain.

incantation, the chanting or reciting of any form of words deemed to have magical power, usually in a brief rhyming spell with an insistent rhythm and other devices of repetition; or the form of words thus recited. Incantation is characteristic of magical charms, curses, prophecies, and the conjuring of spirits: a famous literary example is the witches' chant, 'Double, double, toil and trouble', in *Macbeth*. Poetry that resembles such chants may be called **incantatory.**

incremental repetition, a modern term for a device of repetition commonly found in *ballads. It involves the repetition of lines or *stanzas with small but crucial changes made to a few words from one to the next, and has an effect of *narrative progression or suspense. It is found most often in passages of dialogue, as in the traditional Scottish ballad, 'Lord Randal':

> 'What d' ye leave to your mother, Lord Randal, my son?
> What d'ye leave to your mother, my handsome young man?'
> 'Four and twenty milk kye; mother, mak my bed soon,
> For I'm sick at the heart, and I fain wad lie down.'

'What d' ye leave to your sister, Lord Randal, my son?
What d' ye leave to your sister, my handsome young man?'
'My gold and my silver; mother, mak my bed soon,
For I'm sick at the heart, and I fain wad lie down.'

indeterminacy, (1) in *reader-response criticism, any element of a
*text that requires the reader to decide on its meaning (*see also* ambiguity,
crux, *scriptible*); (2) in *deconstruction, a principle of uncertainty invoked
to deny the existence of any final or determinate meaning that could
bring to an end the play of meanings between the elements of a text (see
différance). To proclaim the ultimate indeterminacy of meaning need not
mean that no decisions can be made about the meaning of anything (or at
least it cannot be determined that it means this), only that there is no final
arbiter of such decisions. Some deconstructionists, however, have the
habit of calling the meanings of literary works 'undecidable'. *See also*
aporia.

index (plural **-dices** or **-dexes**), in the *semiotics of the American
philosopher C. S. Peirce, a *sign that is connected to its object by a
concrete relationship, usually of cause and effect. A finger or signpost
pointing to an object or place is **indexal**; so, in more clearly causal ways,
are many kinds of symptom, mark, or trace: scars, footprints, crumpled
bedclothes etc. Thus smoke may be seen as an index of fire. Peirce
distinguished the index from two other kinds of sign: the *icon and the
*symbol.

Index, the, the name commonly given to the *Index Librorum
Prohibitorum*, a list of the titles of those books that the Roman Catholic
Church forbade its followers to read, from the 16th century to 1966. A
second list, the *Index Expurgatorius*, specified those passages that must be
expurgated from certain works before they could be read by Roman
Catholics.

induction, an older word for the *prologue or introduction to a work.
The introductory episode of Shakespeare's *The Taming of the Shrew*, for
example, is called the induction.

inflection or **inflexion,** the modification of words according to their
grammatical functions, usually by employing variant word-endings to
indicate such qualities as tense, gender, case, and number (*see also*
morphology). English uses inflection for the past tense of many verbs
(usually with the ending -*ed*), for degrees of adjectives (-*er* and -*est*), for

plurals (usually -*es* or -*s*), and other functions; but it is relatively 'uninflected' by comparison with the so-called **inflected languages** such as Latin, in which the use of inflection is far more extensive. In a second sense, the term is sometimes used to denote a change of pitch in the pronunciation of a word (*see* intonation).

inscape and **instress,** two terms coined by the English poet Gerard Manley Hopkins (1844–89) in a not wholly successful attempt to elucidate his poetic method and religious philosophy. Inscape is the unique quality or essential 'whatness' of a thing, while instress is the divine energy that both supports the inscape of all things and brings it alive to the senses of the observer.

intentional fallacy, the name given by the American *New Critics W. K. Wimsatt Jr and Monroe C. Beardsley to the widespread assumption that an author's declared or supposed intention in writing a work is the proper basis for deciding on the meaning and the value of that work. In their 1946 essay 'The Intentional Fallacy' (reprinted in Wimsatt's *The Verbal Icon*, 1954), these critics argue that a literary work, once published, belongs in the public realm of language, which gives it an objective existence distinct from the author's original idea of it: 'The poem is not the critic's own and not the author's (it is detached from the author at birth and goes about the world beyond his power to intend about it or control it). The poem belongs to the public.' Thus any information or surmise we may have about the author's intention cannot in itself determine the work's meaning or value, since it still has to be verified against the work itself. Many other critics have pointed to the unreliability of authors as witnesses to the meanings of their own works, which often have significances wider than their intentions in composing them: as D. H. Lawrence wrote in his *Studies in Classic American Literature* (1923), 'Never trust the artist. Trust the tale.'

interior monologue, the written representation of a character's inner thoughts, impressions, and memories as if directly 'overheard' without the apparent intervention of a summarizing and selecting *narrator. The term is often loosely used as a synonym for *stream of consciousness. However, some confusion arises about the relationship between these two terms when critics distinguish them: some take 'stream of consciousness' as the larger category, embracing all representations of intermingled thoughts and perceptions, within which interior monologue is a special case of 'direct' presentation;

others take interior monologue as the larger category, within which stream of consciousness is a special technique emphasizing continuous 'flow' by abandoning strict logic, *syntax, and punctuation. The second of these alternatives permits us to apply the term 'interior monologue' to that large class of modern poems representing a character's unspoken thoughts and impressions, as distinct from the spoken thoughts imagined in the *dramatic monologue: Browning's 'Soliloquy of the Spanish Cloister' (1842) is an early example. More often, though, the term refers to prose passages employing stream-of-consciousness techniques: the most celebrated instance in English is the final chapter of James Joyce's *Ulysses* (1922). Joyce acknowledged Édouard Dujardin's novel *Les Lauriers sont coupées* (1888) as a precedent in the use of interior monologue. *See also* monologue.

interlude, a short play, of a kind believed to have been performed by small companies of professional actors in the intervals of banquets and other entertainments before the emergence of the London theatres. This rather loose category includes several types of play that are regarded as transitional between the *morality play and Elizabethan comedy: some resemble the morality plays in *didactic intent and are sometimes called 'moral interludes', while others are closer to *farce. Interludes flourished in England from the end of the 15th century to the late 16th century. An early example is Henry Medwall's *Fulgens and Lucres* (1497). The foremost author of interludes was John Heywood, who wrote *The Play of the Weather* (1533) among other works.

internal rhyme, a poetic device by which two or more words rhyme within the same line of verse, as in Kipling's reactionary poem 'The City of Brass' (1909):

> Men swift to see done, and outrun, their extremest commanding—
> Of the tribe which describe with a jibe the perversions of Justice—
> Panders avowed to the crowd whatsoever its lust is.

A special case of internal rhyme between words at the middle and the end of certain lines is *leonine rhyme. *See also* crossed rhyme.

interpolation, a passage inserted into a text by some later writer, usually without the authority of the original author; or the act of introducing such additional material. For example, it was once believed by many critics that the obscene jokes of the drunken porter in Shakespeare's *Macbeth* must have been interpolated by some inferior playwright.

intertextuality, a term coined by Julia Kristeva to designate the various relationships that a given *text may have with other texts. These **intertextual** relationships include anagram, *allusion, adaptation, translation, *parody, *pastiche, imitation, and other kinds of transformation. In the literary theories of *structuralism and *post-structuralism, texts are seen to refer to other texts (or to themselves as texts) rather than to an external reality. The term **intertext** has been used variously for a text drawing on other texts, for a text thus drawn upon, and for the relationship between both. For a fuller account, consult Graham Allen, *Intertextuality* (2000).

intonation, the pattern of variation in pitch during a spoken utterance. Intonation has important expressive functions, indicating the speaker's attitudes (of astonishment, sarcasm, etc.), but it also signals the grammatical status of an utterance, for instance by showing relations between clauses or by marking the difference between a simple statement and a question: in English, a simple assertion like *We are going* can be changed into a question simply by reversing its intonation from a lowering of pitch to a raising of pitch.

intrigue, an older term for the *plot of a play or story, or for its most complicated portion. In another sense closer to modern usage, the term may also refer to the secret scheme ('plot' in the other sense, as conspiracy) that one character or group of characters devises in order to outwit others. Much European comedy of the 17th century is based on complex plots about plotters, and is sometimes called the **comedy of intrigue**, especially where intricacy of plot overshadows the development of character or of satiric theme.

intrusive narrator, an *omniscient narrator who, in addition to reporting the events of a novel's story, offers further comments on characters and events, and who sometimes reflects more generally upon the significance of the story. A device used frequently by the great *realist novelists of the 19th century, notably George Eliot and Leo Tolstoy, the intrusive narrator allows the novel to be used for general moral commentary on human life, sometimes in the form of brief digressive essays interrupting the narrative. An earlier example is the narrator of Henry Fielding's *Tom Jones* (1749).

invective, the harsh denunciation of some person or thing in abusive speech or writing, usually by a succession of insulting *epithets. Among many memorable examples in Shakespeare is Timon's verbal assault upon his false friends in *Timon of Athens*:

> Most smiling, smooth, detested parasites,
> Courteous destroyers, affable wolves, meek bears,
> You fools of fortune, trencher-friends, time's flies,
> Cap-and-knee slaves, vapours, and minute-jacks!

Verb: **inveigh**. *See also* flyting, Juvenalian satire, lampoon.

inversion, the reversal of the normally expected order of words: or, in *prosody, the turning around of a metrical *foot. Inversion of word-order (*syntax) is a common form of *poetic licence allowing a poet to preserve the *rhyme scheme or the *metre of a verse line, or to place special emphasis on particular words. Common forms of inversion in English are the placing of an adjective after its noun (*the body electric*), the placing of the grammatical subject after the verb (*said she*), and the placing of an adverb or adverbial phrase before its verb (*sweetly blew the breeze*). Stronger forms of inversion, where the grammatical object precedes the verb and even the subject, are found in *Latinate styles, notably Milton's. In prosody, the term is applied to a kind of *substitution whereby one foot is replaced by another in which the positions of stressed and unstressed (or of long and short) syllables are exactly reversed: the most common type of **inverted foot** is the *trochee substituted for an *iamb at the beginning of a line.

invocation, an appeal made by a poet to a *muse or deity for help in composing the poem. The invocation of a muse was a *convention in ancient Greek and Latin poetry, especially in the *epic; it was followed later by many poets of the *Renaissance and *neoclassical periods. Usually it is placed at the beginning of the poem, but may also appear in later positions, such as at the start of a new *canto. The invocation is one of the conventions ridiculed in *mock-epic poems: Byron begins the third Canto (1821) of *Don Juan* with the exclamation 'Hail, Muse! *et cetera*'. In terms of *rhetoric, the invocation is a special variety of *apostrophe.

ionic [I-**on**-ik], a Greek metrical *foot consisting of two long syllables followed by two short syllables (known as the greater ionic or ionic *a majore*) or of two short syllables followed by two long syllables (the lesser ionic or ionic *a minore*). Associated with the early religious verse of the Ionians in Asia Minor (now Turkey), the *metre was used by several Greek *lyric poets, by the dramatist Euripides, and in Latin by Horace. It is hardly ever found in English as the basis for whole lines: the Epilogue to Robert Browning's *Asolando* (1889) provides a rare example of the lesser ionic metre adapted to English stresses:

> At the midnight in the silence of the sleep-time

irony a subtly humorous perception of inconsistency, in which an apparently straightforward statement or event is undermined by its *context so as to give it a very different significance. In various forms, irony appears in many kinds of literature, from the *tragedy of Sophocles to the novels of Jane Austen and Henry James, but is especially important in *satire, as in Voltaire and Swift. At its simplest, in **verbal irony**, it involves a discrepancy between what is said and what is really meant, as in its crude form, sarcasm; for the *figures of speech exploiting this discrepancy, *see* antiphrasis, litotes, meiosis. The more sustained **structural irony** in literature involves the use of a naïve or deluded hero or *unreliable narrator, whose view of the world differs widely from the true circumstances recognized by the author and readers; literary irony thus flatters its readers' intelligence at the expense of a character (or fictional narrator). A similar sense of detached superiority is achieved by **dramatic irony**, in which the audience knows more about a character's situation than the character does, foreseeing an outcome contrary to the character's expectations, and thus ascribing a sharply different sense to some of the character's own statements; in *tragedies, this is called **tragic irony**. The term **cosmic irony** is sometimes used to denote a view of people as the dupes of a cruelly mocking Fate, as in the novels of Thomas Hardy. A writer whose works are characterized by an ironic tone may be called an **ironist**. For a fuller account, consult D. C. Muecke, *Irony and the Ironic* (1982).

irregular ode, *see* ode.

Italian sonnet, *see* sonnet.

J

Jacobean [jakŏ-**bee**-an], belonging to the period 1603–25, when James VI of Scotland reigned as King James I of England. The term is formed from the Latin equivalent of his name: *Jacobus*. As a literary period it marks a high point of English drama, including the later plays of Shakespeare, the *masques and major plays of Ben Jonson, and significant works by several other playwrights, notably John Webster's *The Duchess of Malfi* (1623). In non-dramatic poetry, it includes the publication of Shakespeare's *Sonnets* (1609) and of Jonson's *The Forest* (1616). Next to the publication of the First *Folio edition of Shakespeare's plays (1623), the most important literary legacy of this period is the King James Bible (often called the Authorized Version) of 1611, a translation produced by a committee of scholars at James's command.

jeremiad [je-ri-**my**-ad], either a prolonged lamentation or a prophetic warning against the evil habits of a nation, foretelling disaster. The term comes from the name of the Hebrew prophet Jeremiah: the second sense refers to his dire warnings of Jerusalem's coming destruction (fulfilled in 586 BCE) and to his threats against the Egyptians, Chaldeans, Ammonites, Moabites, Philistines, and others, as recorded in the biblical book of Jeremiah; the first sense refers to the sequence of *elegies on Jerusalem's fall in the book of Lamentations. The term has been applied to some literary works that denounce the evils of a civilization: many of the writings of Thomas Carlyle, of H. D. Thoreau, or of D. H. Lawrence would fit this description.

jeu d'esprit [*zher* des-**pri**] (plural *jeux*), a French phrase meaning literally 'play of spirit', perhaps better translated as 'flight of fancy'. The term is applied to light-hearted witticisms and *epigrams such as those of Oscar Wilde, and more generally to any clever piece of writing dashed off in a spirit of fun, such as a *limerick or a short comic novel.

jingle, a brief set of verses with strong, repetitive rhythm and emphatic rhymes, usually similar to a nursery rhyme in being memorable but nonsensical (e.g. 'With a hey, and a ho, and a hey nonino'). Jingles are now used in radio and TV advertisements, but the term was used before the rise of broadcasting to refer, usually unfavourably, to poems—like those of Edgar Allan Poe—that sacrifice meaning to showy effects of sound. *See also* nonsense verse.

jongleur [zho^n^-**gler**], the French term for a kind of wandering entertainer in medieval Europe, especially one who sang or recited works composed by others, such as **chansons de geste*. The term also covered jugglers and acrobats, as did the profession itself—many *jongleurs* seem to have combined various forms of entertainment. Although they appear to have been active across Europe for several hundreds of years before, the *jongleurs* flourished in the 13th century, by which time they were distinguished (not always sharply) from the *troubadours and *trouvères*, who were writers but not necessarily performers, and from the *minstrels, who often had more settled positions at noble courts. One notable *jongleur* is the 13th-century French satirical poet Rutebeuf.

jouissance [zhwee-sah^n^s] the French word for 'enjoyment' (often used in a sexual sense), employed by the critic Roland Barthes in his *Le Plaisir du texte* (1973) to suggest a kind of response to literary works that is different from ordinary *plaisir* (pleasure). Whereas *plaisir* is comfortable and reassuring, confirming our values and expectations, *jouissance*—usually translated as 'bliss' to retain its erotic sense—is unsettling and destabilizing. The distinction seems to stand in parallel with Barthes's preference for those fragmentary or dislocated texts which he called **scriptible* rather than **lisible*, that is, those that challenge the reader to participate in creating them rather than just consume them.

Juvenalian, characteristic of or written in the manner of the Roman poet Juvenal (Decimus Junius Juvenalis, *c.*65 CE—*c.*135), whose sixteen verse *satires are fierce denunciations of his fellow-Romans in general and of women in particular for their mercenary lives. Juvenalian satire is the kind of satire that bitterly condemns human vice and folly, in contrast with the milder and more indulgent kind known as *Horatian satire. In English, Samuel Johnson's poems *London* (1738) and *The Vanity of Human Wishes* (1749) are both imitations of Juvenal, but the satires of Jonathan Swift come closer to Juvenal's uncompromisingly disgusted tone.

juvenilia [joo-vĕ-**nil**-iă], the collective term for those works written during an author's youth. Use of the term commonly implies that the faults of such writings are to be excused as the products of immaturity or lack of experience.

kabuki [ka-boo-ki], a Japanese form of theatrical entertainment which is more popular than the aristocratic *nō plays, and combines song, dance, and stylized gesture in a prolonged spectacle set on a low stage. Scenery and costumes are elaborate, and the female roles are all played by men. Unlike the nō actor, the kabuki performer does not make use of masks, but employs heavy make-up. Kabuki plays are usually based on well-known *legends and *myths.

kenning (plural -**ings** or -**ingar**), a stock phrase of the kind used in Old Norse and Old English verse as a poetic *circumlocution in place of a more familiar word. Examples are *banhus* (bonehouse) for 'body', and *saewudu* (sea-wood) for 'ship'. Similar *metaphoric compounds appear in colloquial speech, e.g. *fire-water* for 'whisky'. A famous Shakespearean example is *the beast with two backs* for 'copulation'. *See also* periphrasis.

kitchen-sink drama, a rather condescending title applied from the late 1950s onwards in Britain to the then new wave of realistic drama depicting the family lives of working-class characters, on stage and in broadcast plays. Such works, by Arnold Wesker, Alun Owen, and others, were at the time a notable departure from the conventions of middle-class drawing-room drama. Wesker's play *Roots* (1959) actually does begin with one character doing the dishes in a kitchen sink.

kitsch, rubbishy or tasteless pseudo-art of any kind. It is most easily recognizable in the products of the souvenir trade, especially those attempting to capitalize on 'high' art (Mona Lisa ashtrays, busts of Beethoven, etc.) or on religion (flesh-coloured Christs that glow in the dark); and is found in many forms of popular entertainment—the films of Cecil B. De Mille, much 'Easy Listening' music. It is harder to identify in written works, but the sentimental *doggerel found in greetings cards is one obvious example, while the trashier end of the science-fiction and sword-and-sorcery fiction markets provide many more pretentious cases.

Knittelvers (plural -*erse*), a German verse form consisting of four-stress lines rhymed as *couplets. Found in the popular poetry of the 15th and 16th centuries either in *accentual metre or in regular *octosyllabic lines, it was rejected by 17th-century poets as too clumsy (the word literally means 'cudgel-verse'), but was revived in the 18th century by Gottsched, Schiller, and Goethe.

Künstlerroman (plural *-mane*), the German term (meaning 'artist-novel') for a novel in which the central character is an artist of any kind, e.g. the musical composer Leverkühn in Thomas Mann's *Doktor Faustus* (1947), or the painter Lantier in Zola's *L'Oeuvre* (1886). Although this category of fiction often overlaps with the *Bildungsroman* in showing the protagonist's development from childhood or adolescence—most famously in Joyce's *A Portrait of the Artist as a Young Man* (1916)—it also includes studies of artists in middle or old age, and sometimes of historical persons: in David Malouf's *An Imaginary Life* (1978), for example, the central character and narrator is the Roman poet Ovid (43 BCE–17CE).

L

lacuna [lă-kew-nă] (plural **-unae** or **-unas**), any gap or missing element in a text, usually in a manuscript. *Adjective*: **lacunal** or **lacunose**. *See also* ellipsis, hiatus.

lai or **lay,** a term from Old French meaning a short *lyric or *narrative poem. The *Contes* (*c*.1175) of Marie de France were narrative *lais* of Arthurian legend and other subjects from Breton folklore, written in *octosyllabic couplets. They provided the model for the so-called 'Breton lays' in English in the 14th century, which include Chaucer's *Franklin's Tale* and the anonymous *Sir Orfeo*. Since the 16th century, the term has applied to songs in general, and to short narrative poems, as in T. B. Macaulay's *Lays of Ancient Rome* (1842).

laisse [less], a subdivision within a medieval French *chanson de geste*. In such poems, the *laisses* were *verse paragraphs of unequal length. *See also* strophe.

lament, any poem expressing profound grief or mournful regret for the loss of some person or former state, or for some other misfortune. *See also* complaint, dirge, elegy, jeremiad, monody, threnody, *ubi sunt*.

lampoon, an insulting written attack upon a real person, in verse or prose, usually involving caricature and ridicule. Among English writers who have indulged in this maliciously personal form of *satire are Dryden, Pope, and Byron. The laws of libel have restricted its further development as a literary form. *See also* flyting, invective.

langue [lahng], the French word for language or tongue, which has had a special sense in linguistics since the Swiss linguist Ferdinand de Saussure, in his *Cours de linguistique générale* (1915), distinguished *langue* from *parole*. In this sense, *langue* refers to the rules and conventions of a given language—its phonological distinctions, its permitted grammatical combinations of elements, etc.—whereas *parole* ('speech') refers to the sphere of actual linguistic events, i.e. utterances. Saussure proposed that because *langue* underlies and makes possible the infinitely varied forms of *parole*, it should be the primary object of linguistic science. The *langue/parole* distinction is one of the theoretical bases of *structuralism, although some structuralist writings have encouraged a confusion between *langue* (the rules of a specific language) and Saussure's distinct third term *langage* (the concept 'language' as such): the power attributed to 'Language' in this tradition has little to do with Saussure's notion of *langue*, and owes more to abstract conceptions of *langage* as a universal 'system'.

lapidary, suitable for engraving in stone. A lapidary inscription is one that is actually carved in stone, while a style of writing—especially in verse—may be called lapidary if it has the dignity or the concision expected of such inscriptions, or otherwise deserves to be passed on to posterity. As a noun, the term also applies to a book about gems, or to a jeweller. *See also* epigram.

Latinate, derived from or imitating the Latin language. Latinate *diction in English is the use of words derived from Latin rather than those originating in Old English, e.g. *suspend* rather than *hang*. A Latinate style may also be marked by prominent syntactic *inversion, especially the delaying of the main verb: while the normal English word-order is subject-verb-object, Milton frequently uses the Latin order object-subject-verb in his poem *Paradise Lost* (1667), as in the line

> His far more pleasant garden God ordained

Milton's is the most notoriously Latinate style in English verse. In English prose, especially of the 18th century, **Latinity** appears both in diction and in the *periodic sentence, which delays the completion of the sense through a succession of subordinate clauses, as in this sentence from Edward Gibbon's *Memoirs* (1796):

> It was at Rome, on the 15th of October, 1764, as I sat musing amidst the ruins of the Capitol, while the barefooted friars were singing vespers in the Temple of Jupiter, that the idea of writing the decline and fall of the city first started to my mind.

Particular instances of words, phrases, or constructions taken from the Latin are called **Latinisms.**

lay, see *lai*.

Leavisites, the name given to followers of the English literary critic F. R. Leavis, who achieved an extensive influence in mid-20th century British culture as co-editor of the journal *Scrutiny* (1932–53), as a teacher in Cambridge, and as the author of *New Bearings in English Poetry* (1932), *Revaluation* (1936), *The Great Tradition* (1948), and several other books. Leavis's attitude to literature and society, strongly influenced by his wife Q. D. Leavis's book *Fiction and the Reading Public* (1932), was marked by an intense moral seriousness and a militant hostility both to Marxism and to the utilitarian values of modern 'commercialism'. He saw the critic's task as one of preserving the values of the best literature—identified with those of 'Life'—against the hostile cultural environment of 'mass' society. His harshly exclusive literary judgements were influenced partly by T. S. Eliot's rejection of 19th-century poetry in favour of the *metaphysical poets, and partly by admiration for the work of D. H. Lawrence. Many of his pronouncements on the decline of English culture followed Eliot's hypothesis of the *dissociation of sensibility and invoked the supposed merits of the 'organic community' of the rural past. The Leavisite influence on the teaching of English literature (which Leavis saw as central to cultural survival) was strong in Britain during the 1950s and 1960s, and produced a detailed version of English literary history in *The Pelican Guide to English Literature* (ed. Boris Ford, 7 vols., 1954–61), but it has declined sharply since Leavis's death in 1978. The Leavisites are sometimes referred to as 'Scrutineers', after the name of their journal. The adjective **Leavisian** is applied more neutrally to ideas characteristic of Leavis's work. *See also* Cambridge school.

legend, a story or group of stories handed down through popular *oral tradition, usually consisting of an exaggerated or unreliable account of some actually or possibly historical person—often a saint, monarch, or popular hero. Legends are sometimes distinguished from *myths in that they concern human beings rather than gods, and sometimes in that they have some sort of historical basis whereas myths do not; but these distinctions are difficult to maintain consistently. The term was originally applied to accounts of saints' lives (*see* hagiography), but is now applied chiefly to fanciful tales of warriors (e.g. King Arthur and his knights), criminals (e.g. Faust, Robin Hood), and other sinners; or more recently to those bodies of biographical rumour and embroidered anecdote surrounding dead film stars and rock musicians (Judy Garland, John Lennon, etc.). *Adjective*: **legendary**. *See also* folklore.

leitmotif [lyt-moh-teef] or **leitmotiv,** a frequently repeated phrase, image, *symbol, or situation in a literary work, the recurrence of which usually indicates or supports a *theme. The term (German, 'leading motif') comes from music criticism, where it was first used to describe the repeated musical themes or phrases that Wagner linked with particular characters and ideas in his operatic works. The repeated references to rings and arches in D. H. Lawrence's novel *The Rainbow* (1915) are examples of the use of a leitmotif; the repetition of set phrases in the novels of Muriel Spark is another example. *See also* motif.

leonine rhyme, a form of *internal rhyme in which a word or syllable(s) in the middle of a verse line rhymes with the final word or syllable(s) of the same line, as in the opening line of Edgar Allan Poe's 'The Raven' (1845):

> Once upon a midnight dreary, while I pondered, weak and weary

The term was once restricted to a particular variety of such rhymes as used by medieval poets in Latin *hexameters and *pentameters, with the first rhyming word immediately preceding the medial *caesura, but it now often refers to similar rhymes in other kinds of line.

lexis, a term used in linguistics to designate the total vocabulary of a language, or sometimes the vocabulary used in a particular text (*see* diction). The adjective **lexical** means 'of vocabulary' or sometimes 'of dictionaries'. A **lexicon** is a dictionary, while a **lexicographer** is a person who compiles dictionaries and is thus a practitioner of **lexicography.**

libretto (plural **-etti** or **-ettos**), the Italian word for a booklet, applied in English to the text of an opera, operetta, or oratorio, that is, to the words as opposed to the music; thus a kind of dramatic work written for operatic or other musical performance. A writer of libretti, such as W. S. Gilbert or W. H. Auden, is known as a **librettist.**

light verse, the general term for various kinds of verse that have no serious purpose and no solemnity of tone. They may deal with trivial subjects, or bring a light-hearted attitude to more serious ones. Light verse is often characterized by a display of technical accomplishment in the handling of difficult rhymes, *metres, and *stanza forms. The many forms of light verse include *Anacreontics, *clerihews, *epigrams, *jingles, *limericks, *mock epics, *nonsense verse, *parodies, and *vers de société*.

limerick [limm-ĕ-rik], an English verse form consisting of five *anapaestic lines rhyming *aabba*, the third and fourth lines having two *stresses and the others three. Early examples, notably those of Edward Lear in his *Book of Nonsense* (1846), use the same rhyming word at the end of the first and last lines, but most modern limericks avoid such repetition. The limerick is almost always a self-contained, humorous poem, and usually plays on rhymes involving the names of people or places. First found in the 1820s, it was popularized by Lear, and soon became a favourite form for the witty obscenities of anonymous versifiers. The following is one of the less offensive examples of the coarse limerick tradition:

> There was a young fellow named Menzies
> Whose kissing sent girls into frenzies;
>   But a virgin one night
>   Crossed her legs in a fright
> And fractured his bi-focal lenses.

lipogram, a written composition that deliberately avoids using a particular letter of the alphabet. Examples have been found in ancient Greek poetry, but the most extravagant curiosities of this pointless game include Alonso Alcalá y Herrera's *Varios effectos de amor* (1641)—a sequence of five novellas each eschewing a different vowel, J. R. Ronden's play *La Pièce sans A* (1816), and Georges Perec's novel *La Disparition* (1969; later translated into English as *A Void*), which dispenses with *e*. Lipograms are extremely rare in English, although one Ernest Wright managed a 50,000-word novel, *Gadsby* (1939), without using *e*.

lisible [liz-eebl], the French word for 'legible', used in a specific sense by the critic Roland Barthes in his book *S/Z* (1970), and usually translated as 'readerly' or 'readable'. Barthes applies this term to texts (usually of the *realist tradition) that involve no true participation from the reader other than the consumption of a fixed meaning. A readerly text can be understood easily in terms of already familiar *conventions and expectations, and is thus reassuringly 'closed'. By contrast, the *texte* *scriptible* ('writerly' text, usually *modernist) challenges the reader to produce its meanings from an 'open' play of possibilities. See also *jouissance*.

litany [litt-ăni], a kind of prayer consisting of a long sequence of chanted supplications and responses; also, by extension, any prolonged or repetitive speech or written composition. Some kinds of *catalogue verse and *incantation resemble the repetitive forms of litany. *Adjective*: **litaneutical.**

literal, confined to the simplest primary meaning of a word, statement, or text, as distinct from any figurative sense (*see* figure) which it may carry—whether *ironic, *allegorical, *metaphoric, or *symbolic.

Thus the literal sense of a text is its most straightforward meaning. **Literalism** is a tendency to interpret texts according to their most obvious meaning, often disregarding their *connotations as well as their figurative senses. A **literal translation** is one that tries as far as possible to transfer each element of a text from one language into the other, without allowance for differences of *idiom between the two languages.

literariness, the sum of special linguistic and formal properties that distinguish literary texts from non-literary texts, according to the theories of *Russian Formalism. The leading Formalist Roman Jakobson declared in 1919 that 'the object of literary science is not literature but *literariness*, that is, what makes a given work a literary work'. Rather than seek abstract qualities like *imagination as the basis of literariness, the Formalists set out to define the observable 'devices' by which literary texts—especially poems—*foreground their own language, in *metre, rhyme, and other patterns of sound and repetition. Literariness was understood in terms of *defamiliarization, as a series of deviations from 'ordinary' language. It thus appears as a relation between different uses of language, in which the contrasted uses are liable to shift according to changed contexts. *See also* function, literature.

literary criticism, *see* criticism.

literati [litt-ĕ-rah-ti], the collective term for educated people, especially those involved in studying, writing, or criticizing literary works. The term is often used disrespectfully. The singular forms, literatus (masculine) and literata (feminine), are rarely used; the French term *littérateur* is more frequently found.

literature, a body of written works related by subject-matter (e.g. the literature of computing), by language or place of origin (e.g. Russian literature), or by prevailing cultural standards of merit. In this last sense, 'literature' is taken to include oral, dramatic, and broadcast compositions that may not have been published in written form but which have been (or deserve to be) preserved. Since the 19th century, the broader sense of literature as a totality of written or printed works has given way to more exclusive definitions based on criteria of imaginative, creative, or artistic value, usually related to a work's absence of factual or practical reference (*see* autotelic). Even more restrictive has been the academic concentration upon poetry, drama, and fiction. Until the mid-20th century, many kinds of non-fictional writing—in philosophy, history, biography, *criticism, topography, science, and politics—were counted as literature; implicit in this broader usage is a definition of literature as that body of works which—for whatever reason—deserves to be preserved as part of the current reproduction of meanings within a given culture (unlike yesterday's newspaper, which belongs in the disposable category of ephemera). This sense seems more tenable than the later attempts to divide literature—as creative, imaginative, fictional, or non-practical—from factual writings or practically effective works of propaganda, *rhetoric, or *didactic writing. The *Russian Formalists' attempt to define *literariness in terms of linguistic deviations is important in the theory of *poetry, but has not addressed the more difficult problem of the non-fictional prose forms. See also *belles-lettres*, canon, paraliterature. For a fuller account, consult Peter Widdowson, *Literature* (1998).

litotes [**ly**-toh-teez], a *figure of speech by which an affirmation is made indirectly by denying its opposite, usually with an effect of understatement: common examples are *no mean feat* and *not averse to a drink*. This figure is *not uncommon* in all kinds of writing. For example, William Wordsworth in his autobiographical poem *The Prelude* (1850) frequently uses the phrase 'not seldom' to mean 'fairly often'. *See also* meiosis.

littérateur [lit-er-at-**er**], a person occupied with literature, usually as a professional writer or critic. The term is often used with a disparaging suggestion of pretentiousness. *See also* literati.

liturgical drama, a form of religious drama performed within a church as an extension of the liturgy (i.e. the established form of Christian worship in the Mass or Eucharist). In medieval Europe, the introduction of chanted responses to the Easter services seems to have evolved into a more recognizably dramatic form of *passion play, while the Christmas service gave rise to the first Nativity plays. Liturgical drama is generally thought to be the origin of *mystery plays and *miracle plays, which came to be performed by lay actors in sites away from the churches themselves, and in the *vernacular rather than in Latin.

local color writing, a kind of fiction that came to prominence in the USA in the late 19th century, and was devoted to capturing the unique customs, manners, speech, folklore, and other qualities of a particular regional community, usually in humorous short stories. The most famous of the local colorists was Mark Twain; others included Bret Harte, George Washington Cable, Joel Chandler Harris, Kate Chopin, and Sarah Orne Jewett. The trend has some equivalents in European fiction, notably in the attention given by Zola and Hardy to the settings of their stories.

loco-descriptive, *see* topographical poetry.

logocentrism, the term used by Jacques Derrida and other exponents of *deconstruction to designate the desire for a centre or original guarantee of all meanings, which in Derrida's view has characterized Western philosophy since Plato. The Greek word *logos* can just mean 'word', but in philosophy it often denotes an ultimate principle of truth or reason, while in Christian theology it refers to the Word of God as the origin and foundation of all things. Derrida's critique of logocentric thinking shows how it attempts to repress difference (see *différance*) in favour of identity and presence: the philosophical 'metaphysics of presence' craves a 'transcendental signified' or ultimately self-sufficient meaning (e.g. God, Man, Truth). The most significant case of logocentrism is the enduring *phonocentrism that privileges speech over writing because speech is held to guarantee the full 'presence' and integrity of meaning.

log-rolling, a disreputable form of collusion in the reviewing of books, whereby one author writes a glowing appraisal of his or her friend's book, and the friend repays the favour by endorsing the first author's books too. The term arises from the proverbial phrase 'You roll my log and I'll roll yours'. *See also* claque.

long measure or **long metre,** *see* common measure.

longueur [long-ger], the French word for 'length', applied to any tediously prolonged passage or scene in a literary work.

lyric [li-rik], in the modern sense, any fairly short poem expressing the personal mood, feeling, or meditation of a single speaker (who may sometimes be an invented character, not the poet). In ancient Greece, a lyric was a song for accompaniment on the lyre, and could be a **choral lyric** sung by a group (*see* chorus), such as a *dirge or *hymn; the modern sense, current since the *Renaissance, often suggests a song-like quality in the poems to which it refers. Lyric poetry is the most extensive category of verse, especially after the decline—since the 19th century in the West—of the other principal kinds: *narrative and dramatic verse. Lyrics may be composed in almost any *metre and on almost every subject, although the most usual emotions presented are those of love and grief. Among the common lyric forms are the *sonnet, *ode, *elegy, *haiku, and the more personal kinds of hymn. **Lyricism** is the emotional or song-like quality, the **lyrical** property, of lyric poetry. A writer of lyric poems may be called a **lyric poet,** a **lyricist,** or a **lyrist.** In another sense, **the lyrics** of a popular song or other musical composition are the words as opposed to the music; these may not always be lyrical in the poetic sense (e.g. in a narrative song like a *ballad).

macaronic verse, poetry in which two or more languages are mixed together. Strictly, the term denotes a kind of comic verse in which words from a *vernacular language are introduced into Latin (or other foreign-language) verses and given Latin *inflections; such verse had a vogue among students in Europe in the 16th and 17th centuries, but is rare in English. More loosely, the term is applied to any verses in which phrases or lines in a foreign language are frequently introduced: several medieval English poems have Latin *refrains or alternating Latin and English lines, and in modern times the poems of Ezra Pound and T. S. Eliot have been called macaronic for their use of lines in several languages.

Machiavel [mak-yă-vel], a type of stage *villain found in Elizabethan and *Jacobean drama, and named after the Florentine political theorist Niccolò Machiavelli, whose notorious book *Il Principe* (*The Prince*, 1513) justified the use of dishonest means to retain state power. Exaggerated accounts of Macchiavelli's views led to the use of his name—sometimes directly referred to in speeches—for a broad category of ruthless schemers, atheists, and poisoners. Shakespeare's Iago and Richard III are the most famous examples of the type.

machinery, the collective term applied since the 18th century to the supernatural beings—gods, angels, devils, nymphs, etc.—who take part in the action of an *epic or *mock-epic poem or in a dramatic work. The term is taken from the Greek dramatic convention of the *deus ex machina*, and is also applied in a more familiar sense to the cranes, moving sets, and other contraptions used in the theatre.

madrigal, a short *lyric poem, usually of love or *pastoral life, often set to music as a song for several voices without instrumental accompaniment. As a poetic form, it originated in 14th-century Italy, but it was revived and adopted by composers throughout Europe in the 16th century; the English madrigal flourished from the 1580s to the 1620s. There is no fixed metrical form or *rhyme scheme, but the madrigal usually ends with a rhyming *couplet. *Adjective*: **madrigalian**.

magic realism, a kind of modern fiction in which fabulous and
fantastical events are included in a *narrative that otherwise maintains
the 'reliable' tone of objective realistic report. The term was once applied
to a trend in German fiction of the early 1950s, but is now associated
chiefly with certain leading novelists of Central and South America,
notably Miguel Ángel Asturias, Alejo Carpentier, and Gabriel García
Márquez. The latter's *Cien años de soledad* (*One Hundred Years of Solitude*,
1967) is often cited as a leading example, celebrated for the moment at
which one character unexpectedly ascends to heaven while hanging her
washing on a line. The term has also been extended to works from very
different cultures, designating a tendency of the modern novel to reach
beyond the confines of *realism and draw upon the energies of *fable,
*folktale and *myth while retaining a strong contemporary social
relevance. Thus Günter Grass's *Die Blechtrommel* (*The Tin Drum*, 1959),
Milan Kundera's *The Book of Laughter and Forgetting* (1979), and Salman
Rushdie's *Midnight's Children* (1981) have been described as magic realist
novels along with Angela Carter's *Nights at the Circus* (1984) and Rushdie's
The Satanic Verses (1988). The fantastic attributes given to characters in
such novels—levitation, flight, telepathy, telekinesis—are among the
means that magic realism adopts in order to encompass the often
phantasmagoric political realities of the 20th century. *See also* fabulation.

malapropism [mal-ă-prop-izm], a confused, comically inaccurate
use of a long word or words. The term comes from the character Mrs
Malaprop (after the French *mal à propos*, 'inappropriately') in Sheridan's
play *The Rivals* (1775): her bungled attempts at learned speech include a
reference to another character as 'the very pine-apple of politeness',
instead of 'pinnacle'. This kind of joke, though, is older than the name:
Shakespeare's Dogberry in *Much Ado About Nothing* (*c*.1598) makes similar
errors. *Adjective*: **malapropian**. *Verb*: **malaprop**.

mannerism, a vague term for the self-conscious cultivation of
peculiarities of style—usually elaborate, ingenious, and ornate—in
literary works of any period. Like the *baroque, with which it often
overlaps, mannerism is a concept more clearly defined in art history than
in literary studies: art historians have marked out a Mannerist period
(roughly 1520–1610) between the High Renaissance and the Baroque,
characterized by distortions of figure and perspective. Clear equivalents
in English literature of this period would be the **mannered** style of
*euphuism and the elaborate *conceits of the Elizabethan *sonnet.
But mannered styles can be found in many later periods, from the

*Latinate style of Milton to the far-fetched similes of Raymond Chandler. A common indicator of literary mannerism is that the elaborate manner is maintained, whatever the nature of the matter treated.

Märchen [mairh-yen], the German term for tales of enchantment and marvels, usually translated as 'fairy tales' despite the absence of actual fairies from most examples; also for a single such tale (the singular and plural forms being the same). *Märchen* have been divided into two categories: the *Volksmärchen* are *folktales of the kind collected by Jacob and Wilhelm Grimm in their celebrated *Kinder- und Hausmärchen* (1812), while *Kunstmärchen* are 'art tales', that is, literary creations like the uncanny tales of E. T. A. Hoffmann.

Martian poets, the term applied in the 1980s to a small group of poets in Britain whose work is marked by the prominence of surprising visual *metaphors, *similes, and *conceits. The leading figures are Christopher Reid and Craig Raine, who both published important collections in 1979: Reid's *Arcadia* and Raine's *A Martian Sends a Postcard Home* both transform everyday objects, in a playful kind of *defamiliarization. The term comes from the title poem of Raine's book, in which we are shown familiar earthly sights through the inexperienced eyes of a visiting Martian ('Rain is when the earth is television'). Similar effects are achieved by David Sweetman in *Looking Into the Deep End* (1981) and by Oliver Reynolds in *Skevington's Daughter* (1985).

marvellous, the (*US* **marvelous**), a category of fiction in which supernatural, magical, or other wondrous impossibilities are accepted as normal within an imagined world clearly separated from our own reality. The category includes fairy tales, many *romances, and most *science fiction, along with various other kinds of *fantasy with 'other-worldly' settings, like J. R. R. Tolkein's *The Lord of the Rings* (1954–5). Modern theorists have distinguished marvellous tales from those of the *uncanny in terms of the explanations offered for strange events: in the marvellous, these are explained as magic, while in the uncanny they are given psychological causes.

masculine ending, the ending of a metrical verse line on a stressed syllable, as in Emily Brontë's regular *iambic line:

> And who can fight against despair?

Masculine endings are also common in *trochaic verse, where the final unstressed syllable expected in the regular pattern is frequently abandoned (*see* catalectic). In French, a masculine line is any line not ending in mute *e, es*, or *ent*. A masculine *caesura is one that immediately follows a stressed syllable, usually in the middle of a line. *See also* metre, stress.

masculine rhyme, the commonest kind of rhyme, between single stressed syllables (e.g. de*lay/stay*) at the ends of verse lines. In contrast with *feminine rhyme, which adds further unstressed syllables after the rhyming stressed syllables, masculine rhyme matches only the final syllable with its equivalent in the paired line, as in Christina Rossetti's *couplet:

> And all the rest forget,
> But one remembers yet.

In French verse, the alternation of masculine and feminine rhymes became the norm from the 16th century onwards.

masque or **mask,** a spectacular kind of indoor performance combining poetic drama, music, dance, song, lavish costume, and costly stage effects, which was favoured by European royalty in the 16th and early 17th centuries. Members of the court would enter disguised, taking the parts of mythological persons, and enact a simple *allegorical plot, concluding with the removal of masks and a dance joined by members of the audience. Shakespeare included a short masque scene in *The Tempest* (1611), and Milton's play *Comus* (1634) is loosely related to the masque; these are now the best-known examples, but at the courts of James I and Charles I the highest form of the masque proper was represented by the quarrelsome collaboration of Ben Jonson with the designer Inigo Jones from 1605 to 1631 in the hugely expensive *Oberon* (1611) and other works. The parliamentary Revolution of the 1640s brought this form of extravagance to an abrupt end.

matter of Britain, the *legends of King Arthur and his Knights of the Round Table, which form the subject-matter for a number of medieval *romances—usually known as Arthurian romances. These are often distinguished from the romances dealing with the matter of France (i.e. legends of Charlemagne and his knights) or the matter of Rome (classical Roman legends or myths).

maxim, a short and memorable statement of a general principle; thus an *aphorism or *apophthegm, especially one that imparts advice or guidance. The French writer La Rochefoucauld published his aphorisms as *Maximes* (1665), while Benjamin Franklin included several celebrated examples in his *Poor Richard's Almanack* (1733–58), including the maxim 'Three may keep a secret, if two of them are dead.'

measure, an older word for *metre. The term is also used to refer to any metrical unit such as a *foot, a *dipody, or a line.

medievalism or **mediaevalism,** enthusiasm for or imitation of the arts and customs of Europe during the Middle Ages—that is, from about the 8th century to the 15th. In literature, this may manifest itself in the use of *archaisms, in the choice of medieval settings for *narrative works, or more broadly in an ideological attachment to values associated with medieval societies (e.g. chivalry, religious faith, social hierarchy). Antiquarian interest in *ballads and other aspects of medieval art grew in the late 18th century, influencing the *Gothic novel and the strongly medievalist nostalgia of *Romanticism. Medievalism is a significant current in 19th-century literature from Walter Scott's novel *Ivanhoe* (1819) and Keats's poem 'The Eve of St Agnes' (1820) to the prose and verse *romances of William Morris. Important works of Victorian social criticism, notably Thomas Carlyle's *Past and Present* (1843) and John Ruskin's *The Stones of Venice* (1851–3), contrasted medieval social conditions favourably with those of the modern industrial city. A **medievalist** is usually a scholar studying some aspect of medieval history or culture.

medium (plural -**dia**), the material or the technical process employed in an art or a communication. In literature, the medium is language, although further distinctions are also made between the media of speech and print, between theatre and cinema, and between prose and poetry. A misleading implication in some uses of the term is that the meaning of a work already exists as a complete entity only requiring transmission through the medium of language; this notion is resisted by most modern theorists of literature.

meiosis [my-oh-sis] (plural -**oses**) the Greek term for understatement or 'belittling': a rhetorical *figure by which something is referred to in terms less important than it really deserves, as when Mercutio in *Romeo and Juliet* calls his mortal wound a 'scratch'. Usually the effect is one of *irony or *anticlimax, but it may be disparaging, as when a writer is called a scribbler. The favoured form of meiosis is *litotes, in which an affirmation is made indirectly by denying its opposite, e.g. *it was no mean feat*. Adjective: **meiotic**.

Meistersinger or **Mastersinger,** a singing poet belonging to the musical guilds that flourished in the towns of southern Germany in the 15th and 16th centuries, claiming descent from the medieval *Minnesänger*. The *Meistersinger* were craftsmen (e.g. Hans Sachs, a cobbler) whose singing and poetic composition, both secular and religious, were governed by strict and secretive rules. Their form of composition for unaccompanied singing is known as *Meistersang* or *Meistergesang*.

melodrama, a popular form of sensational drama that flourished in the 19th-century theatre, surviving in different forms in modern cinema and television. The term, meaning 'song-drama' in Greek, was originally applied in the European theatre to scenes of mime or spoken dialogue accompanied by music. In early 19th-century London, many theatres were only permitted to produce musical entertainments, and from their simplified plays—some of them adapted from *Gothic novels—the modern sense of melodrama derives: an emotionally exaggerated conflict of pure maidenhood and scheming villainy in a plot full of suspense. Well-known examples are Douglas Jerrold's *Black-Ey'd Susan* (1829), the anonymous *Maria Marten* (c.1830), and *Sweeney Todd, the Demon Barber of Fleet Street* (1842); the Irish playwright Dion Boucicault wrote several melodramas from the 1850s onwards, notably *The Colleen Bawn* (1860). Similar plots and simplified characterization in fiction, as in Dickens, can also be described as melodramatic. See also *drame, Grand Guignol*. For a fuller account, consult James L. Smith, *Melodrama* (1973).

memoir-novel, a kind of novel that pretends to be a true autobiography or memoir. It was an important form in the emergence of the modern novel during the 18th century, in such works as Daniel Defoe's *Moll Flanders* (1722) and John Cleland's *Memoirs of a Lady of Pleasure* (1748–9; usually known as *Fanny Hill*). A similar pseudo-autobiographical mode of *first-person narrative is found in very many later novels, but the pretence that the real author was only an 'editor' of a true account did not outlive the 18th century.

Menippean satire or **Varronian satire,** a form of intellectually humorous work characterized by miscellaneous contents, displays of curious erudition, and comical discussions on philosophical topics. The name comes from the Greek Cynic philosopher Menippus (3rd century BCE), whose works are lost, but who was imitated by the Roman writer Varro (1st century BCE) among others. The Canadian critic Northrop Frye revived the term in *Anatomy of Criticism* (1957) while also introducing the overlapping term *anatomy after a famous example of Menippean satire, Robert Burton's *Anatomy of Melancholy* (1621). The best-known example of the form is Lewis Carroll's *Alice's Adventures in Wonderland* (1865); other examples include the novels of Thomas Love Peacock, and John Barth's *campus novel *Giles Goat-Boy* (1966). The humour in these works is more cheerfully intellectual and less aggressive than in those works which we would usually call *satires, although it holds up contemporary intellectual life to gentle ridicule.

metacriticism, criticism of *criticism; that is, the examination of the principles, methods, and terms of criticism either in general (as in critical theory) or in the study of particular critics or critical debates. The term usually implies a consideration of the principles underlying critical interpretation and judgement.

metadrama or **metatheatre,** drama about drama, or any moment of self-consciousness by which a play draws attention to its own fictional status as a theatrical pretence. Normally, direct addresses to the audience in *prologues, *epilogues, and *inductions are metadramatic in that they refer to the play itself and acknowledge the theatrical situation; a similar effect may be achieved in *asides. In a more extended sense, the use of a play-within-the-play, as in *Hamlet*, allows a further metadramatic exploration of the nature of theatre, which is taken still further in plays *about* plays, such as Luigi Pirandello's *Sei personaggi in cerca d'autore* (*Six Characters in Search of an Author*, 1921). *See also* foregrounding, self-reflexive.

metafiction, fiction about fiction; or more especially a kind of fiction that openly comments on its own fictional status. In a weak sense, many modern novels about novelists having problems writing their novels may be called metafictional in so far as they discuss the nature of fiction; but the term is normally used for works that involve a significant degree of self-consciousness about themselves as fictions, in ways that go beyond occasional apologetic addresses to the reader. The most celebrated case is Sterne's *Tristram Shandy* (1760–7), which makes a continuous joke of its own digressive form. A notable modern example is John Fowles's *The*

French Lieutenant's Woman (1969), in which Fowles interrupts the narrative to explain his procedures, and offers the reader alternative endings. Perhaps the finest of modern metafictions is Italo Calvino's *Se una notte d'inverno un viaggatore* (*If on a winter's night a traveler*, 1979), which begins 'You are about to begin reading Italo Calvino's new novel, *If on a winter's night a traveler.*' See also *mise-en-abyme*, postmodernism, self-reflexive. For a fuller account, consult Patricia Waugh, *Metafiction* (1984).

metalanguage, any use of language about language, as for instance in *glosses, definitions, or arguments about the usage or meaning of words. Linguistics sometimes describes itself as a metalanguage because it is a 'language' about language; and so on the same assumption *criticism is a metalanguage about literature. Some theorists of *structuralism have spoken of metalanguages as if they were clearly separate from or standing above the 'object-languages' they describe, but this claim is denied by *post-structuralism, which points out that linguistics, criticism, etc., are still within the same general language, albeit as specialized uses with their own terminologies. Thus there is in principle no absolute distinction between criticism and literature. Roman Jakobson in his listing of linguistic *functions describes the 'metalingual' (or **metalinguistic**) function as that by which speakers check that they understand one another. In a wider sense, literary works often have a metalinguistic aspect in which they highlight uses of language: a very clear case of this is Shaw's *Pygmalion* (1913). It is also possible to have a **meta-metalanguage**, i.e. a 'third-level' discourse such as an analysis of linguistics, or a work of *metacriticism.

metalepsis, a term used in different senses in *rhetoric and *narratology. In rhetoric, the precise sense of metalepsis is uncertain, but it refers to various kinds of complex *figure or *trope that are figurative to the second or third degree; that is, they involve a figure that either refers us to yet another figure or requires a further imaginative leap to establish its reference, usually by a process of *metonymy. Extended *similes and *rhetorical questions sometimes show a **metaleptic** multiplication of figures. Thus Marlowe's famous lines from *Dr Faustus* combine metaleptically a rhetorical question with *synecdoche and *hyperbole:

> Was this the face that launched a thousand ships
> And burnt the topless towers of Ilium?

These same lines illustrate a slightly different sense of metalepsis as a figure that brings together two distantly related facts (here, Helen's beauty and the destruction of Troy), metonymically joining cause and effect while jumping or compressing the intervening steps in the causal chain. In narratology, metalepsis is a breaking of the boundaries that separate distinct 'levels' of a narrative, usually between an *embedded tale and its *frame story (*see* diegesis). An example occurs in Chaucer's *Merchant's Tale*, when a fictional character within the tale told by the Merchant refers to the Wife of Bath, who should be unknown to him since she exists on another level as one of the pilgrims listening to the Merchant. Narrative metalepsis, sometimes called 'frame-breaking', has become common in modern experimental fiction.

metaphor, the most important and widespread *figure of speech, in which one thing, idea, or action is referred to by a word or expression normally denoting another thing, idea, or action, so as to suggest some common quality shared by the two. In metaphor, this resemblance is assumed as an imaginary identity rather than directly stated as a comparison: referring to a man as *that pig*, or saying *he is a pig* is metaphorical, whereas *he is like a pig* is a *simile. Metaphors may also appear as verbs (a talent may *blossom*) or as adjectives (a novice may be *green*), or in longer *idiomatic phrases, e.g. *to throw the baby out with the bath-water*. The use of metaphor to create new combinations of ideas is a major feature of *poetry, although it is quite possible to write poems without metaphors. Much of our everyday language is also made up of metaphorical words and phrases that pass unnoticed as 'dead' metaphors, like the *branch* of an organization. A **mixed metaphor** is one in which the combination of qualities suggested is illogical or ridiculous (*see also* catachresis), usually as a result of trying to apply two metaphors to one thing: *those vipers stabbed us in the back*. Modern analysis of metaphors and similes distinguishes the primary literal term (called the '*tenor') from the secondary figurative term (the 'vehicle') applied to it: in the metaphor *the road of life*, the tenor is life, and the vehicle is the road. For a fuller account, consult Terence Hawkes, *Metaphor* (1972).

metaphysical poets, the name given to a diverse group of 17th-century English poets whose work is notable for its ingenious use of intellectual and theological concepts in surprising *conceits, strange *paradoxes, and far-fetched *imagery. The leading metaphysical poet was John Donne, whose colloquial, argumentative abruptness of rhythm and tone distinguishes his style from the *conventions of Elizabethan love-lyrics. Other poets to whom the label is applied include Andrew

Marvell, Abraham Cowley, John Cleveland, and the predominantly religious poets George Herbert, Henry Vaughan, and Richard Crashaw. In the 20th century, T. S. Eliot and others revived their reputation, stressing their quality of *wit, in the sense of intellectual strenuousness and flexibility rather than smart humour. The term **metaphysical poetry** usually refers to the works of these poets, but it can sometimes denote any poetry that discusses **metaphysics**, that is, the philosophy of knowledge and existence.

metatheatre, *see* metadrama.

meter, *see* metre.

metonymy [met-on-ĭmi], a *figure of speech that replaces the name of one thing with the name of something else closely associated with it, e.g. *the bottle* for alcoholic drink, *the press* for journalism, *skirt* for woman, *Mozart* for Mozart's music, *the Oval Office* for the US presidency. A well-known metonymic saying is *the pen is mightier than the sword* (i.e. writing is more powerful than warfare). A word used in such metonymic expressions is sometimes called a **metonym** [met-ŏnim]. An important kind of metonymy is *synecdoche, in which the name of a part is substituted for that of a whole (e.g. *hand* for worker), or vice versa. Modern literary theory has often used 'metonymy' in a wider sense, to designate the process of association by which metonymies are produced and understood: this involves establishing relationships of *contiguity* between two things, whereas *metaphor establishes relationships of *similarity* between them. The metonym/metaphor distinction has been associated with the contrast between *syntagm and *paradigm. *See also* antonomasia.

metre (*US* **meter**), the pattern of measured sound-units recurring more or less regularly in lines of verse. Poetry may be composed according to one of four principal **metrical** systems:

(i) in *quantitative metre*, used in Greek and Latin, the pattern is a sequence of long and short syllables counted in groups known as feet (*see* foot, quantitative verse);

(ii) in *syllabic metre*, as in French and Japanese, the pattern comprises a fixed number of syllables in the line (*see* syllabic verse);

(iii) in *accentual metre* (or 'strong-stress metre'), found in Old English and in later English popular verse, the pattern is a regular number of stressed syllables in the line or group of lines, regardless of the number of unstressed syllables (*see* accentual verse);

(iv) in *accentual-syllabic metre*, the pattern consists of a regular number of stressed syllables appropriately arranged within a fixed total number of syllables in the line (with permissible variations including *feminine endings), both stressed and unstressed syllables being counted.

The fourth system—accentual-syllabic metre—is the one found in most English verse in the literary tradition since Chaucer; some flexible uses of it incline towards the accentual system. However, the descriptive terms most commonly used to analyse it have, confusingly, been inherited from the vocabulary of the very different Greek and Latin quantitative system. Thus the various English metres are named after the classical feet that their groupings of stressed and unstressed syllables resemble, and the length of a metrical line is still often expressed in terms of the number of feet it contains: a *dimeter has two feet, a *trimeter three, a *tetrameter four, a *pentameter five, a *hexameter six, and a *heptameter seven. A simpler and often more accurate method of description is to refer to lines in either accentual or accentual-syllabic metre according to the number of stressed syllables: thus an English tetrameter is a 'four-stress line', a pentameter a 'five-stress line' (these being the commonest lines in English).

English accentual-syllabic metres fall into two groups, according to the way in which stressed (●) and unstressed (○) syllables alternate: in *duple metres*, stressed syllables alternate more or less regularly with single unstressed syllables, and so the line is traditionally described as a sequence of disyllabic (2-syllable) feet; while in *triple metres*, stressed syllables alternate with pairs of unstressed syllables, and the line is seen as a sequence of trisyllabic (3-syllable) feet.

Of the two duple metres, by far the more common in English is the *iambic metre*, in which the stressed syllables are for the most part perceived as following the unstressed syllables with which they alternate (○●○●○● etc.), although some variations on this pattern are accepted. In traditional analysis by feet, iambic verse is said to be composed predominantly of *iambs (○●). This iambic pentameter by John Dryden illustrates the metre:

> And doom'd to death, though fated not to die.

The other duple metre, used in English less frequently than the iambic, is *trochaic metre*, in which the iambic pattern is reversed so that the stressed syllables are felt to be preceding the unstressed syllables with which they alternate (●○●○●○ etc.); in terms of classical feet, trochaic verse is said to be made up predominantly of *trochees (●○). This trochaic tetrameter from Longfellow illustrates the metre:

> Dark behind it rose the forest

It is common, though, for poets using trochaic metre to begin and end the line on a stressed syllable (*see* catalectic), as in Blake's line:

> Tyger, tyger, burning bright

In such cases it is hard to distinguish trochaic and iambic metres.

   The triple metres are far less common in English, although sometimes found. In *dactylic metre*, named after the *dactyl (●○○), the stressed syllables are felt to precede the intervening pairs of unstressed syllables:

> Cannon in front of them   (Tennyson: dactylic dimeter)

In *anapaestic metre*, named after the *anapaest (○○●), the pattern is reversed:

> Of your fainting, dispirited race   (Arnold: anapaestic trimeter)

Dactylic and anapaestic verse is not usually composed purely of dactyls and anapaests, however: other feet or additional syllables are frequently combined with or substituted for them.

   All these patterns are open to different kinds of variation, of which the most common is traditionally called *substitution of one foot for another (but *see also* demotion, promotion); for the other feet sometimes mentioned in the context of substitution, *see* foot. Other variations include the addition or subtraction of syllables to alter the line's length. The theory and practice of metrical verse is known as *prosody or metrics, while the detailed analysis of the metrical pattern in lines of verse is called *scansion. For a fuller account, consult Derek Attridge, *Poetic Rhythm: An Introduction* (1995).

metrics, another word for *prosody, that is, the theory and practice of poetic *metre. A poet composing metrical verse, or a theorist of metre, may be called a **metrist** or **metrician**.

Miltonic sonnet, *see* sonnet.

mime, in the modern sense, a dramatic performance or scene played with bodily movement and gesture and without words; thus a non-literary art. However, in ancient Greece and Rome the mime was a kind of crude *farce about domestic life, including dialogue as well as gesture, both often obscene. A performer in such a play could also be called a mime. *See also* dumb show, pantomime.

mimesis [my-**mees**-is], the Greek word for imitation, a central term in aesthetic and literary theory since Aristotle. A literary work that is understood to be reproducing an external reality or any aspect of it is described as **mimetic**, while **mimetic criticism** is the kind of *criticism that assumes or insists that literary works reflect reality. *See also* diegesis, reflectionism, *ut pictura poesis*.

minimalism, a literary or dramatic style or principle based on the extreme restriction of a work's contents to a bare minimum of necessary elements, normally within a short form, e.g. a *haiku, *epigram, brief dramatic *sketch, or *monologue. Minimalism is often characterized by a bareness or starkness of vocabulary or of dramatic setting, and a reticence verging on or even becoming silence. The term has been borrowed from modern sculpture and painting, and applied especially to the later dramatic work of the Irish writer Samuel Beckett, whose 30-second play *Breath* (1969), for example, has no characters and no words.

Minnesänger [min-ĕ-zeng-er] or **Minnesingers,** the poets of *courtly love (*Minne*) who flourished in southern Germany in the late 12th and early 13th centuries, composing their love-lyrics to be sung at aristocratic courts, where several of the *Minnesänger* were themselves noblemen. They are the German equivalents of the Provençal *troubadours and French *trouvères*. Their form of love poetry is known as *Minnesang*, a term sometimes extended to cover other *lyrics of this period. Among the foremost Minnesingers were Dietmar von Aist, Hartmann von Aue, and Walther von der Vogelweide.

minstrel, a professional entertainer of late medieval Europe, either itinerant or settled at a noble court. Minstrels of the 13th and 14th centuries, the descendants of the *jongleurs*, sang and recited lyrics and narrative poems including *chansons de geste* and *ballads. Their art, sometimes called **minstrelsy,** declined with the advent of printing. They are distinguished from the *troubadours, who were educated amateur poets of higher social rank. In the USA, the **minstrel show** was a 19th-century form of entertainment with white performers in blackface presenting stereotyped impressions of black American folk culture, and playing banjos.

miracle play, a kind of medieval religious play representing non-scriptural legends of saints or of the Virgin Mary. The term is often confusingly applied also to the *mystery plays, which form a distinct body of drama based on biblical stories. Thanks to the book-burning zeal of the English Reformation, no significant miracle plays survive in English, but there is a French cycle of forty *Miracles de Notre-Dame* probably dating from the 14th century.

mise-en-abyme [meez on ab-**eem**], a term coined by the French writer André Gide, supposedly from the language of heraldry, to refer to an internal reduplication of a literary work or part of a work. Gide's own novel *Les Faux-Monnayeurs* (*The Counterfeiters*, 1926) provides a prominent example: its central character, Édouard, is a novelist working on a novel called *Les Faux-Monnayeurs* which strongly resembles the very novel in which he himself is a character. The 'Chinese box' effect of *mise-en-abyme* often suggests an infinite regress, i.e. an endless succession of internal duplications. It has become a favoured device in *postmodernist fictions by Jorge Luis Borges, Italo Calvino, and others. *See also* metafiction.

mise en scène [meez ah^n sen], the French term for the staging or visual arrangement of a dramatic production, comprising scenery, properties, costume, lighting, and human movement. The term is also used in film-making for the staging of the action in front of the camera, i.e. for the combination of setting, lighting, acting, and costume, as distinct from camerawork and editing.

misprision, misreading or misunderstanding. Harold Bloom, in his theory of the *anxiety of influence, uses the term to mean a kind of defensive distortion by which a poet creates a poem in reaction against another poet's powerful 'precursor' poem, and which is also necessarily involved in all readers' interpretations of poetry.

mixed metaphor, *see* metaphor.

mnemonic [ni-**mon**-ik], helpful in remembering something; or (as a noun) a form of words or letters that assists the memory, e.g. the rhyme beginning 'Thirty days hath September'. Rhyming verse is often employed for mnemonic purposes, and it is sometimes claimed that this was poetry's original function.

mock epic, a poem employing the lofty style and the conventions of *epic poetry to describe a trivial or undignified series of events; thus a kind of *satire that mocks its subject by treating it in an inappropriately grandiose manner, usually at some length. Mock epics incidentally make fun of the elaborate conventions of epic poetry, including *invocations, battles, supernatural *machinery, *epic similes, and *formulaic descriptions (e.g. of funeral rites or of warriors arming for combat). The outstanding examples in English are Alexander Pope's *The Rape of the Lock* (1712–14) and *The Dunciad* (1728–43), while Boileau's *Le Lutrin* (1674–83) is an important French example. *Adjective*: **mock-epic** or ***mock-heroic.** *See also* burlesque, irony, parody.

mock-heroic, written in an ironically grand style that is comically incongruous with the 'low' or trivial subject treated. This adjective is commonly applied to *mock epics, but serves also for works or parts of works using the same comic method in various forms other than that of the full-scale mock-epic poem: Swift's prose satire *The Battle of the Books* (1704) is an important case, as is Byron's intermittently mock-heroic poem *Don Juan* (1819–24). Shorter satirical poems employing fewer epic conventions, such as Ben Jonson's 'On the Famous Voyage' (1616) and Dryden's *Mac Flecknoe* (1682), are probably better described as mock-heroic poems rather than mock epics, partly because they are not long enough to be divided into *cantos. Theatrical *burlesques of *heroic drama, such as Henry Fielding's *Tom Thumb* (1730) are also referred to as mock-heroic. *See also* heroic poetry, parody, satire.

mode, an unspecific critical term usually designating a broad but identifiable kind of literary method, mood, or manner that is not tied exclusively to a particular *form or *genre. Examples are the *satiric mode, the *ironic, the *comic, the *pastoral, and the *didactic.

modernism, a general term applied retrospectively to the wide range of experimental and **avant-garde* trends in the literature (and other arts) of the early 20th century, including *Symbolism, *Futurism, *Expressionism, *Imagism, *Vorticism, *Dada, and *Surrealism, along with the innovations of unaffiliated writers. Modernist literature is characterized chiefly by a rejection of 19th-century traditions and of their consensus between author and reader: the conventions of *realism, for instance, were abandoned by Franz Kafka and other novelists, and by expressionist drama, while several poets rejected traditional *metres in favour of *free verse. Modernist writers tended to see themselves as an *avant-garde* disengaged from bourgeois values, and disturbed their readers by adopting complex and difficult new forms and styles. In fiction, the accepted continuity of chronological development was upset by Joseph Conrad, Marcel Proust, and William

Faulkner, while James Joyce and Virginia Woolf attempted new ways of tracing the flow of characters' thoughts in their *stream-of-consciousness styles. In poetry, Ezra Pound and T. S. Eliot replaced the logical exposition of thoughts with *collages of fragmentary images and complex *allusions. Luigi Pirandello and Bertolt Brecht opened up the theatre to new forms of abstraction in place of realist and *naturalist representation. Modernist writing is predominantly cosmopolitan, and often expresses a sense of urban cultural dislocation, along with an awareness of new anthropological and psychological theories. Its favoured techniques of juxtaposition and multiple *point of view challenge the reader to reestablish a coherence of meaning from fragmentary forms. In English, its major landmarks are Joyce's *Ulysses* and Eliot's *The Waste Land* (both 1922). In Hispanic literature the term has a special sense: *modernismo* denotes the new style of poetry in Spanish from 1888 to *c.*1910, strongly influenced by the French *Symbolists and *Parnassians and introduced by the Nicaraguan poet Rubén Darío and the Mexican poet Manuel Gutiérrez Nájera. For a fuller account, consult Peter Childs, *Modernism* (2000).

monodrama, a play or dramatic scene in which only one character speaks; or a sequence of *dramatic monologues all spoken by the same single character. The second sense is rarely used, except of Tennyson's *Maud* (1855), to which the author attached the subtitle *A Monodrama* in 1875. In the first sense, some German playwrights of the late 18th century wrote monodramas that had musical accompaniment, notably J. C. Brandes's *Ariadne auf Naxos* (1774). Modern writers of monodramas include Samuel Beckett in *Krapp's Last Tape* (1958) and Alan Bennett, who has written several monodramas for television. *See also* monologue.

monody, an *elegy, *dirge, or *lament uttered by a single speaker, or presented as if to be spoken by a single speaker. In ancient Greek poetry, the term referred to an *ode sung by a single performer, as distinct from a choral ode. Milton applied the term to his elegy 'Lycidas' (1637), and Arnold used it in the subtitle of his 'Thyrsis' (1867). A composer or singer of monodies is a **monodist.** *Adjective*: **monodic.** *See also* threnody.

monologic or **monological,** *see* dialogic.

monologue, an extended speech uttered by one speaker, either to others or as if alone. Significant varieties include the *dramatic monologue (a kind of poem in which the speaker is imagined to be addressing a silent audience), and the *soliloquy (in which the speaker is supposed to be 'overheard' while alone). Some modern plays in which only one character speaks, like Beckett's *Krapp's Last Tape* (1958), are known either as *monodramas or as monologues. In prose fiction, the *interior monologue is a representation of a character's unspoken thoughts, sometimes rendered in the style known as *stream of consciousness. The speaker of a monologue is sometimes called a **monologuist**.

monometer [mon-om-iter], a verse line consisting of only one *foot (or, in some classical Greek and Latin *metres, one *dipody, i.e. one linked pair of feet). Monometers are rarely used as the basis for whole poems. *Adjective*: **monometric**.

monorhyme, a poem or poetic passage in which every line ends on the same rhyme; rare in English, but found more commonly in Welsh, in medieval Latin, and in Arabic.

morality play, a kind of religious drama popular in England, Scotland, France, and elsewhere in Europe in the 15th and early 16th centuries. Morality plays are dramatized *allegories, in which personified virtues, vices, diseases, and temptations struggle for the soul of Man as he travels from birth to death. They instil a simple message of Christian salvation, but often include comic scenes, as in the lively obscenities of *Mankind* (c.1465). The earliest surviving example in English is the long *Castle of Perseverance* (c.1420), and the best-known is *Everyman* (c.1510). Most are anonymous, but *Magnyfycence* (c.1515) was written by John Skelton. Echoes of the morality plays can be found in Elizabethan drama, especially Marlowe's *Dr Faustus* and the character of Iago in Shakespeare's *Othello*, who resembles the sinister tempter known as the *Vice in morality plays. *See also* interlude, psychomachy.

morpheme, a linguistic term for a minimal unit of grammatical meaning in a language. Words are composed of one or more morphemes (e.g. *tables* = *table* + *s*). Prefixes, suffixes, plural endings etc. are called 'bound morphemes' because they do not occur on their own. *Adjective:* **morphemic**. *See also* inflection.

morphology, a branch of linguistics concerned with analysing the structure of words. The morphology of a given word is its structure or form.

mosaic rhyme, *see* feminine rhyme, triple rhyme.

motif [moh-**teef**], a situation, incident, idea, image, or character-type that is found in many different literary works, folktales, or myths; or any element of a work that is elaborated into a more general *theme. The fever that purges away a character's false identity is a recurrent motif in Victorian fiction; and in European *lyric poetry the *ubi sunt* motif and the *carpe diem* motif are commonly found. Where an image, incident, or other element is repeated significantly within a single work, it is more commonly referred to as a *leitmotif. *See also* archetype, stock character, topos.

Movement, the, the term applied since 1954 to a loose group of English poets whose work subsequently appeared in the anthology *New Lines* (1956) edited by Robert Conquest. Apart from Conquest himself, the group included Kingsley Amis, Donald Davie, D. J. Enright, Thom Gunn, Elizabeth Jennings, Philip Larkin, and John Wain. Their common ground was limited to an avoidance of romantic postures in favour of ironic detachment, a reaction against the excesses of *modernism, and a cultivation of poetry as a disciplined craft. The central figures—Larkin and Amis (who both also wrote as novelists)—are associated with a defiantly provincial Englishness, for which the term 'movement' is singularly inappropriate, but others—notably Davie, Enright, and Gunn—had or later acquired a more international perspective.

multi-accentuality, the ability of words and other linguistic signs to carry more than one meaning according to the contexts in which they are used. The concept was introduced in an important Russian critique of Saussure's abstract theory of la *langue*: Valentin Voloshinov's *Marxism and the Philosophy of Language* (1929; sometimes alleged to have been written by Mikhail Bakhtin) accused Saussure of attributing fixed meanings to signs, when in actual practice the meaning of words is open to continual redefinition within the struggles between social classes and groups. In certain historical circumstances, particular words become objects of struggle between groups for whom they have different meanings: the meaning of *freedom* is constantly contested, while recent examples would include *terrorist*, among many others. *See also* dialogic, polysemy.

muse, a source of inspiration to a poet or other writer, usually represented as a female deity, and conventionally called upon for assistance in a poet's *invocation. In ancient Greek religion, the muses were nine sister-goddesses, the daughters of Zeus and Mnemosyne (the goddess of memory), who presided over various arts and some branches of learning. Their cult was associated particularly with the Pierian Spring on Mount Olympus, with Mount Parnassus near Delphi, and with Mount Helicon in Boeotia. Their names and responsibilities are as follows: Calliope (*epic poetry); Clio (history); Erato (*lyric love poetry); Euterpe (flute music); Melpomene (*tragedy); Polyhymnia (*hymns); Terpsichore (choral dance and song); Thalia (*comedy); and Urania (astronomy). Later poets of the *Renaissance, however, often referred to the women praised in their love poems as muses who inspired their verse; and in modern *criticism the term has often been extended to any cause or principle underlying a writer's work.

mystery play, a major form of popular medieval religious drama, representing a scene from the Old or New Testament. Mystery plays— also known as *pageants or as Corpus Christi plays—were performed in many towns across Europe from the 13th century to the 16th (and later, in Catholic Spain and Bavaria). They seem to have developed gradually from Latin *liturgical drama into civic occasions in the local languages, usually enacted on Corpus Christi, a holy feast day from 1311 onwards. Several English towns had *cycles of mystery plays, in which wagons stopping at different points in the town were used as stages for the various episodes, each presented by a trade guild (then known as a 'mystery'). A full cycle, like the 48 plays enacted at York, would represent the entire scheme of Christian cosmology from the Creation to Doomsday. Other English cycles survive from Chester, Wakefield, and the unidentified 'N-town'; the plays of the anonymous 'Wakefield Master', notably the *Second Shepherds' Play*, are the most celebrated. *See also* miracle play, passion play.

myth, a kind of story or rudimentary *narrative sequence, normally traditional and anonymous, through which a given culture ratifies its social customs or accounts for the origins of human and natural phenomena, usually in supernatural or boldly imaginative terms. The term has a wide range of meanings, which can be divided roughly into 'rationalist' and 'romantic' versions: in the first, a myth is a false or unreliable story or belief (*adjective*: **mythical**), while in the second, 'myth' is a superior intuitive mode of cosmic understanding (*adjective*: **mythic**). In most literary contexts, the second kind of usage prevails, and myths are regarded as fictional stories containing deeper truths, expressing collective attitudes to fundamental matters of life, death, divinity, and existence (sometimes deemed to be 'universal'). Myths are usually distinguished from *legends in that they have less of an historical basis, although they seem to have a similar mode of existence in oral transmission, re-telling, literary adaptation, and *allusion. A **mythology** is a body of related myths shared by members of a given people or religion, or sometimes a system of myths evolved by an individual writer, as in the 'personal mythologies' of William Blake and W. B. Yeats; the term has sometimes also been used to denote the study of myths. *Verb*: **mythicize** or **mythologize**. *See also* archetype, myth criticism, mythopoeia. For a fuller account, consult Laurence Coupe, *Myth* (1997).

myth criticism, a kind of literary interpretation that regards literary works as expressions or embodiments of recurrent mythic patterns and structures, or of 'timeless' *archetypes. Myth criticism, which flourished in the 1950s and 1960s, is less interested in the specific qualities of a given work than in those features of its *narrative structure or *symbolism that seem to connect it to ancient myths and religions. An important precedent for many myth-critical studies was J. G. Frazer's speculative anthropological work *The Golden Bough* (1890–1915), which proposed a cycle of death and rebirth found in fertility cults as the common basis for several mythologies. The most influential modern myth critic, Northrop Frye, translated this hypothesis into a universal scheme of literary history in his *Anatomy of Criticism* (1957), in which the major narrative *genres are related to the seasonal cycle. Other leading myth critics have included Gaston Bachelard, Richard Chase, and Leslie Fiedler. More recently, myth criticism has been widely dismissed as a form of *reductionism that neglects cultural and historical differences as well as the specific properties of literary works.

mythopoeia [mith-oh-**pee**-ă] or **mythopoesis** [mith-ŏ-poh-**ees**-is], the making of myths, either collectively in the *folklore and religion of a given (usually pre-literate) culture, or individually by a writer who elaborates a personal system of spiritual principles as in the writings of William Blake. The term is often used in a loose sense to describe any kind of writing that either draws upon older myths or resembles myths in subject-matter or imaginative scope. *Adjective*: **mythopoeic** or **mythopoetic**.

mythos, *see* plot.

narratee, the imagined person whom the *narrator is assumed to be addressing in a given *narrative. The narratee is a notional figure within the 'space' of the *text itself, and is thus not to be confused either with the real reader or with the *implied reader (who is addressed by the *implied author at a separate 'level'). Narratees are often hard to identify clearly, since they are not usually described or characterized explicitly. In some works, though, they appear as minor characters, especially in a *frame story (e.g. the Wedding Guest in Coleridge's 'The Rime of the Ancient Mariner'), and in some they even function as narrators as well: Lockwood, the narratee of Nelly's *embedded narratives in *Wuthering Heights*, is the narrator of the story as a whole.

narration, the process of relating a sequence of events; or another term for a *narrative. In the first sense, narration is often distinguished from other kinds of writing (*dialogue, description, commentary) which may be included in a narrative; it is also distinguished from the events recounted, i.e. from the *story, and from the narrative itself. *Verb:* **narrate.**

narrative [na-ră-tiv], a telling of some true or fictitious event or connected sequence of events, recounted by a *narrator to a *narratee (although there may be more than one of each). Narratives are to be distinguished from descriptions of qualities, states, or situations, and also from dramatic enactments of events (although a dramatic work may also include narrative speeches). A narrative will consist of a set of events (the *story) recounted in a process of narration (or *discourse), in which the events are selected and arranged in a particular order (the *plot). The category of narratives includes both the shortest accounts of events (e.g. *the cat sat on the mat*, or a brief news item) and the longest historical or biographical works, diaries, travelogues, etc., as well as novels, ballads, epics, short stories, and other fictional forms. In the study of fiction, it is usual to divide novels and shorter stories into *first-person narratives and *third-person narratives. As an adjective, 'narrative' means 'characterized by or relating to story-telling': thus **narrative technique** is the method of telling stories, and **narrative poetry** is the class of poems (including ballads, epics, and verse romances) that tell stories, as distinct from dramatic and *lyric poetry. Some theorists of *narratology have attempted to isolate the quality or set of properties that distinguishes narrative from non-narrative writings: this is called **narrativity**. For a fuller account, consult Michael J. Toolan, *Narrative* (1988).

narratology, a term used since 1969 to denote the branch of literary study devoted to the analysis of *narratives, and more specifically of forms of narration and varieties of *narrator. Narratology as a modern theory is associated chiefly with European *structuralism, although older studies of narrative forms and devices, as far back as Aristotle's *Poetics* (4th century BCE) can also be regarded as narratological works. Modern narratology may be dated from Vladimir Propp's *Morphology of the Folktale* (1928), with its theory of narrative *functions.

narrator [nă-ray-ter], one who tells, or is assumed to be telling, the story in a given *narrative. In modern analysis of fictional narratives, the narrator is the imagined 'voice' transmitting the story, and is distinguished both from the real author (who may have written other tales with very different narrators) and from the *implied author (who does not recount the story, but is inferred as the authority responsible for selecting it and inventing a narrator for it). Narrators vary according to their degree of participation in the story: in *first-person narratives they are involved either as witnesses or as participants in the events of the story, whereas in *third-person narratives they stand outside those events; an *omniscient narrator stands outside the events but has special privileges such as access to characters' unspoken thoughts, and knowledge of events happening simultaneously in different places. Narrators also differ in the degree of their overtness: some are given noticeable characteristics and personalities (as in first-person narratives and in some third-person narratives; *see* intrusive narrator), whereas 'covert' narrators are identified by no more than a 'voice' (as in most third-person narratives). Further distinctions are made between reliable narrators, whose accounts of events we are obliged to trust, and *unreliable narrators, whose accounts may be partial, ill-informed, or otherwise misleading: most third-person narrators are reliable, but some first-person narrators are unreliable. In a dramatic work, a narrator is a performer who recounts directly to the audience a summary of events preceding or during a scene or act. *See also* point of view.

naturalism, a more deliberate kind of *realism in novels, stories, and plays, usually involving a view of human beings as passive victims of natural forces and social environment. As a literary movement, naturalism was initiated in France by Jules and Edmond Goncourt with their novel *Germinie Lacerteux* (1865), but it came to be led by Émile Zola, who claimed a 'scientific' status for his studies of impoverished characters miserably subjected to hunger, sexual obsession, and hereditary defects in *Thérèse Raquin* (1867), *Germinal* (1885), and many other novels. Naturalist fiction aspired to a sociological objectivity, offering detailed and fully researched investigations into unexplored corners of modern society—railways in Zola's *La Bête humaine* (1890), the department store in his *Au Bonheur des dames* (1883)—while enlivening this with a new sexual sensationalism. Other novelists and storytellers associated with naturalism include Alphonse Daudet and Guy de Maupassant in France, Theodore Dreiser and Frank Norris in the United States, and George Moore and George Gissing in England; the most significant work of naturalism in English being Dreiser's *Sister Carrie* (1900). In the theatre, Henrik Ibsen's play *Ghosts* (1881), with its stress on heredity, encouraged an important tradition of dramatic naturalism led by August Strindberg, Gerhart Hauptmann, and Maxim Gorky; in a somewhat looser sense, the realistic plays of Anton Chekhov are sometimes grouped with the naturalist phase of European drama at the turn of the century. The term **naturalistic** in drama usually has a broader application, denoting a very detailed illusion of real life on the stage, especially in speech, costume, and sets. *See also* verisimilitude, *verismo*. For a fuller account, consult Lilian R. Furst and Peter. N. Skrine, *Naturalism* (1971).

negative capability, the phrase used by the English poet John Keats to describe the quality of selfless receptivity necessary to a true poet. In a letter to his brothers (December 1817), he writes

> at once it struck me, what quality went to form a Man of Achievement especially in Literature & which Shakespeare possessed so enormously— I mean *Negative Capability*, that is when man is capable of being in uncertainties, Mysteries, doubts, without any irritable reaching after fact & reason.

He goes on to criticize Coleridge for not being 'content with half knowledge'; and in later letters complains of the 'egotistical' and philosophical bias of Wordsworth's poetry. By negative capability, then, Keats seems to have meant a poetic capacity to efface one's own mental identity by immersing it sympathetically and spontaneously within the subject described, as Shakespeare was thought to have done.

négritude [nay-gri-tood], the slogan (literally 'negro-ness') of a cultural movement launched by black students in Paris in 1932, subsequently influencing many black writers, especially in the French-speaking world. The movement aimed to re-assert traditional African cultural values against the French colonial policy of assimilating blacks into white culture. Its two most important figures were the Senegalese poet and politician Léopold Sédar Senghor and the Martiniquan poet and politician Aimé Césaire, and its literary masterpiece is Césaire's *Cahier d'un retour au pays natal* (1938). Senghor defined *négritude* very broadly as 'the sum total of the values of the civilization of the African world,' understood in terms of 'intuitive reason' and 'cosmic rhythm'. The influential journal *Présence Africaine*, founded in 1947, promoted this ideal. A later, more politically radical generation of black writers, however, questioned the movement's limited aims: as Wole Soyinka wrote, 'the tiger does not proclaim his tigritude—he pounces'.

nemesis [nem-ĭ-sis] (plural **-eses**), retribution or punishment for wrongdoing; or the agent carrying out such punishment, often personified as Nemesis, a minor Greek goddess responsible for executing the vengeance of the gods against erring humans. The term is applied especially to the retribution meted out to the *protagonist of a *tragedy for his or her insolence or *hubris. *See also* poetic justice.

neoclassicism, the literary principle according to which the writing and *criticism of poetry and drama were to be guided by rules and precedents derived from the best ancient Greek and Roman authors; a codified form of *classicism that dominated French literature in the 17th and 18th centuries, with a significant influence on English writing, especially from *c*.1660 to *c*.1780. In a more general sense, often employed in contrast with *Romanticism, the term has also been used to describe the characteristic world-view or value-system of this 'Age of Reason', denoting a preference for rationality, clarity, restraint, order, and *decorum, and for general truths rather than particular insights. In its more immediately literary sense as a habitual deference to Greek and Roman models in literary theory and practice, neoclassicism emerged from the rediscovery of Aristotle's *Poetics* (4th century BCE) by Italian scholars in the 16th century, notably by J. C. Scaliger, whose dogmatic interpretation of the dramatic *unities in his *Poetica* (1561) profoundly affected the course of French drama. Along with Aristotle's theory of poetry as imitation and his classification of *genres, the principles of the Roman poet Horace as expounded in his *Ars Poetica* (*c*.20 BCE) dominated the **neoclassical** or **neoclassic** view of literature: these included the principle of decorum by which the style must suit the subject-matter, and the belief that art must both delight and instruct. The central assumption of neoclassicism was that the ancient authors had already attained perfection, so that the modern author's chief task was to imitate them—the imitation of Nature and the imitation of the ancients amounting to the same thing. Accordingly, the approved genres of classical literature—*epic, *tragedy, *comedy, *elegy, *ode, *epistle, *eclogue, *epigram, *fable, and *satire—were adopted as the favoured forms in this period. The most influential summary of neoclassical doctrine is Boileau's verse treatise *L'Art poétique* (1674); its equivalent in English is Alexander Pope's *Essay on Criticism* (1711). In England, neoclassicism reached its height in the *Augustan Age, when its general view of the world was presented memorably in Pope's *Essay on Man* (1733–4). Some modern critics refer to the period 1660–1780 in England as the 'Neoclassical period', but as an inclusive label this is misleading in that one very important development in this period—the emergence of the *novel—falls outside the realm of neoclassicism, there being no acknowledged classical model for the new form.

neologism [ni-ol-ŏ-jizm], a word or phrase newly invented or newly introduced into a language. *Verb*: **neologize**. *See also* coinage, nonce word, portmanteau word.

Neoplatonism, a philosophical and religious system that both rivalled and influenced Christianity from the 3rd to the 6th century, and was derived from the work of the Greek philosopher Plato (427–347 BCE) along with elements of oriental mysticism. The founder of Neoplatonism was Plotinus (205–270 CE), who constructed an elaborate hierarchy of spiritual levels through which the individual soul could ascend from physical existence to merge with the One. Interest in Neoplatonic philosophy, often associated with magic and demonology, was revived in the *Renaissance. *See also* Platonism.

neo-realism, any revival of *realism in fiction, especially in novels and stories describing the lives of the poor in a contemporary setting. The term is associated especially with the dominant trend of Italian fiction in the 1940s and 1950s, led by Cesare Pavese, Alberto Moravia, and Elio Vittorini, and with the parallel movement in Italian cinema of the same period, led by Roberto Rossellini and Vittorio de Sica. See also *verismo*.

New Comedy, the name given to the kind of *comedy that superseded the *Old Comedy of Aristophanes in Athens from the late 4th century BCE, providing the basis for later Roman comedy and eventually for the comic theatre of Molière and Shakespeare. Preceded by a phase of 'middle comedy' (of which almost nothing has survived), New Comedy abandoned topical *satire in favour of fictional plots based on contemporary life: these portrayed the tribulations of young lovers caught up among *stock characters such as the miserly father and the boastful soldier. The *chorus was reduced to a musical interlude. The chief exponent of New Comedy was Menander, of whose many works only one complete play, *Dyskolos (The Bad-Tempered Man*, 317 BCE), survives, along with several fragments. Greek New Comedy was further adapted and developed in Rome by Plautus and Terence in the early 2nd century BCE. *See also* romantic comedy.

New Criticism, a movement in American literary *criticism from the 1930s to the 1960s, concentrating on the verbal complexities and ambiguities of short poems considered as self-sufficient objects without attention to their origins or effects. The name comes from John Crowe Ransom's book *The New Criticism* (1941), in which he surveyed the theories developed in England by T. S. Eliot, I. A. Richards, and William Empson, together with the work of the American critic Yvor Winters. Ransom called for a more 'objective' criticism focusing on the intrinsic qualities of a work rather than on its biographical or historical context; and his students Cleanth Brooks and Robert Penn Warren had already provided a very influential model of such an approach in their college textbook *Understanding Poetry* (1938), which helped to make New Criticism the academic orthodoxy for the next twenty years. Other critics grouped under this heading, despite their differences, include Allen Tate, R. P. Blackmur, W. K. Wimsatt Jr, and Kenneth Burke. Influenced by T. S. Eliot's view of poetry's *autotelic status, and by the detailed *semantic analyses of I. A. Richards in *Practical Criticism* (1929) and Empson in *Seven Types of Ambiguity* (1930), the American New Critics repudiated 'extrinsic' criteria for understanding poems, dismissing them under such names as the *affective fallacy and the *intentional fallacy. Moreover, they sought to overcome the

traditional distinction between *form and *content: for them, a poem
was ideally an 'organic unity' in which tensions were brought to
equilibrium. Their favoured terms of analysis—*irony, *paradox,
*imagery, *metaphor, and *symbol—tended to neglect questions of
*genre, and were not successfully transferred to the study of dramatic
and *narrative works. Many later critics—often unsympathetic to the
New Critics' Southern religious conservatism—accused them of cutting
literature off from history, but their impact has in some ways been
irreversible, especially in replacing biographical source-study with text-
centred approaches. The outstanding works of New Criticism are
Brooks's *The Well-Wrought Urn* (1947) and Wimsatt's *The Verbal Icon* (1954).

Newgate novel, a term applied to certain popular English novels of
the 1830s that are based on legends of 18th-century highwaymen and
other notorious criminals as recorded in the *Newgate Calendar* (c.1773).
Edward Bulwer's *Paul Clifford* (1830) and *Eugene Aram* (1832), along with
W. H. Ainsworth's *Rookwood* (1834) and *Jack Sheppard* (1840) were the
principal examples, and all came under fierce attack from critics,
including W. M. Thackeray, who accused them of encouraging crime.
Dickens's *Oliver Twist* (1838) shares many features of Newgate fiction, but
it managed to escape the censure meted out to Ainsworth and Bulwer.

new historicism, a term applied to a trend in American academic
literary studies in the 1980s that emphasized the historical nature of
literary texts and at the same time (in contrast with older historicisms)
the 'textual' nature of history. As part of a wider reaction against purely
formal or linguistic critical approaches such as the *New Criticism and
*deconstruction, the new historicists, led by Stephen Greenblatt, drew
new connections between literary and non-literary texts, breaking down
the familiar distinctions between a text and its historical 'background' as
conceived in established historical forms of criticism. Inspired by Michel
Foucault's concepts of *discourse and power, they attempted to show
how literary works are implicated in the power-relations of their time,
not as secondary 'reflections' of any coherent world-view but as active
participants in the continual remaking of meanings. New historicism is
less a system of interpretation than a set of shared assumptions about the
relationship between literature and history, and an essayistic style that
often develops general reflections from a startling historical or
anthropological anecdote. Greenblatt's books *Renaissance Self-Fashioning*
(1980) and *Shakespearean Negotiations* (1988) are the exemplary models.

Other scholars of Early Modern ('Renaissance') culture associated with him include Jonathan Goldberg, Stephen Orgel, Lisa Jardine, and Louis Montrose. The term has been applied to similar developments in the study of *Romanticism, such as the work of Jerome McGann and Marjorie Levinson. A major concern of new historicism, following Foucault, is the cultural process by which subversion or dissent is utimately contained by 'power'. For a fuller account, consult Paul Hamilton, *Historicism* (1996).

nō or **noh,** a traditional form of Japanese drama characterized by highly ritualized chant and gesture, and its use of masked actors. Combining music, dance, and speech in prose and verse, the *nō* play derives from religious rituals, and is performed by an all-male cast, originally for an aristocratic audience. More than 200 such plays survive from as early as the 14th century, mostly on religious and mythological subjects. English translations appeared in the early 20th century, influencing the work of Ezra Pound, W. B. Yeats, and Bertolt Brecht.

nom de plume, a pen-name, i.e. a pseudonym under which a writer's work is published, as Marian Evans's novels appeared under the name of 'George Eliot'.

nonce word, a word invented to be used for a single specific occasion; or an old word of which only one occurrence has been found. *See also* coinage, neologism, portmanteau word.

nonsense verse, a kind of humorous poetry that amuses by deliberately using strange non-existent words and illogical ideas. Its masters in English are Edward Lear and Lewis Carroll, followed by G. K. Chesterton and Ogden Nash. Classics of the genre are Lear's 'The Owl and the Pussy-Cat' (1871) and his *limericks, along with the songs in Carroll's *Through the Looking-Glass* (1871), including 'The Walrus and the Carpenter' and the celebrated 'Jabberwocky'. *See also* doggerel, jingle, light verse.

nouveau roman, le [noo-voh roh-mah^n], the French term ('new novel') applied since the mid-1950s to experimental novels by a group of French writers who rejected many of the traditional elements of novel-writing, such as the sequential *plot and the analysis of characters' motives. The leading light of this group was Alain Robbe-Grillet, whose essays on the novel in *Pour un nouveau roman* (1963) argue for a neutral registering of sensations and things rather than an interpretation of

events or a study of characters: these principles were put into practice
most famously in his *anti-novel *La Jalousie* (1957). Other notable
nouveaux romans include Nathalie Sarraute's *Le Planétarium* (1959) and
Michel Butor's *La Modification* (1957); Sarraute's *Tropismes* (1938) is often
cited as the first *nouveau roman*.

nouvelle, *see* novella.

novel, nearly always an extended fictional prose *narrative, although
some novels are very short, some are non-fictional, some have been
written in verse, and some do not even tell a story. Such exceptions help
to indicate that the novel as a literary *genre is itself exceptional: it
disregards the constraints that govern other literary forms, and
acknowledges no obligatory structure, style, or subject-matter. Thriving
on this openness and flexibility, the novel has become the most
important literary genre of the modern age, superseding the *epic, the
*romance, and other narrative forms. Novels can be distinguished from
*short stories and *novellas by their greater length, which permits
fuller, subtler development of characters and themes. (Confusingly, it is
a shorter form of tale, the Italian *novella*, that gives the novel its name in
English.) There is no established minimum length for a novel, but it is
normally at least long enough to justify its publication in an independent
volume, unlike the short story. The novel differs from the prose romance
in that a greater degree of *realism is expected of it, and that it tends to
describe a recognizable secular social world, often in a sceptical and
prosaic manner inappropriate to the marvels of romance. The novel has
frequently incorporated the structures and languages of non-fictional
prose forms (history, autobiography, journalism, travel writing), even to
the point where the non-fictional element outweighs the fictional. It is
normally expected of a novel that it should have at least one character,
and preferably several characters shown in processes of change and
social relationship; a *plot, or some arrangement of narrated events, is
another normal requirement. Special *subgenres of the novel have
grown up around particular kinds of character (the *Künstlerroman, the
spy novel), setting (the *historical novel, the *campus novel), and plot
(the detective novel); while other kinds of novel are distinguished either
by their structure (the *epistolary novel, the *picaresque novel) or
by special emphases on character (the *Bildungsroman) or ideas (the
*roman à thèse). Although some ancient prose narratives like Petronius'
Satyricon (1st century CE) can be called novels, and although some
significant forerunners of the novel—including François Rabelais's

Gargantua (1534)—appeared in the 16th century, it is the publication in Spain of the first part of Miguel de Cervantes's *Don Quixote de la Mancha* in 1605 that is most widely accepted as announcing the arrival of the true novel. In France the inaugural landmark was Madame de Lafayette's *La Princesse de Clèves* (1678), while in England Daniel Defoe is regarded as the founder of the English novel with his *Robinson Crusoe* (1719) and *Moll Flanders* (1722). The novel achieved its predominance in the 19th century, when Charles Dickens and other writers found a huge audience through serial publication, and when the conventions of realism were consolidated. In the 20th century a division became more pronounced between the popular forms of novel and the various experiments of *modernism and *postmodernism—from the *stream of consciousness to the *anti-novel; but repeated reports of the 'death of the novel' have been greatly exaggerated. *Adjective*: **novelistic**. *See also* fiction.

novelette, a trivial or cheaply sensational novel or *romance; or (in a neutral sense, especially in the USA) a short novel or extended short story, i.e. a *novella. The adjective **novelettish** carries the unfavourable connotations of the first sense.

novella [nŏ-vel-ă], a fictional tale in prose, intermediate in length and complexity between a *short story and a *novel, and usually concentrating on a single event or chain of events, with a surprising turning point. Joseph Conrad's *Heart of Darkness* (1902) is a fine example; Henry James and D. H. Lawrence also favoured the novella form. The term comes from the Italian word *novella* ('novelty'; plural *novelle*), which was applied to the much shorter stories found in Boccaccio's *Decameron* (1349–53), until it was borrowed at the end of the 18th century by Goethe and other writers in Germany, where the novella (German, *Novelle) in its modern sense became established as an important literary *genre. In France it is known as the *nouvelle*. See also *conte*, novelette.

Novelle [no-vel-ĕ] (plural *-ellen*), the German term for a fictional prose tale that concentrates on a single event or situation, usually with a surprising conclusion. The term, adopted from the Italian (*see* novella), was introduced in 1795 by J. W. von Goethe. The outstanding German tradition of *Novellen* includes works by Tieck, Kleist, and Thomas Mann, most of which conform (in terms of length) to the English sense of 'novella'.

numbers, a term—now obsolete—formerly applied to poetry in general, by association with the counting of feet or syllables in regular verse *metres.

nursery rhyme, a traditional verse or set of verses chanted to infants by adults as an initiation into rhyme and verbal rhythm. Most are hundreds of years old, and derive from songs, proverbs, riddles, *ballads, street cries, and other kinds of composition originally intended for adults, which have become almost meaningless outside their original contexts. Their exact origins are often obscure, although a few more recent examples are by known authors: 'Mary had a little lamb' was written by Sarah Josepha Hale in 1830. *See also* jingle, nonsense verse.

obiter dicta, the Latin phrase ('things said in passing') sometimes used to refer to the table-talk or incidental remarks made by a writer or other person, of the kind recalled in biographies.

objective correlative, an external equivalent for an internal state of mind; thus any object, scene, event, or situation that may be said to stand for or evoke a given mood or emotion, as opposed to a direct subjective expression of it. The phrase was given its vogue in modern criticism by T. S. Eliot in the rather tangled argument of his essay 'Hamlet and His Problems' (1919), in which he asserts that Shakespeare's *Hamlet* is an 'artistic failure' because Hamlet's emotion does not match the 'facts' of the play's action. The term is symptomatic of Eliot's preference—similar to that of *Imagism—for precise and definite poetic images evoking particular emotions, rather than the effusion of vague yearnings which Eliot and Ezra Pound criticized as a fault of 19th-century poetry.

occasional verse, poetry written for or prompted by a special occasion, e.g. a wedding, funeral, anniversary, birth, military or sporting victory, or scientific achievement. Poetic forms especially associated with occasional verse are the *epithalamion, the *elegy, and the *ode. Occasional verse may be serious, like Andrew Marvell's 'An Horation Ode upon Cromwell's Return from Ireland' (1650) and Walt Whitman's 'Passage to India' (1871), or light, like William Cowper's 'On the Death of Mrs Throckmorton's Bullfinch' (1789). Significant modern examples of occasional verse in English are W. B. Yeats's 'Easter, 1916', and W. H. Auden's 'September 1, 1939', 'August 1968', and 'Moon Landing'.

occupatio, a rhetorical device (also known under the Greek name *paralipsis*) by which a speaker emphasizes something by pretending to pass over it: 'I will not mention the time when...' The device was favoured by Chaucer, who uses it frequently in his *Canterbury Tales*.

octave or **octet,** a group of eight verse lines forming the first part of a *sonnet (in its Italian or Petrarchan form); or a *stanza of eight lines. In the first and most frequently used sense, an octave usually rhymes *abbaabba*. In the second sense, it may also be called an **octastich**. *See also huitain, ottava rima*, triolet.

octavo [ok-**tay**-voh], a book size resulting from folding a printer's sheet of paper three times to make eight leaves (i.e. 16 pages): thus a size smaller than *quarto but bigger than *duodecimo.

octosyllabic [ok-toh-**sī**-**lab**-ik], having eight syllables to the line. Octosyllabic verse in English is usually written in the form of iambic or trochaic *tetrameters. It appears in various forms including the *In Memoriam* stanza, but is most commonly found in *couplets, both in light *Hudibrastic verse and in more serious works such as Wordsworth's poem beginning

> She was a phantom of delight
> When first she gleamed upon my sight

In medieval French poetry, octosyllabic couplets were used in *lais, *fabliaux, and other kinds of poem.

ode, an elaborately formal *lyric poem, often in the form of a lengthy ceremonious address to a person or abstract entity, always serious and elevated in tone. There are two different classical models: Pindar's Greek **choral odes** devoted to public praise of athletes (5th century BCE), and Horace's more privately reflective odes in Latin (*c*.23–13 BCE). Pindar composed his odes for performance by a *chorus, using lines of varying length in a complex three-part structure of *strophe, *antistrophe, and *epode corresponding to the chorus's dancing movements (*see* Pindaric), whereas Horace wrote literary odes in regular *stanzas. Close English imitations of Pindar, such as Thomas Gray's 'The Progress of Poesy' (1754), are rare, but a looser **irregular ode** with varying lengths of strophes was introduced by Abraham Cowley's 'Pindarique Odes' (1656) and followed by John Dryden, William Collins, William Wordsworth (in 'Ode: Intimations of Immortality' (1807)), and S. T. Coleridge, among others; this irregular form of ode is sometimes called the **Cowleyan ode**. Odes in which the same form of stanza is repeated regularly (*see* homostrophic) are called **Horatian odes**: in English, these include the celebrated odes of John Keats, notably 'Ode on a Grecian Urn' and 'Ode to a Nightingale' (both 1820). *Adjective*: **odic**.

oeuvre [ervr], the French word for a work, often used to refer instead to the total body of works produced by a given writer. *See also* canon, corpus.

Old Comedy, the kind of *comedy produced in Athens during the 5th century BCE, before the emergence of the *New Comedy. Old Comedy is distinguished by its festive, farcical mood, by its *lampooning of living persons in topical *satire, and by its prominent use of a *chorus in grotesque masks and costumes. Its leading exponent, and the only one whose plays have survived, was Aristophanes, author of *The Clouds* (423 BCE) and *The Frogs* (405 BCE).

omniscient narrator [om-**nish**-ěnt], an 'all-knowing' kind of *narrator very commonly found in works of fiction written as *third-person narratives. The omniscient narrator has a full knowledge of the story's events and of the motives and unspoken thoughts of the various characters. He or she will also be capable of describing events happening simultaneously in different places—a capacity not normally available to the limited *point of view of *first-person narratives. *See also* intrusive narrator.

onomatopoeia [on-ŏ-mat-ŏ-**pee**-ă], the use of words that seem to imitate the sounds they refer to (whack, fizz, crackle, hiss); or any combination of words in which the sound gives the impression of echoing the sense. This *figure of speech is often found in poetry, sometimes in prose. It relies more on conventional associations between verbal and non-verbal sounds than on the direct duplication of one by the other. *Adjective*: **onomatopoeic**.

oral tradition, the passing on from one generation (and/or locality) to another of songs, chants, proverbs, and other verbal compositions within and between non-literate cultures; or the accumulated stock of works thus transmitted by word of mouth. *Ballads, *folktales, and other works emerging from an oral tradition will often be found in several different versions, because each performance is a fresh improvisation based around a 'core' of narrative incidents and *formulaic phrases. The state of dependence on the spoken word in oral cultures is known as **orality**.

oratory [o-**ră**-tri], the art of public speaking; or the exercise of this art in **orations**—formal speeches for public occasions. A literary style resembling public speech and its formal devices may be called **oratorical**. *See also* rhetoric.

organic form, a concept that likens literary works to living organisms forming themselves by a process of 'natural' growth. The doctrine of organic form, promoted in the early 19th century by S. T. Coleridge and subsequently favoured by American *New Criticism, argues that in an artistic work the whole is more than the mere sum of its component parts, and that *form and *content fuse indivisibly in an 'organic unity'. It rejects as 'mechanical' the *neoclassical concept of conformity to rules, along with the related assumption that form or style is an 'ornament' to a pre-existing content. It tends to be hostile to conceptions of *genre and *convention, as it is to the practice of *paraphrase. Carried to a dogmatic conclusion, its emphasis on unity condemns any literary analysis as a destructive abstraction; this attitude is sometimes referred to as **organicism**.

Ossianism, the craze for Celtic *folklore and *myth that was prompted by the appearance of two *epic poems, *Fingal* (1762) and *Temora* (1763), supposedly composed by Ossian (i.e. Oisin, the legendary 3rd-century Gaelic warrior and *bard, son of Finn or Fingal) and 'translated' by James Macpherson, a Scottish schoolteacher. The supposed discovery of an ancient northern epic had a great imaginative impact in Europe after the translation of 'Ossian' into German (1768–9) and French (1777): Goethe, Herder, and Napoleon Bonaparte were among the leading Ossianic enthusiasts. Even after 1805, when investigators found the epics to be forgeries concocted around some genuine Gaelic folklore, Macpherson's vision of the misty and melancholy Celtic world lived on in the Romantic imagination. *See also* Romanticism, preromanticism.

ostranenie, *see* defamiliarization.

ottava rima [ot-**ahv**-ă-**ree**-mă], a form of verse *stanza consisting of eight lines rhyming *ababab cc*, usually employed for *narrative verse but sometimes used in *lyric poems. In its original Italian form ('eighth rhyme'), pioneered by Boccaccio in the 14th century and perfected by Ariosto in the 16th, it used *hendecasyllables; but the English version uses iambic *pentameters. It was introduced into English by Thomas Wyatt in the 16th century, and later used by Byron in *Don Juan* (1819–24) as well as by Keats, Shelley, and Yeats.

oxymoron [oksi-**mor**-on] (plural **-mora**), a *figure of speech that combines two usually contradictory terms in a compressed *paradox, as in the word *bittersweet* or the phrase *living death*. Oxymoronic phrases, like Milton's 'darkness visible', were especially cultivated in 16th- and

17th-century poetry. Shakespeare has his Romeo utter several in one speech:

> Why then, O brawling love, O loving hate,
> O anything of nothing first create;
> O heavy lightness, serious vanity,
> Misshapen chaos of well-seeming forms,
> Feather of lead, bright smoke, cold fire, sick health,
> Still-waking sleep, that is not what it is!

paean [pee-ăn] (also spelt **pean**), a song or chant of triumphant rejoicing usually after a military victory. Originally choral hymns of thanksgiving to the Greek god Apollo, paeans were later extended to other gods and to military leaders.

paeon [pee-on], a Greek metrical unit (*foot) consisting of one long syllable and three short syllables, usually in that order (– ⌣ ⌣ ⌣, known as the 'first paeon' from the position of the long syllable). Named after its use in *paeans, it occurs in some classical Greek comedy. In English, the paeon combines one stressed syllable with three unstressed syllables; but the foot is rarely found outside the poetry of Gerard Manley Hopkins, who used the second (○●○○) and third (○○●○) paeons in combination with other feet in his 'The Windhover' and other poems. *Adjective*: **paeonic**.

pageant, a wagon used as a mobile stage on which were performed *mystery plays and related dramas in the Middle Ages. The term is sometimes also applied to a play performed on such a movable stage, usually a mystery play. In a later sense, a pageant is a public procession displaying *tableaux and costumes appropriate to the commemoration of some historical event or tradition, sometimes involving short dramatic scenes.

palaeography [pal-i-og-răfi], the study and deciphering of old manuscripts.

palimpsest, a manuscript written on a surface from which an earlier text has been partly or wholly erased. Palimpsests were common in the Middle Ages before paper became available, because of the high cost of parchment and vellum. In a figurative sense, the term is sometimes applied to a literary work that has more than one 'layer' or level of meaning.

palindrome, a word (like *deed, eye,* or *tenet*) that remains the same if read backwards; or a sentence or verse in which the order of letters is the same reading backwards or forwards, disregarding punctuation and spaces between words: *Madam, I'm Adam*. Adjective: **palindromic**.

palinode, a poem or song retracting some earlier statement by the poet. A notable example in English is Chaucer's *The Legend of Good Women*, written to recant his earlier defamation of women in *Troilus and Criseyde*.

panegyric [pan-ĕ-**ji**-rik], a public speech or written composition devoted to the prolonged, effusive praise of some person, group of people, or public body (e.g. a government or army). This branch of *rhetoric was particularly cultivated in ancient Greece and Rome. A composer or speaker of a panegyric is known as a **panegyrist**. *Verb*: **panegyrize**. *See also* encomium.

pantomime, now a theatrical entertainment for children, based on a fairy tale but including songs, dances, topical jokes, and the playing of the hero's part by a woman. In ancient Rome, however, a pantomime was a play on a mythological subject, in which a single performer mimed all the parts while a *chorus sang the story. The term is sometimes also used as a *synonym for *mime or *dumb show. *Adjective*: **pantomimic**.

parable, a brief tale intended to be understood as an *allegory illustrating some lesson or moral. The forty parables attributed to Jesus of Nazareth in Christian literature have had a lasting influence upon the Western tradition of *didactic allegory. A modern instance is Wilfred Owen's poem 'The Parable of the Old Man and the Young' (1920), which adapts a biblical story to the 1914–18 war; a longer prose parable is John Steinbeck's *The Pearl* (1948). *Adjective*: **parabolic**. *See also* fable.

paradigm [pa-**ră**-dym], in the general sense, a pattern or model in which some quality or relation is illustrated in its purest form; but in the terminology of *structuralism, a set of linguistic or other units that can be substituted for each other in the same position within a sequence or structure. A paradigm in this sense may be constituted by all words sharing the same grammatical function, since the substitution of one for another does not disturb the *syntax of a sentence. Linguists often refer to the **paradigmatic** [pa-ră-dig-**mat**-ik] dimension of language as the 'vertical axis' of selection, whereas the syntagmatic dimension governing the combination of linguistic units is the 'horizontal axis' (*see* syntagm). Thus any *sign has two kinds of relation to other signs: a paradigmatic relation to signs of the same class (which are absent in any given utterance), and a syntagmatic relation to signs present in the same sequence.

paradox, a statement or expression so surprisingly self-contradictory as to provoke us into seeking another sense or context in which it would be true (although some paradoxes cannot be resolved into truths, remaining flatly self-contradictory, e.g. *Everything I say is a lie*). Wordsworth's line 'The Child is father of the Man' and Shakespeare's 'the truest poetry is the most feigning' are notable literary examples. Ancient theorists of *rhetoric described paradox as a *figure of speech, but 20th-century critics have given it a higher importance as a mode of understanding by which poetry challenges our habits of thought. Paradox was cultivated especially by poets of the 17th century, often in the verbally compressed form of *oxymoron. It is also found in the prose *epigram; and is pervasive in the literature of Christianity, a notoriously paradoxical religion. In a wider sense, the term may also be applied to a person or situation characterized by striking contradictions. A person who utters paradoxes is a **paradoxer.**

paraliterature, the category of written works relegated to the margins of recognized *literature and often dismissed as subliterary despite evident resemblances to the respectable literature of the official *canon. Paraliterature thus includes many modern forms of popular fiction and drama: children's adventure stories, most detective and spy thrillers, most *science fiction and *fantasy writing, *pornography and women's *romances, along with much television and radio drama.

parallelism, the arrangement of similarly constructed clauses, sentences, or verse lines in a pairing or other sequence suggesting some correspondence between them. The effect of parallelism is usually one of balanced arrangement achieved through repetition of the same syntactic forms (*see* syntax). In classical *rhetoric, this device is called parison or isocolon. These lines from Shakespeare's *Richard II* show parallelism:

> I'll give my jewels for a set of beads,
> My gorgeous palace for a hermitage,
> My gay apparel for an almsman's gown,
> My figured goblets for a dish of wood ...

Parallelism is an important device of 18th-century English prose, as in Edward Gibbon's sentence from his *Memoirs* (1796): 'I was neither elated by the ambition of fame, nor depressed by the apprehension of contempt.' Where the elements arranged in parallel are sharply opposed, the effect is one of *antithesis. In a more extended sense, the term is applied to correspondences between larger elements of dramatic or narrative works, such as the relation of *subplot to main *plot in a play.

paraphrase, a restatement of a text's meaning in different words, usually in order to clarify the sense of the original. Paraphrase involves the separation or abstraction of *content from *form, and so has been resisted strongly by *New Criticism and other schools of modern critical opinion: Cleanth Brooks in *The Well-Wrought Urn* (1947) issued a notable denunciation of the 'heresy of paraphrase', i.e. the idea that a poem is **paraphrasable.** This is a necessary theoretical warning, since the particular form and *diction of a poem (or other work) give it meanings that are not reducible to simple statements and that do not survive the substitution of *synonyms; but the practice of paraphrase can help to establish this very fact, and is an analytic procedure too useful to be outlawed. *Adjective*: **paraphrastic.**

pararhyme, *see* half-rhyme.

paratactic, marked by the juxtaposition of clauses or sentences, without the use of connecting words: *I'll go; you stay here.* A paratactic style has the effect of abruptness, because the relationship between one statement and the next is not made explicit. This passage from H. D. Thoreau's *Walden* (1854) displays **parataxis** in the lack of obvious connection between sentences:

> I think that we may safely trust a good deal more than we do. We may waive just so much care of ourselves as we honestly bestow elsewhere. Nature is as well adapted to our weakness as our strength. The incessant anxiety and strain of some is a well nigh incurable form of disease.

The opposite, explicitly connected style is called *hypotactic. *See also* asyndeton, polysyndeton.

parison, *see* parallelism.

Parnassians, a group of French poets who set a new standard of formal precision in *lyric poetry from the 1860s to the 1890s, partly in reaction against the emotional extravagance of *Romanticism. Adopting Leconte de Lisle as their leader, they followed Théophile Gautier's principle of *art for art's sake, sometimes championing the virtues of impersonality and of traditional verse-forms. Their work appeared in the anthology *La Parnasse contemporain* (1866), which was followed by two further collections with the same title in 1871 and 1876. The leading figures in the group included José-Maria de Hérédia—whose sonnets in *Les Trophées* (1893) constitute the foremost achievement of Parnassianism—along with R.-F.-A. Sully-Prudhomme, Catulle Mendès, Léon Dierx, and François Coppée. Their name refers to Mount Parnassus, a site associated with the Greek *muses.

parody, a mocking imitation of the *style of a literary work or works, ridiculing the stylistic habits of an author or school by exaggerated mimicry. Parody is related to *burlesque in its application of serious styles to ridiculous subjects, to *satire in its punishment of eccentricities, and even to *criticism in its analysis of style. The Greek dramatist Aristophanes parodied the styles of Aeschylus and Euripides in *The Frogs* (405 BCE), while Cervantes parodied *chivalric romances in *Don Quixote* (1605). In English, two of the leading parodists are Henry Fielding and James Joyce. Poets in the 19th century, especially William Wordsworth and Robert Browning, suffered numerous parodies of their works. *Adjective*: **parodic.** *See also* mock-heroic, travesty. For a fuller account, consult Simon Dentith, *Parody* (2000).

parole, see *langue*.

paronomasia [pa-rŏ-noh-**may**-ziă], punning; the term used in ancient *rhetoric to refer to any play on the sounds of words. *Adjective*: **paronomastic.** *See* pun.

passion play, a religious play representing the trials, crucifixion, and resurrection of Jesus of Nazareth. Performances of such plays are recorded in various parts of Europe from the early 13th century onwards, in Latin and in the *vernaculars. Some formed part of the cycles of *mystery plays, others were performed separately, usually on Good Friday. The most famous example today is the *Oberammergauer Passionsspiel* still performed by the villagers of Oberammergau in Bavaria at ten-year intervals; this custom originated in a vow made during an outbreak of plague in 1633.

passus (plural **passus**) a section of a longer poem or story, especially a medieval work such as William Langland's *Piers Plowman*. The term is borrowed from the Latin word for a 'step'. *See also* canto.

pastiche [pas-**teesh**], a literary work composed from elements borrowed either from various other writers or from a particular earlier author. The term can be used in a derogatory sense to indicate lack of originality, or more neutrally to refer to works that involve a deliberate and playfully imitative tribute to other writers. Pastiche differs from *parody in using imitation as a form of flattery rather than mockery, and from *plagiarism in its lack of deceptive intent. A well-known modern example is John Fowles's novel *The French Lieutenant's Woman* (1969), which is partly a pastiche of the great Victorian novelists. The frequent resort to pastiche has been cited as a characteristic feature of *post-modernism. A writer of pastiches is sometimes called a **pasticheur**. *Verb*: **pastiche.**

pastoral, a highly conventional mode of writing that celebrates the innocent life of shepherds and shepherdesses in poems, plays, and prose *romances. Pastoral literature describes the loves and sorrows of musical shepherds, usually in an idealized Golden Age of rustic innocence and idleness; paradoxically, it is an elaborately artificial cult of simplicity and virtuous frugality. The pastoral tradition in Western literature originated with the Greek *idylls of Theocritus (3rd century BCE), who wrote for an urban readership in Alexandria about shepherds in his native Sicily. His most influential follower, the Roman poet Virgil, wrote *eclogues (42–37 BCE) set in the imagined tranquillity of *Arcadia. In the 3rd century CE, the prose romance *Daphnis and Chloe* by Longus continued the tradition. An important revival of pastoral writing in the 16th century was led by Italian dramatists including Torquato Tasso and Battista Guarini, while long prose romances also appeared in other languages, notably Sir Philip Sidney's *Arcadia* (1590) and Honoré d'Urfé's *L'Astrée* (1607–27). English pastorals were written in several forms, from the eclogues of Edmund Spenser's *The Shephearde's Calender* (1579) and the comedy of Shakespeare's *As You Like It* (c.1599) to *lyrics like Marlowe's 'The Passionate Sheepeard to his Love' (1600). A significant form within this tradition is the pastoral *elegy, in which the mourner and the mourned are represented as shepherds in decoratively mythological surroundings: the outstanding English example is John Milton's 'Lycidas' (1637). While most forms of pastoral literature died out during the 18th century, Milton's influence secured for the pastoral elegy a longer life: P. B. Shelley's 'Adonais' (1821) and Matthew Arnold's 'Thyrsis' (1867) are both elegiac imitations of 'Lycidas'. By the late 18th century, pastoral poetry had been overshadowed by the related but distinct fashions for *georgics and *topographical poetry, and it came to be superseded by the more realistic poetry of country life written by George Crabbe, William Wordsworth, and John Clare. For a fuller account, consult Terry Gifford, *Pastoral* (1999).

pastourelle, a short *narrative poem in which a knight relates his encounter with a humble shepherdess whom he attempts (with or without success) to seduce in the course of their amusing *dialogue. Such poems were fashionable in France, Italy, and Germany in the 13th century.

pathetic fallacy, the poetic convention whereby natural phenomena which cannot feel as humans do are described as if they could: thus rain-clouds may 'weep', or flowers may be 'joyful' in sympathy with the poet's (or imagined speaker's) mood. The pathetic fallacy normally involves the use of some *metaphor which falls short of full-scale *personification in its treatment of the natural world. The rather odd term was coined by the influential Victorian art critic John Ruskin in the third volume of his *Modern Painters* (1856). Ruskin's strict views about the accurate representation of nature led him to distinguish great poets like Shakespeare, who use the device sparingly, from lesser poets like Wordsworth and Shelley, whose habitual use of it becomes 'morbid'. Later critics, however, employ the term in a neutral sense. *See also* apostrophe, poetic licence.

pathos [pay-thoss], the emotionally moving quality or power of a literary work or of particular passages within it, appealing especially to our feelings of sorrow, pity, and compassionate sympathy. *Adjective:* **pathetic.**

patronage, the provision of financial or other material assistance to a writer by a wealthy person or public institution, in return for entertainment, prestige, or homage. Dr Johnson defined a patron as 'a wretch who supports with insolence, and is paid with flattery'. The system of patronage has had several varieties, from the accommodation of a poet in a royal household to the payment of a single fee for a flattering dedication. Its importance declined sharply in the 18th century with the appearance of a publishing market, but patronage continues in some modern forms such as business sponsorship of dramatic performances.

pattern poetry, verse that is arranged in an unusual shape on the page so as to suggest some object or movement matching the ideas or mood of the words. Pattern poems were known in Greece in the 4th century BCE.

A well-known English example is George Herbert's 'Easter Wings' (1633); later poets who have used this form in English include e. e. cummings and Dylan Thomas. Since the 1950s, pattern poetry has often been referred to as *concrete poetry.

penny dreadful, the name given in the Victorian age to a kind of cheaply produced book containing bloodthirsty narratives of crime, sometimes merely *plagiarisms from *Gothic novels. In the later 19th century the term was extended to include tamer adventure stories for boys in cheap formats.

pentameter [pen-**tamm**-it-er], a metrical verse line having five main *stresses, traditionally described as a line of five 'feet' (*see* foot). In English poetry since Chaucer, the pentameter—almost always an *iambic line normally of 10 syllables—has had a special status as the standard line in many important forms including *blank verse, the *heroic couplet, *ottava rima*, *rhyme royal, and the *sonnet. In its pure iambic form, the pentameter shows a regular alternation of stressed and unstressed syllables, as in this line by Percy Bysshe Shelley:

>   If Winter comes, can Spring be far behind?

There are, however, several permissible variations in the placing of stresses, which help to avoid the monotony of such regular alternation (*see* demotion, promotion, inversion); and the pentameter may be lengthened from 10 syllables to 11 by a *feminine ending. In classical Greek and Latin poetry, the second line of the elegiac *distich, commonly but inaccurately referred to as a 'pentameter' is in fact composed of two half-lines of two and a half feet each, with *dactyls or *spondees in the first half and dactyls in the second.

performative, a kind of utterance that performs with language the deed to which it refers (e.g. *I promise to come*), instead of describing some state of affairs. The term was coined by the philosopher J. L. Austin in *How to Do Things with Words* (1962) as part of his *speech act theory. Austin distinguishes 'constative' utterances, which state that something is or is not the case, from performatives, which are verbal actions rather than true or false statements; however, he goes on to argue that constatives are also implicitly performative, in that they perform the act of asserting something. The concept has been adapted in *Queer theory and related discussions of gender, notably by Judith Butler, who has argued that a person's gender is continually and variably performed rather than given as a fact. *See also* illocutionary act.

periodic sentence, a long sentence in which the completion of the *syntax and sense is delayed until the end, usually after a sequence of balanced subordinate clauses. The effect is a kind of suspense, as the reader's attention is propelled forward to the end, as in this sentence from Ann Radcliffe's *Romance of the Forest* (1791), describing the heroine's response to an unwelcome sexual advance:

> While he was declaring the ardour of his passion in such terms, as but too often make vehemence pass for sincerity, Adeline, to whom this declaration, if honourable, was distressing, and if dishonourable, was shocking, interrupted him and thanked him for the offer of a distinction, which, with a modest, but determined air, she said she must refuse.

See also hypotactic, Latinate.

periodical, a magazine published at regular intervals, usually weekly, fortnightly, monthly, or quarterly.

peripeteia [pe-ri-pĕ-tee-ă] or **peripety** [pe-**rip**-ĕti], a sudden reversal of a character's circumstances and fortunes, usually involving the downfall of the *protagonist in a *tragedy, and often coinciding with the 'recognition' or *anagnorisis. In a *comedy, however, the peripeteia abruptly restores the prosperity of the main character(s). See also *coup de théâtre*.

periphrasis [pe-**rif**-ră-sis] (plural -ases), a roundabout way of referring to something by means of several words instead of naming it directly in a single word or phrase. Commonly known as *'circumlocution', periphrasis is often used in euphemisms like *passed away* for 'died', but can have a more emphatic effect in poetry, as in the use of *kennings. It was especially cultivated by 18th-century poets whose principle of *decorum discouraged them from using commonplace words: thus fish were called *the finny tribe*, and in Robert Blair's poem 'The Grave' (1743) a telescope is *the sight-invigorating tube*. The 17th-century French fashion for *préciosité* cultivated periphrasis to excess. *Adjective*: **periphrastic**. *See also* antonomasia, litotes, poetic diction.

perlocutionary act, a term used in *speech act theory to designate an utterance that has an effect upon the actions, thoughts, or feelings of the listener, e.g. convincing, alarming, insulting, boring. The perlocutionary effect of an utterance may differ from the intended effect of the speaker's *illocutionary act. *See also* affective.

peroration [pe-rŏ-**ray**-shŭn], the conclusion of a formal speech (or written argument), in which the previous points are summed up in a forceful appeal to the audience; or any formal and impassioned speech, in its entirety. *Verb*: **perorate**. *Adjective*: **perorational** or **perorative**. *See also* epilogue.

persona [per-**soh**-nă] (plural **-onae**), the assumed identity or fictional 'I' (literally a 'mask') assumed by a writer in a literary work; thus the speaker in a *lyric poem, or the *narrator in a fictional narrative. In a *dramatic monologue, the speaker is evidently not the real author but an invented or historical character. Many modern critics, though, insist further that the speaker in any poem should be referred to as the persona, to avoid the unreliable assumption that we are listening to the true voice of the poet. One reason for this is that a given poet may write different poems in which the speakers are of distinct kinds: another is that our identification of the speaking voice with that of the real poet would confuse imaginative composition with autobiography. Some theorists of narrative fiction have preferred to distinguish between the narrator and the persona, making the persona equivalent to the *implied author.

personification, a *figure of speech by which animals, abstract ideas, or inanimate things are referred to as if they were human, as in Sir Philip Sidney's line:

> Invention, Nature's child, fled stepdame Study's blows

This figure or *trope, known in Greek as *prosopopoeia*, is common in most ages of poetry, and particularly in the 18th century. It has a special function as the basis of *allegory. In drama, the term is sometimes applied to the impersonation of non-human things and ideas by human actors. *Verb*: **personify**. *See also* pathetic fallacy.

Petrarchan [pet-**rar**-kăn] characteristic of, or derived from, the work of the major Italian poet Petrarch (Francesco Petrarca, 1304–74), especially his *sonnets and other love *lyrics in Italian. The **Petrarchan sonnet**, also known as the Italian sonnet, is divided into an *octave rhyming *abbaabba* and a *sestet normally rhyming *cdecde*, and thus avoids the final *couplet found in the English or 'Shakespearean' sonnet. The **Petrarchan conceit** is an exaggerated comparison or striking *oxymoron of the kind found in sonnets written under Petrarch's influence: common varieties are the comparison of a lady's eyes with the sun, and the description of love in terms of its pleasurable pains. The widespread imitation of Petrarch's love poetry in Europe, reaching its height in the 16th century, is known as **Petrarchism.** This important imitative tradition is marked by the increasingly conventional presentation of *courtly love, in which the despairing poet speaks in fanciful and paradoxical terms of his torments as the worshipper of a disdainful mistress. A notable Petrarchan *convention is the *blazon or catalogue of the lady's physical beauties: coral lips, pearly teeth, alabaster neck etc. Petrarchism is evident in French poets of the *Pléiade and in the English sonneteers from Wyatt to Shakespeare.

phenomenology, a philosophical movement based on the investigation of 'phenomena' (i.e. things as apprehended by consciousness) rather than on the existence of anything outside of human consciousness. Phenomenology was founded in the early years of the 20th century by the German philosopher Edmund Husserl, who hoped to return philosophy to concrete experience and to reveal the essential structures of consciousness. In an amended form, Husserl's phenomenology was developed by his student Martin Heidegger, and became an important influence on *existentialism and the modern tradition of *hermeneutics. Its impact on literary studies is most evident in the work of the *Geneva school on authors' characteristic modes of awareness; but other kinds of phenomenological criticism—such as that of the Polish theorist Roman Ingarden—place more emphasis on the reader's consciousness of literary works. In this sense, phenomenology has prepared the ground for *reception theory. For a more extended account, consult Robert R. Magliola, *Phenomenology and Literature* (1977).

philistine, a person devoted narrow-mindedly to material prosperity at the expense of intellectual and artistic awareness; or (as an adjective) ignorantly uninterested in culture and ideas. This sense of the term comes from the insulting label *Philister* applied by German students to their non-academic neighbours in university towns, likening them to the enemies of the chosen people in the Hebrew scriptures; it was given wide currency in English by the poet and critic Matthew Arnold in his book *Culture and Anarchy* (1869), which attacks the **philistinism** of the British middle class. Arnold usually applied the term 'the Philistines' to the prosperous bourgeoisie, especially to its nonconformist Liberal representatives.

philology, an older term for linguistics, and especially for the branch of linguistic study devoted to comparative and historical research into the development of languages. In a wider sense, the term sometimes also covers the study of literary texts. A researcher in this scholarly field is a **philologist**.

philosophes [feel-o-zof], the French word ('philosophers') applied especially to the sceptical thinkers of the 18th-century *Enlightenment in France, who subjected the established institutions and beliefs of their time to rational criticism. The foremost *philosophes* included Voltaire, Montesquieu, Helvétius, and the *Encyclopédistes* led by Diderot, d'Alembert and d'Holbach. Their sceptical undermining of religious dogma and political injustice is often regarded as a factor contributing to the downfall of the *ancien régime* in the French Revolution.

phoneme [foh-neem], a minimal unit of potentially meaningful sound within a given language's system of recognized sound distinctions. Each phoneme in a language acquires its identity by contrast with other phonemes, for which it cannot be substituted without potentially altering the meaning of a word: our recognition of a difference between the words *level* and *revel* indicates a phonemic distinction in English between /l/ and /r/. (It is usual for phonemic symbols to be printed between oblique strokes in this fashion.) However, the actual *phonetic* difference between the two /l/ sounds in most pronunciations of the word *level* is disregarded by speakers of English, who treat them as 'allophones' (i.e. phonetic variations) of the same phoneme. Each language divides up the infinite number of possible sounds into a fairly small number of distinct phonemes, in ways which do not always match the distinctions observed in other languages (/l/ and /r/ are not distinguished in Chinese, for example). The concept of the phoneme has great significance for *structuralism, because it suggests that meanings are dependent on an abstract system of differences. The branch of linguistics that analyses the sound systems of languages is known as **phonemics**. *See also* grapheme, morpheme, phonology.

phonetics [fŏ-net-iks], the science devoted to the physical analysis of the sounds of human speech, including their production, transmission, and perception. A pure science connected to acoustics and anatomy, phonetics is concerned with the accurate description of speech sounds as sounds, rather than with the way languages divide sounds up into meaningful units (this being the domain of *phonology). A person practising the science of phonetics is a **phonetician**.

phonocentrism, the term employed in *deconstruction to refer to an alleged bias in Western thinking about language, whereby writing is regarded suspiciously as an untrustworthy parasite upon the authenticity of speech. According to Jacques Derrida in his book *De la grammatologie* (1967), the preference for speech—whose truth seems to be guaranteed by the presence of the speaker—is still upheld even in the modern linguistic theories of Ferdinand de Saussure (*see* sign), despite Saussure's demonstration that language is a system of abstract differences. Derrida's argument equates 'writing' with difference, and speech with illusory presence; he can thus claim that speech actually relies upon a prior 'writing'—that is, upon that system of differences which produces meanings in a language. Phonocentrism is one important aspect of a more general attachment to stability of meanings, which Derrida calls *logocentrism.

phonology [fŏ-**nol**-ŏji], the branch of linguistics concerned with the analysis of sound-systems as they function in languages (rather than with physical sounds as such, as in *phonetics). The term is sometimes also applied to the sound-system itself, in a given language: the 'phonology of English' is the system of distinctions and rules governing the speech of this language. The founding concept of phonology is that of the *phoneme.

picaresque novel [pik-ă-**resk**], in the strict sense, a *novel with a **picaroon** (Spanish, *picaró*: a rogue or scoundrel) as its hero or heroine, usually recounting his or her escapades in a *first-person narrative marked by its *episodic structure and realistic low-life descriptions. The picaroon is often a quick-witted servant who takes up with a succession of employers. The true Spanish picaresque novel is represented by the anonymous *Lazarillo de Tormes* (1554) and by Mateo Alemán's more widely influential *Guzmán de Alfarache* (1599–1604); its imitators include Johann Grimmelhausen's *Simplicissimus* (1669) in German, Alain-René Lesage's *Gil Blas* (1715–35) in French, and Daniel Defoe's *Moll Flanders* (1722) in English. In the looser sense now more frequently used, the term is applied to *narratives that do not have a picaroon as their central character, but are loosely structured as a sequence of episodes united only by the presence of the central character, who is often involved in a long journey: Cervantes' *Don Quixote* (1605), Henry Fielding's *Tom Jones* (1749), and Mark Twain's *Adventures of Huckleberry Finn* (1884) are examples of novels that are referred to as being wholly or partly picaresque in this sense, while Byron's narrative poem *Don Juan* (1819–24) is a rare case of a picaresque story in verse.

Pindaric [pin-**da**-rik], characteristic of or derived from the work of the Greek poet Pindar (Pindaros, 518–438 BCE), a writer of public choral *odes. The **Pindaric ode** has an unfixed number of *stanzas arranged in groups of three, in which a *strophe and *antistrophe sharing the same length and complex metrical pattern are followed by an *epode of differing length and pattern. This triadic arrangement matches the movements of the *chorus that would have performed Pindar's works on public occasions. In English, two rare examples of 'regular' odes conforming to this Pindaric model are Thomas Gray's 'The Progress of Poesy' and 'The Bard' (both 1747). More common, though, is the 'irregular' or 'Cowleyan' ode comprising a number of strophes that do not correspond in length or in the arrangement of their lines: Abraham Cowley's 'Pindarique Odes' (1656) began this kind of departure from strict Pindaric precedent. A more clearly distinct tradition in the composition of odes is represented by the *Horatian ode, which employs a regularly repeated stanza form.

pirated, published without the author's permission by some other person who thereby steals part of the author's potential income from a written work. Literary piracy was often a problem for writers before the enforcement of international copyright agreements in the late 19th century.

plagiarism [**play**-jă-rizm], the theft of ideas (such as the plots of narrative or dramatic works) or of written passages or works, where these are passed off as one's own work without acknowledgement of their true origin; or a piece of writing thus stolen. Plagiarism is not always easily separable from imitation, adaptation, or *pastiche, but is usually distinguished by its dishonest intention. A person practising this form of literary theft is a **plagiarist**. The older term **plagiary** was applied both to plagiarisms and to plagiarists. *Verb*: **plagiarize**.

Platonism [**play**-tŏn-izm], the doctrines of the Greek philosopher Plato (Platon, 427–347 BCE), especially the idealist belief that the perceptible world is an illusory shadow of some higher realm of transcendent Ideas or Forms. Despite Plato's hostility to poets as misleading imitators of worldly illusions, **Platonic** ideas have repeatedly been adopted in Western literature: in the *Renaissance his view of physical beauty as an outward sign of spiritual perfection is prevalent in love poetry, while in the age of *Romanticism his idealist philosophy was absorbed by many poets, notably Percy Bysshe Shelley. The **Cambridge Platonists** were a group of theologians associated with Cambridge University in the mid-17th century, who sought to reconcile the Anglican faith with human Reason while promoting religious tolerance; their leading writers were Henry More and Ralph Cudworth. *See also* Neoplatonism.

Pléiade, la [play-ahd], the name given to an important group of 16th-century French poets led by Pierre de Ronsard. The name, taken from the constellation of seven stars known in English as the Pleiades, had formerly been applied to a group of Greek *Alexandrian poets; Ronsard himself adopted it for his group in 1556. The group of seven comprised Ronsard, Joachim du Bellay, Pontus de Tyard, Jean-Antoine de Baïf, Etienne Jodelle, Remy Belleau, and either Jacques Peletier or Jean Dorat (according to differing lists). Devoted students of the Greek and Latin classics, the poets of the *Pléiade* were nevertheless strongly committed to developing the French language as a medium for major poetry. Rejecting the popular traditions and forms of medieval verse, they transformed French poetry by establishing the *alexandrine as the major verse line, and by introducing the *ode and the *sonnet into the language. Their most important manifestos are Du Bellay's *Deffence et illustration de la langue francoyse* (1549) and Ronsard's Preface to his *Odes* (1550).

pleonasm [plee-ŏn-azm], the use of unnecessary additional words; or a phrase in which such needless repetition occurs, e.g. *at this moment in time*. Adjective: **pleonastic**.

ploce or **ploche** [ploh-kay], a very common *figure of speech that consists in a delayed repetition of the same word or words. By contrast with *epizeuxis (immediate repetition), it interposes some other words between the two occurrences of the terms emphasized. *See also* epanalepsis.

plot, the pattern of events and situations in a narrative or dramatic work, as selected and arranged both to emphasize relationships— usually of cause and effect—between incidents and to elicit a particular kind of interest in the reader or audience, such as surprise or suspense. Although in a loose sense the term commonly refers to that sequence of chief events which can be summarized from a story or play, modern criticism often makes a stricter distinction between the plot of a work and its *story: the plot is the selected version of events as presented to the reader or audience in a certain order and duration, whereas the story is the full sequence of events as we imagine them to have taken place in their 'natural' order and duration. The story, then, is the hypothetical 'raw material' of events which we reconstruct from the finished product of the plot. The critical discussion of plots originates in Aristotle's *Poetics* (4th century BCE), in which his term *mythos* corresponds roughly with our 'plot'. Aristotle saw plot as more than just the arrangement of incidents: he assigned to plot the most important function in a drama, as a governing principle of development and coherence to which other elements (including character) must be subordinated. He insisted that a plot should have a beginning, a middle, and an end, and that its events should form a coherent whole. Plots vary in form from the fully integrated or 'tightly knit' to the loosely *episodic. In general, though, most plots will trace some process of change in which characters are caught up in a developing conflict that is finally resolved. *See also* intrigue, subplot.

plurisignation, *see* ambiguity.

poetaster [poh-it-as-ter], a writer of verse who does not deserve to be called a poet, despite his or her pretensions; an inferior poet lacking in ability. Trivial or worthless verse may sometimes be called **poetastery**.

poète maudit [poh-et moh-dee], a French phrase for an 'accursed' poet, usually a brilliant but self-destructive writer misunderstood by an indifferent society. The name for this romantic stereotype comes from the title of Paul Verlaine's collection of essays on Mallarmé, Rimbaud, and other French poets, *Les poètes maudits* (1884).

poetic diction, in the most general sense, the choice of words and *figures in poetry. The term is more often used, however, to refer to that specialized language which is peculiar to poetry in that it employs words and figures not normally found in common speech or prose. Some elements of poetic diction, such as *kennings, compound *epithets, and *archaisms, occur widely in earlier periods of poetry, but the most elaborate system of poetic diction in English is found among poets of the 18th century, when the principle of *decorum required the use of *periphrasis to avoid naming 'common' things: thus Pope refers to a pair of scissors as 'the glitt'ring Forfex'. Poetic diction in the 18th century is also marked by *Latinate vocabulary, conventional epithets and archaisms, and frequent use of *personification; it was rejected as 'gaudy and inane phraseology' by William Wordsworth, whose Preface to the second edition (1800) of *Lyrical Ballads* argues for a plainer diction closer to 'the real language of men'. *See also* poeticism.

poetic drama, the category of plays written wholly or mainly in verse. This includes most *tragedies and other serious plays from the earliest times to the 19th century, along with most *comedy up to the late 17th century. Strictly speaking, the term is not identical with dramatic poetry (*see* drama), which also includes verse compositions not suited for the stage, such as *closet dramas.

poetic justice, the morally reassuring allocation of happy and unhappy fates to the virtuous and the vicious characters respectively, usually at the end of a *narrative or dramatic work. The term was coined by the critic Thomas Rymer in his *The Tragedies of the Last Age Consider'd* (1678) with reference to Elizabethan *poetic drama: such justice is 'poetic', then, in the sense that it occurs more often in the fictional plots of plays than in real life. As Miss Prism explains in Oscar Wilde's *The Importance of Being Earnest*, 'The good ended happily, and the bad unhappily. That is what Fiction means.' In a slightly different but commonly used sense, the term may also refer to a strikingly appropriate reward or punishment, usually a 'fitting retribution' by which a villain is ruined by some process of his own making. *See also* nemesis.

poetic licence (*US* **license**), the imaginative and linguistic freedom granted to poets, allowing them to depart from normal prose standards of factual accuracy, *syntax, grammar, or pronunciation where this may produce a more satisfying imaginative or metrical effect. Depending upon prevailing aesthetic conventions, this may permit the use of *elision or of syntactic *inversion to fit the *metre of a line, of *eye rhyme or *broken rhyme to fit a *rhyme scheme, of unusual *diction, of illogical *figures (e.g. *catachresis, *hyperbole), or of other imaginative 'liberties' ranging from *personification and the *pathetic fallacy to inaccuracies of chronology (*anachronism), geography, or natural science.

poeticism [poh-**et**-is-izm], a word or phrase that survives only within a tradition of *poetic diction, usually an *archaism like *of yore* or a conventional *syncope such as *o'er*.

poetics [poh-**et**-iks], the general principles of *poetry or of *literature in general, or the theoretical study of these principles. As a body of theory, poetics is concerned with the distinctive features of poetry (or literature as a whole), with its languages, forms, *genres, and modes of composition. A theorist of poetry or literature may be called a **poetician**. *See also* aesthetics, criticism.

poetry, language sung, chanted, spoken, or written according to some pattern of recurrence that emphasizes the relationships between words on the basis of sound as well as sense: this pattern is almost always a rhythm or *metre, which may be supplemented by *rhyme or *alliteration or both. The demands of verbal patterning usually make poetry a more condensed medium than *prose or everyday speech, often involving variations in *syntax, the use of special words and phrases (*poetic diction) peculiar to poets, and a more frequent and more elaborate use of *figures of speech, principally *metaphor and *simile. All cultures have their poetry, using it for various purposes from sacred ritual to obscene insult, but it is generally employed in those utterances and writings that call for heightened intensity of emotion, dignity of expression, or subtlety of meditation. Poetry is valued for combining pleasures of sound with freshness of ideas, whether these be solemn or comical. Some critics make an evaluative distinction between poetry, which is elevated or inspired, and *verse, which is merely clever or mechanical. The three major categories of poetry are *narrative, dramatic, and *lyric, the last being the most extensive.

point of view, the position or vantage-point from which the events of a story seem to be observed and presented to us. The chief distinction usually made between points of view is that between *third-person narratives and *first-person narratives. A third-person *narrator may be *omniscient, and therefore show an unrestricted knowledge of the story's events from outside or 'above' them; but another kind of third-person narrator may confine our knowledge of events to whatever is observed by a single character or small group of characters, this method being known as 'limited point of view' (*see* focalization). A first-person narrator's point of view will normally be restricted to his or her partial knowledge and experience, and therefore will not give us access to other characters' hidden thoughts. Many modern authors have also used 'multiple point of view', in which we are shown the events from the positions of two or more different characters.

polemic [pŏ-**lemm**-ik], a thorough written attack on some opinion or policy, usually within a theological or political dispute, sometimes also in philosophy or *criticism. Notable **polemicists** in English are John Milton, whose *Areopagitica* (1644) attacks censorship, and H. D. Thoreau, whose 'Slavery in Massachusetts' (1854) berates upholders of the Fugitive Slave Law. *Adjective*: **polemical**.

polyphonic [poli-**fon**-ik], literally 'many-voiced', a term found in the writings of the Russian literary theorist Mikhail Bakhtin, where it is equivalent to *dialogic. Thus a polyphonic novel is one in which several different voices or points of view interact on more or less equal terms. The term **polyphonic prose** has been applied to a kind of *free verse printed as if it were prose and showing similarities to the *prose poem, as in Amy Lowell's *Can Grande's Castle* (1918). *Noun*: **polyphony**.

polyptoton, a *figure of speech in which a partial repetition arises from the use in close proximity of two related words having different forms, e.g. singular and plural forms of the same word: 'Going, going, gone.'

polysemy [poli-**see**-mi], a linguistic term for a word's capacity to carry two or more distinct meanings, e.g. *grave*: 'serious' or 'tomb' (*see also* homonym). In some modern linguistic and literary theory, it is argued that all *signs are polysemic, and the term has been extended to larger units including entire literary works. *See also* ambiguity, multi-accentuality.

polysyndeton [poli-**sin**-dĕ-ton], a rhetorical term for the repeated use of conjunctions to link together a succession of words, clauses, or sentences, as in Keats's *Endymion* (1818):

> And soon it lightly dipped, and rose, and sank,
> And dipped again ...

Polysyndeton is the opposite of *asyndeton.

pornography, a kind of fictional writing composed so as to arouse sexual excitement in its readers, usually by the repeated and explicit description of sexual acts in abstraction from their emotional and other interpersonal contexts; also visual images having the same purpose. The distinction between pornography and literary *eroticism* is open to continued debate, but it is commonly accepted that eroticism treats sexuality within some fuller human and imaginative context, whereas pornographic writing tends to be narrowly functional and often physiologically improbable. Further confusion arises from the questionable assimilation of the term into the distinct legal concept of *obscenity*, which usually governs the public mention or display of specific acts, organs, words, and supposed 'perversions'. Several works of serious literary merit, including Radclyffe Hall's *The Well of Loneliness* (1928) and James Joyce's *Ulysses* (1922), have been legally condemned as obscene although they do not fit most definitions of pornography. The term's etymology is of little help: it is a rather bogus 19th-century coinage combining Greek words to mean 'writing about prostitutes'.

portmanteau word, a word concocted by fusing two different words together into one: a common example is *brunch*, from 'breakfast' and 'lunch'. The term was coined by Lewis Carroll in *Through the Looking-Glass* (1871), where he invents the word *slithy* from 'lithe' and 'slimy'; the portmanteau referred to is a kind of suitcase composed of two halves. The most extended literary use of portmanteau words is found in James Joyce's novel *Finnegans Wake* (1939). *See also* coinage, neologism, nonce word, pun.

postcolonial literature, a category devised to replace and expand upon what was once called Commonwealth Literature. As a label, it thus covers a very wide range of writings from countries that were once colonies or dependencies of the European powers. There has been much debate about the scope of the term: should predominantly white ex-colonies like Ireland, Canada, and Australia be included? why are the United States exempted both from the accepted list of former colonies and from the category of colonizing powers? In practice, the term is applied most often to writings from Africa, the Indian sub-continent, the Caribbean, and other regions whose histories during the 20th century are marked by colonialism, anti-colonial movements, and subsequent transitions to post-Independence society. Critical attention to this large body of work in academic contexts is often influenced by a distinct school of **postcolonial theory** which developed in the 1980s and 1990s, under the influence of Edward W. Said's landmark study *Orientalism* (1978). Postcolonial theory considers vexed cultural-political questions of national and ethnic identity, 'otherness', race, imperialism, and language, during and after the colonial periods. It draws upon *post-structuralist theories such as those of *deconstruction in order to unravel the complex relations between imperial 'centre' and colonial 'periphery', often in ways that have been criticized for being excessively abstruse. The principal luminaries of postcolonial theory after Said have been Gayatri C. Spivak and Homi K. Bhabha. For fuller accounts, consult

A. Loomba, *Colonialism/Postcolonialism* (1998) and Bart Moore-Gilbert, *Postcolonial Theory* (1997).

postmodernism, a disputed term that has occupied much recent debate about contemporary culture since the early 1980s. In its simplest and least satisfactory sense it refers generally to the phase of 20th-century Western culture that succeeded the reign of high *modernism, thus indicating the products of the age of mass television since the mid-1950s. More often, though, it is applied to a cultural condition prevailing in the advanced capitalist societies since the 1960s, characterized by a superabundance of disconnected images and styles—most noticeably in television, advertising, commercial design, and pop video. In this sense, promoted by Jean Baudrillard and other commentators, **postmodernity** is said to be a culture of fragmentary sensations, eclectic nostalgia, disposable simulacra, and promiscuous superficiality, in which the traditionally valued qualities of depth, coherence, meaning, originality, and authenticity are evacuated or dissolved amid the random swirl of empty signals.

As applied to literature and other arts, the term is notoriously ambiguous, implying either that modernism has been superseded or that it has continued into a new phase. Postmodernism may be seen as a continuation of modernism's alienated mood and disorienting techniques and at the same time as an abandonment of its determined quest for artistic coherence in a fragmented world: in very crude terms, where a modernist artist or writer would try to wrest a meaning from the world through myth, symbol, or formal complexity, the postmodernist greets the *absurd or meaningless confusion of contemporary existence with a certain numbed or flippant indifference, favouring self-consciously 'depthless' works of *fabulation, *pastiche, *bricolage, or *aleatory disconnection. The term cannot usefully serve as an inclusive description of all literature since the 1950s or 1960s, but is applied selectively to those works that display most evidently the moods and formal disconnections described above. It seems to have little relevance to modern poetry, and limited application to drama outside the 'absurdist' tradition, but is used widely in reference to fiction, notably to the novels (or *anti-novels) and stories of Thomas Pynchon, Kurt Vonnegut, Italo Calvino, Vladimir Nabokov, William S. Burroughs, Angela Carter, Salman Rushdie, Peter Ackroyd, Julian Barnes, Jeanette Winterson, and many of their followers. Some of their works, like Pynchon's *Gravity's Rainbow* (1973) and Nabokov's *Ada* (1969), employ devices reminiscent of *science fiction, playing with contradictory orders of reality or the irruption of the fabulous into the secular world.

Opinion is still divided, however, on the value of the term and of the phenomenon it purports to describe. Those who most often use it tend to welcome 'the postmodern' as a liberation from the hierarchy of 'high' and 'low' cultures; while sceptics regard the term as a symptom of irresponsible academic euphoria about the glitter of consumerist capitalism and its moral vacuity. For more extended discussions, consult Jean-François Lyotard, *The Postmodern Condition* (1986); H. Bertens and D. Fokkema (eds.), *Approaching Postmodernism* (1986); and Brian McHale, *Postmodernist Fiction* (1987). *See also* post-structuralism.

post-structuralism, a school of thought that emerged partly from within French *structuralism in the 1960s, reacting against structuralist pretensions to scientific objectivity and comprehensiveness. The term covers the philosophical *deconstruction practised by Jacques Derrida and his followers, along with the later works of the critic Roland Barthes, the psychoanalytic theories of Jacques Lacan and Julia Kristeva, the historical critiques of Michel Foucault, and the cultural-political writings of Jean-François Lyotard and Gilles Deleuze. These thinkers emphasized the instability of meanings and of intellectual categories (including that of the human 'subject'), and sought to undermine any theoretical system that claimed to have universal validity—such claims being denounced as 'totalitarian'. They set out to dissolve the fixed *binary oppositions of structuralist thought, including that between language and *metalanguage—and thus between literature and criticism. Instead they favoured a non-hierarchical plurality or 'free play' of meanings, stressing the *indeterminacy of texts. Although waning in French intellectual life by the end of the 1970s, post-structuralism's delayed influence upon literary and cultural theory in the English-speaking world has persisted. For a fuller account, consult Madan Sarup, *An Introductory Guide to Post-Structuralism and Postmodernism* (1988).

pot-boiler, a derogatory term for a work written solely or mainly to earn money.

poulter's measure, an English poetic *metre composed of alternate lines of 12 and 14 syllables (iambic *hexameters and *heptameters), usually in rhyming *couplets, as shown in these lines by the Earl of Surrey, a 16th-century poet:

> Then comes a sudden fear, that riveth all my rest,
> Lest absence cause forgetfulness to sink within her breast.

Although popular in the 16th century, the metre was rarely used
thereafter, because of its clumsiness. It seems to be related to *short
measure and to the *limerick, despite differences in *rhyme scheme. Its
name comes from the poulterer's former custom of providing eggs in
'dozens' of twelve and fourteen. *See also* fourteener.

practical criticism, in the general sense, the kind of *criticism that
analyses specific literary works, either as a deliberate application of a
previously elaborated theory or as a supposedly non-theoretical
investigation. More specifically, the term is applied to an academic
procedure devised by the critic I. A. Richards at Cambridge University in
the 1920s and illustrated in his book *Practical Criticism* (1929). In this
exercise, students are asked to analyse a short poem without any
information about its authorship, date, or circumstances of composition,
thus forcing them to attend to the 'words on the page' rather than refer
to biographical and historical contexts. This discipline, enthusiastically
adopted by the *Cambridge school, became a standard model of rigorous
criticism in British universities, and its style of 'close reading' influenced
the *New Criticism in America. *See also* explication.

préciosité, la, a cult of refined language and manners that established
itself in French high society of the mid-17th century, led by the *salon of
Catherine de Vivonne, Marquise de Rambouillet from about 1618 to
1650. The *précieuses* devised elegant expressions to remedy what they felt
to be the indelicacies of French speech; many of these are recorded in A.
B. de Somaize's *Dictionnaire des précieuses* (1660). This sometimes excessive
fashion for *periphrasis was satirized by Molière in his one-act comedy
Les Précieuses ridicules (1659). The English term **preciosity** has a less
specific sense, referring to any kind of affectation.

Pre-Raphaelites, a group of English artists and writers of the Victorian
period, associated directly or indirectly with the self-styled Pre-
Raphaelite Brotherhood of young artists founded in 1848 by Dante
Gabriel Rossetti, John Everett Millais, and William Holman Hunt. The
PRB (as it is usually abbreviated) rebelled against the conventional
academic styles of painting modelled upon Raphael (1483–1520), seeking
a freshness and simplicity found in earlier artists, along with a closer
fidelity to Nature. The organized Brotherhood itself lasted only a few
years, but **Pre-Raphaelitism** as a broader current survived in the

paintings of Edward Burne-Jones, the designs of William Morris, and the art criticism of John Ruskin, as well as in the poetry of Christina Rossetti, D. G. Rossetti, Morris, and A. C. Swinburne—the last three being dubbed 'The Fleshly School of Poetry' in a hostile review by Robert Buchanan (*Contemporary Review*, 1871). Pre-Raphaelite poetry is often characterized by dreamy *medievalism, mixing religiosity and sensuousness, notably in D. G. Rossetti's 'The Blessed Damozel' (1850), Morris's *The Defence of Guenevere* (1858), and Swinburne's *Poems and Ballads* (1866).

preromanticism, a general term applied by modern literary historians to a number of developments in late 18th-century culture that are thought to have prepared the ground for *Romanticism in its full sense. In various ways, these are all departures from the orderly framework of *neoclassicism and its authorized *genres. The most important constituents of preromanticism are the *Sturm und Drang* phase of German literature; the *primitivism of Jean-Jacques Rousseau and of *Ossianism; the cult of *sensibility in the *sentimental novel; the taste for the *sublime and the picturesque in landscape; the sensationalism of the early *Gothic novels; the melancholy of English *graveyard poetry; and the revival of interest in old *ballads and *romances. These developments seem to have helped to give a new importance to subjective and spontaneous individual feeling.

prescriptive, seeking to lay down rules and instructions. Prescriptive *criticism formulates the norms according to which literary works ought to be written, whereas descriptive criticism tries to account for the ways in which they actually have been written. In discussions of language, **prescriptivism** is the attitude that tries to impose an unchanging standard of 'correct' usage in language, especially in grammar; it is rejected as a misconceived dogma by most modern linguists.

primitivism, a preference for the supposedly free and contented existence found in a 'primitive' way of life as opposed to the artificialities of urban civilization. Often connected with a nostalgia for a lost Eden or Golden Age (as in much *pastoral literature), primitivism is found in the literature of many periods, but it had a particular prominence in 18th-century Europe and 19th-century America, contributing to the values of *Romanticism. The most influential primitivist, Jean-Jacques Rousseau, argued in his *Discours sur l'origine de l'inégalité* (1755) and other writings that the freedom and dignity of the 'noble savage' had become stifled by the constraints of civilized society. The popularity of the supposedly ancient epic poems of 'Ossian' (*see* Ossianism) encouraged this view, which was given a new form by William Wordsworth in his exaltation of rural simplicity, and by several American writers including James Fenimore Cooper, H. D. Thoreau, and Herman Melville in the mid-19th century. Later, D. H. Lawrence maintained a strongly primitivist stance against industrial society and its crushing of individual spontaneity.

problem play, usually a play dealing with a particular social problem in a realistic manner designed to change public opinion; also called a thesis play. Significant examples are Henrik Ibsen's *A Doll's House* (1879), on women's subordination in marriage, and George Bernard Shaw's *Mrs Warren's Profession* (1902) on prostitution. In studies of Shakespeare, however, the term has been used to designate a group of his plays written in the first years of the 17th century: the 'dark comedies' *Measure for Measure* and *All's Well That Ends Well*, and the *tragicomedy *Troilus and Cressida*. Critics have often been disturbed by the sombre and cynical mood of these plays, which seems to clash oddly with their comic conventions. *See also* discussion play.

proem, a preface or introduction to a work. *Adjective*: **proemial.**

prolepsis (plural -**epses**), the Greek word for 'anticipation', used in three senses: (i) in a speech, the trick of answering an opponent's objections before they are even made; (ii) as a *figure of speech, the application of an *epithet or description before it actually becomes applicable, e.g. the wounded Hamlet's exclamation 'I am dead, Horatio'; (iii) in narrative works, a 'flashforward' by which a future event is related as an interruption to the 'present' time of the narration, as in this passage from Muriel Spark's *The Prime of Miss Jean Brodie* (1961) about the school-girl Mary:

> '... Speech is silver but silence is golden. Mary, are you listening? What was I saying?'
>   Mary Macgregor, lumpy, with merely two eyes, a nose and a mouth like a snowman, who was later famous for being stupid and always to blame and who, at the age of twenty-three, lost her life in a hotel fire, ventured, 'Golden.'

In this third sense, prolepsis is an *anachrony which is the opposite of 'flashback' or *analepsis. *Adjective* **proleptic.**

proletcult, an abbreviation for 'proletarian culture' (Russian, *proletar-skaya kul'tura*), the slogan and title adopted by a movement of cultural revolution and popular education in the Soviet Union, launched in 1917 by A. A. Bogdanov. It claimed to be initiating a new working-class culture uncontaminated by the bourgeois artistic heritage, and it promoted the publication of works by proletarian writers.

prologue [proh-log], an introductory section of a play, speech, or other literary work. The term is also sometimes applied to the performer who makes an introductory speech in a play.

promotion, the use of an unstressed syllable to realize the rhythmic 'beat' in a position normally occupied within a metrical verse line by a stressed syllable (*see* metre). This common device of metrical variation in English verse occurs where an unstressed syllable appears between two other unstressed syllables, or between an unstressed syllable and a line-break. In Keats's line:

His soul shall taste the sadness of her might.

the syllable *of* has been promoted to a 'beat' position between two other unstressed syllables; this does not mean, though, that it should be heavily stressed in reading aloud. Where promotion occurs on the last syllable of an *iambic line, it sometimes produces a *weak ending. *See also* demotion.

propagandism, the tendency to compose literary works chiefly to serve the purpose of propaganda, that is, writing to persuade people to support a particular religious or political cause. Propagandist writing is thus a kind of *didactic literature directed toward changing or confirming readers' and audiences' allegiances. In liberal criticism, the term is used disparagingly of left-wing literary forms such as *agitprop, *socialist realism, or the *epic theatre of Brecht, with the suggestion that these are betrayals of true Art.

props, the usual abbreviation for stage 'properties', i.e. those objects that are necessary to the action of a dramatic work (other than scenery, costumes, and fixed furnishings): weapons, documents, cigarettes, items of food and drink, etc.

proscenium arch [prŏ-seen-iŭm], the structure separating the main acting area from the auditorium in most Western theatres of the 19th and early 20th centuries. It usually forms a rectangular 'picture frame', the 'picture' being revealed by opening a curtain. Its associated dramatic *conventions often involve the illusion of looking into a room through an invisible 'fourth wall'.

prose, the form of written language that is not organized according to the formal patterns of *verse; although it will have some sort of rhythm and some devices of repetition and balance, these are not governed by a regularly sustained formal arrangement, the significant unit being the sentence rather than the line. Some uses of the term include spoken language as well, but it is usually more helpful to maintain a distinction at least between written prose and everyday speech, if not formal *oratory. Prose has as its minimum requirement some degree of continuous coherence beyond that of a mere list. The adjectives **prosaic** and **prosy** have a derogatory meaning of dullness and ordinarinesss; the neutral adjective is simply 'prose', as in 'prose writings'.

prose poem, a short composition employing the rhythmic *cadences and other devices of *free verse (such as poetic *imagery and *figures) but printed wholly or partly in the format of prose, i.e. with a right-hand margin instead of regular line-breaks. This *genre emerged in France during the 19th century, notably in Charles Baudelaire's *Spleen de Paris* (1869) and Arthur Rimbaud's *Les Illuminations* (1886); a significant English sequence of prose poems is Geoffrey Hill's *Mercian Hymns* (1971). A prose poem is a self-contained work usually similar to a *lyric, whereas **poetic prose** may occur intermittently within a longer prose work.

prosody [pros-ŏdi], the systematic study of *versification, covering the principles of *metre, *rhythm, *rhyme, and *stanza forms; or a particular system of versification. In linguistics, the term is applied to patterns of *stress and *intonation in ordinary speech. Prosody in the literary sense is also known as *metrics. *Adjective*: **prosodic.** *See also* scansion.

prosopopoeia [pros-ŏ-pŏ-**pee**-ă], the Greek rhetorical term for a *trope consisting either of the *personification of some non-human being or idea, or of the representation of an imaginary, dead, or absent person as alive and capable of speech and hearing, as in an *apostrophe. *Adjective*: **prosopopoeial.**

protagonist [proh-**tag**-ŏn-ist], the chief character in a play or story, who may also be opposed by an *antagonist. Originally, in ancient Greek theatre, the protagonist was the principal actor in a drama. *See also* hero.

prothalamion [proh-thă-**lam**-iŏn], a marriage-poem. The term, invented by Edmund Spenser for the title of his poem celebrating the weddings of Katherine and Elizabeth Somerset in 1596, is derived from *epithalamion, literally meaning 'before the bridal chamber'.

proverb, a short popular saying of unknown authorship, expressing some general truth or superstition: 'Too many cooks spoil the broth.' Proverbs are found in most cultures, and are often very ancient. The Hebrew scriptures include a book of Proverbs. Many poets—notably Chaucer—incorporate proverbs into their works, and others imitate their condensed form of expression: William Blake's 'Proverbs of Hell' in *The Marriage of Heaven and Hell* (1793) are, strictly speaking, *aphorisms, since they originate from a known author. *Adjective*: **proverbial**.

psalm, a sacred song or *hymn. The term usually refers to the Hebrew verses in the biblical book of Psalms, traditionally (but unreliably) attributed to King David. These psalms, notably in the English translation attributed to Miles Coverdale and found in the *Book of Common Prayer*, have had an important place in Christian worship, in English religious poetry, and in the development of *free verse. The art of singing psalms is called **psalmody**, while a collection of psalms is known as a **psalter**. *Adjective*: **psalmic** or **psalmodic**.

pseudo-statement, a term invented by the British critic I. A. Richards in *Science and Poetry* (1926) in an attempt to distinguish the special kind of 'truth' provided by poetry and fiction: whereas scientific or ordinary 'referential' language makes statements that are either true or false, poetry's 'emotive' language gives us pseudo-statements, i.e. utterances that are not subject to factual verification but which are valuable in 'organizing our attitudes'. The term proved to be controversial, partly because it was misunderstood to mean 'falsehood', and partly because it implied that poetry can have no cognitive status; but the idea itself is traditional: Sir Philip Sidney's *Apology for Poetry* (1595) argued that the poet 'nothing affirms, and therefore never lieth'. A somewhat similar distinction is involved in the later concept of the *performative.

psychomachy [sy-kom-ăki], a battle for the soul. The term comes from the Latin poem *Psychomachia* (*c.*400 CE) by Prudentius, describing a battle between virtues and vices for the soul of Man. This depiction of moral conflict had an important influence on medieval *allegory, especially in the *morality plays. Later echoes of medieval psychomachy can be found in Shakespeare's 144th sonnet and in Tennyson's poem 'The Two Voices' (1842).

pun, an expression that achieves emphasis or humour by contriving an *ambiguity, two distinct meanings being suggested either by the same word (*see* polysemy) or by two similar-sounding words (*see* homophone). In the terminology of *rhetoric, punning is regarded as a *figure of speech, and known as *paranomasia. See also *double entendre*, equivoque.

purple patch, an over-written passage in which the writer has strained too hard to achieve an impressive effect, by elaborate *figures or other means. The phrase (Latin, *purpureus pannus*) was first used by the Roman poet Horace in his *Ars Poetica* (*c*.20 BCE) to denote an irrelevant and excessively ornate passage; the sense of irrelevance is normally absent in modern usage, although such passages are usually incongruous. By extension, 'purple prose' is lavishly figurative, rhythmic, or otherwise overwrought. *See also* bombast, fustian.

pyrrhic, a hypothetical metrical unit sometimes invoked in traditional *scansion: it consists of two unstressed syllables (or, in *quantitative verse, two short syllables), and is rather questionably referred to as a *foot. It has been called upon in many attempts to clear up problems of traditional scansion by feet, as a device of *substitution. Some modern systems of scansion, however, have abolished it by considering pairs of unstressed syllables in terms of *promotion and other concepts. *See also* metre.

quantitative verse, verse in which the *metre is based on the principle of **quantity** (i.e. the duration of a syllable's sound), and in which the basic metrical unit, the *foot, is composed of syllables classified either as 'long' or as 'short'. This metrical system is found in Greek and Latin, as well as in Arabic and some other languages, but does not apply to English verse, which uses patterns of stress rather than quantitatively measured syllables and feet. Some unfruitful attempts were, however, made in the 16th and 17th centuries to write quantitative verse in English.

quarto, a size of book or page that results from folding a standard printer's sheet twice, forming four leaves (i.e. eight pages). Many of Shakespeare's plays first appeared in quarto editions, most of these being textually unreliable. For other book sizes, *see* duodecimo, folio, octavo.

quatrain, a verse *stanza of four lines, rhymed or (less often) unrhymed. The quatrain is the most commonly used stanza in English and most modern European languages. Most *ballads and many *hymns are composed in quatrains in which the second and fourth lines rhyme (*abcb* or *abab*); the 'heroic quatrain' of iambic *pentameters also rhymes *abab*. A different *rhyme scheme (*abba*) is used in the *In Memoriam* stanza and some other forms. The rhyming four-line groups that make up the first eight or twelve lines of a *sonnet are also known as quatrains.

Queer theory, a body of academic writings that has since the early 1990s attempted to redefine and de-stabilize categories of sexuality in the light of *post-structuralist theory, and especially under the influence of Michel Foucault's *La Volonté de savoir* (1976). Rooted in the lesbian and gay activism of the 1970s but now more sceptical about inherited conceptions of 'gay' and 'lesbian' as simple or given 'identities', certain gay and lesbian intellectuals and activists adopted the more controversial but also more inclusive label 'queer' to cover a range of sexual orientations and sub-cultures. Queer theory stresses the historical variability, fluidity, and provisional or 'performed' nature of sexualities (*see* performative), notably in the writings of Judith Butler, whose book *Gender Trouble* (1990) is a key text of this school. The pursuit of these concerns in the reading of literary texts is more often associated with the work of Eve Kosofsky Sedgwick, whose *Between Men* (1985) and *Epistemology of the Closet* (1990) investigate the paradoxes of 'homosocial' male bonding and homophobia in English fiction. For a fuller account, consult Annamarie Jogose, *Queer Theory* (1996).

quintain or **quintet,** a verse *stanza of five lines. It appears in various forms, from the English *limerick to the Japanese *tanka. A significant Spanish form is the *quintilla*, which uses *octosyllabic lines and only two rhymes without a final *couplet (e.g. *abbab* or *ababa*).

raisonneur, a character in a play who appears to act as a mouthpiece for the opinons of the play's author, usually displaying a superior or more detached view of the action than the other characters.

readerly, see *lisible*.

reader-response criticism, a general term for those kinds of modern *criticism and literary theory that focus on the responses of readers to literary works, rather than on the works themselves considered as self-contained entities. It is not a single agreed theory so much as a shared concern with a set of problems involving the extent and nature of readers' contribution to the meanings of literary works, approached from various positions including those of *structuralism (*see* competence), psychoanalysis, *phenomenology, and *hermeneutics. The common factor is a shift from the description of *texts in terms of their inherent properties to a discussion of the production of meanings within the reading process. Important contributions to this debate include Wolfgang Iser's *The Act of Reading* (1978), which sees readers as 'actualizing' texts by filling in their 'gaps' or *indeterminacies of meaning, and Stanley Fish's *Is There a Text in this Class?* (1980), which gives the reader an even more active role as the text's true producer. A somewhat distinct line of historical investigation is represented by the *reception theory of Hans Robert Jauss. For a fuller account, consult Elizabeth Freund, *The Return of the Reader* (1987).

realism, a mode of writing that gives the impression of recording or 'reflecting' faithfully an actual way of life. The term refers, sometimes confusingly, both to a literary method based on detailed accuracy of description (i.e. *verisimilitude) and to a more general attitude that rejects idealization, escapism, and other extravagant qualities of *romance in favour of recognizing soberly the actual problems of life. Modern criticism frequently insists that realism is not a direct or simple reproduction of reality (a 'slice of life') but a system of *conventions producing a lifelike illusion of some 'real' world outside the text, by processes of selection, exclusion, description, and manners of addressing the reader. In its methods and attitudes, realism may be found as an element in many kinds of writing prior to the 19th century (e.g. in Chaucer or Defoe, in their different ways); but as a dominant literary trend it is associated chiefly with the 19th-century novel of middle- or lower-class life, in which the problems of ordinary people in unremarkable circumstances are rendered with close attention to the details of physical setting and to the complexities of social life. The outstanding works of realism in 19th-century fiction include Honoré de Balzac's *Illusions perdues* (1837–43), Gustave Flaubert's *Madame Bovary* (1857), and George Eliot's *Middlemarch* (1871–2). In France, a self-consciously realist school announced itself in 1857 with the publication of Champfleury's *Le Réalisme*, but the term normally refers to the general convention rather than to this barely significant group. In the work of some novelists, realism passes over into the movement of *naturalism, in which sociological investigation and determinist views of human behaviour predominate. Realism also established itself as an important tradition in the theatre in the late 19th and early 20th centuries, in the work of Henrik Ibsen, Bernard Shaw, and others; and it remains a standard convention of film and television drama. Despite the radical attempts of *modernism to displace the realist emphasis on external reality (notably in the movements of *expressionism and *surrealism), realism survived as a major current within 20th-century fiction, sometimes under the label of *neo-realism. For a fuller account, consult Damian Grant, *Realism* (1970).

recension, a version of a literary work arrived at by a process of *revision or *textual criticism; or the process of reconstructing the most reliable readings from variant versions of a text. *See also* edition.

reception theory, a branch of modern literary studies concerned with the ways in which literary works are received by readers. The term has sometimes been used to refer to *reader-response criticism in general, but it is associated more particularly with the 'reception-aesthetics' (German, *Rezeptionsästhetik*) outlined in 1970 by the German literary historian Hans Robert Jauss. Drawing on philosophical *hermeneutics, Jauss argued that literary works are received against an existing *horizon of expectations consisting of readers' current knowledge and presuppositions about literature, and that the meanings of works change as such horizons shift. Unlike most varieties of reader-response theory, then, reception theory is interested more in historical changes affecting the reading public than in the solitary reader.

recessive accent, a *stress placed on the first syllable of a two-syllable word that is normally pronounced with the stress on its second syllable. This sometimes occurs in English verse when such a word is followed by a stressed syllable: for the sake of conformity to the *metre, the stress is shifted to the initial position, as in John Donne's line

> But éxtreme sense hath made them desperate

The recessive accent is thus a specific type of 'wrenched accent' (*see* accent).

récit [ray-see], the French word for an 'account' or *narrative of events. As used in modern French *narratology, the term refers to the actual narrative *text itself, as opposed both to the *story and to its *narration.

recognition, *see* anagnorisis.

recto, the front side of a printed sheet; thus the right-hand (and odd-numbered) page in a book, as opposed to the *verso*, which is the left-hand, even-numbered page on the other side.

redaction, the editing or revising of a work for publication; or a new (sometimes shortened) *edition of a work. An editor is sometimes called a **redactor**. *Verb*: **redact**.

reductionism, the tendency to explain away the complexities of a literary work as the products of a single, much simpler cause. A **reductive** interpretation of a work reduces or 'collapses' its actual complexity into a reassuring simplicity, seeing it as the direct expression of some originating element such as a personal motive, a psychological defect, a national or social identity, or a mythic *archetype.

referent, that to which a linguistic expression refers. Usually this means some thing, process, or state of affairs in the world outside language. The Saussurean theory of the *sign, however, regards external reality as an unnecessary complication, preferring to replace the notion of the referent with the purely conceptual notion of the *signified. A distinction has sometimes been made in modern criticism between the **referential** language of factual information and the 'emotive' language of poetry (*see* pseudo-statement).

reflectionism, a term sometimes used to refer to the common assumption that literary works reflect (or, in the well-worn *metaphor, 'hold a mirror up to') a pre-existing reality. This view is often challenged in modern literary theory, on the grounds that it denies the active nature of language and of the writer's transforming work. *See also* mimesis, realism.

refrain, a line, group of lines, or part of a line repeated at regular or irregular intervals in a poem, usually at the end of each *stanza. It may recur in exactly the same form, or may be subject to slight variations (*see* incremental repetition). It may form part of a stanza, as in the *ballade or *villanelle; or it may appear separately, as in many songs and *ballads, in which case it may be called a *burden, and, if intended for group singing, a *chorus. *See also* repetend.

register, a term used in *stylistics to refer to a variety of language used in specified kinds of social situation: thus a formal register is different from an informal one.

Renaissance, the 'rebirth' of literature, art, and learning that progressively transformed European culture from the mid-14th century in Italy to the mid-17th century in England, strongly influenced by the rediscovery of classical Greek and Latin literature, and accelerated by the development of printing. The Renaissance is commonly held to mark the close of the Middle Ages and the beginning of the modern Western world, although the problems of dating this process have caused much debate: the existence of a significant renaissance of European learning in the 12th century is now accepted, while the 18th-century *Enlightenment is a direct continuation of the Renaissance's intellectual tendencies. However, the term normally refers to the combined intellectual and artistic transformations of the 15th and 16th centuries, including the emergence of *humanism, Protestant individualism, Copernican astronomy, and the discovery of America. In literary terms, the Renaissance may be seen as a new tradition running from Petrarch and Boccaccio in Italy to Jonson and Milton in England, embracing the work of the French *Pléiade and of Sidney, Spenser, and Shakespeare; it is marked by a new self-confidence in *vernacular literatures, a flourishing of *lyric poetry, and a revival of such classical forms as *epic and *pastoral literature. The term 'Renaissance' has also been extended to various literary revivals in specific times and places: for examples, *see* American Renaissance, Harlem Renaissance.

repartee [rep-ar-**tee**], a rapid and witty response in conversation, especially one that turns an insult back on its originator; or a succession of such replies in a *dialogue between characters (usually in a drama). The term may also be applied to a person's talent for making witty replies.

repetend [rep-ĕt-end], a word, phrase, or line that recurs in a poem. As distinct from a *refrain, a repetend is repeated only partially or only at irregular intervals.

Restoration comedy, a kind of English *comedy, usually in the form of the *comedy of manners, that flourished during the Restoration period in England (i.e. from the Restoration of the Stuart monarchy in 1660 to about 1700), when actresses were first employed on the London stage. Appealing to a fairly narrow audience of aristocrats in the recently reopened theatres, Restoration comedy relied upon sophisticated *repartee and a knowledge of the exclusive code of manners in high society, the plots being based on the complex *intrigues of the marriage-market. The characters can often be divided between the young aristocrats who can understand and manipulate the rules of the social game, and the middle-class upstarts who wish to be thought fashionable and witty but expose their ignorance in a series of blunders. The frequently cynical approach to marriage and sexual infidelity in Restoration comedy invited accusations of immorality. Significant examples are George Etheredge's *The Man of Mode* (1676), William Wycherley's *The Country Wife* (1675), and William Congreve's *The Way of the World* (1700).

revenge tragedy, a kind of *tragedy popular in England from the 1590s to the 1630s, following the success of Thomas Kyd's sensational play *The Spanish Tragedy* (c.1589). Its action is typically centred upon a leading character's attempt to avenge the murder of a loved one, sometimes at the prompting of the victim's ghost; it involves complex intrigues and disguises, and usually some exploration of the morality of revenge. Drawing partly on precedents in *Senecan tragedy, the English revenge tragedy is far more bloodthirsty in its explicit presentation of premeditated violence, and so the more gruesome examples such as Shakespeare's *Titus Andronicus* are sometimes called 'tragedies of blood'. Notable examples of plays that are fully or partly within the revenge tradition are Christopher Marlowe's *The Jew of Malta*, Cyril Tourneur's *The Revenger's Tragedy*, John Webster's *The Duchess of*

Malfi, and John Ford's *'Tis Pity She's a Whore*. A more famous play drawing on the revenge *conventions is Shakespeare's *Hamlet*. For a fuller account, consult John Kerrigan, *Revenge Tragedy* (1996).

reverdie, a kind of medieval French dancing song celebrating the arrival of spring. The term is sometimes extended to include any poem or poetic passage that welcomes spring's return.

reversal, *see* peripeteia.

revision, the process of amending an earlier version (published or unpublished) of a work; or the newly amended text thus produced. *Adjective*: **revisionary** or **revisional**. *Verb*: **revise**.

revue, a theatrical entertainment consisting of a series of songs, dances, and comic *sketches. It is often devoted to topical *satire, although another kind of revue concentrates on spectacular costumes and dancing. *See also* burlesque.

Rezeptionsästhetik, *see* reception theory.

rhapsody, in the modern sense, a work or passage expressing ecstatic or uncontrolled emotion, often in a loosely structured fashion. In ancient Greece, a rhapsody was a selection of *epic poetry sung by a **rhapsode** or **rhapsodist**—literally a 'stitcher' who combined memorized passages with his own improvisations, although this kind of *minstrel was later required chiefly to recite Homer's *Iliad* and *Odyssey* in their established versions. *Adjective*: **rhapsodic**. *Verb*: **rhapsodize**.

rhetoric [ret-er-ik], the deliberate exploitation of eloquence for the most persuasive effect in public speaking or in writing. It was cultivated as an important art and science in antiquity, and was an essential element of medieval university education, involving the elaborate categorizing of *figures of speech together with the arts of memory, arrangement, and oratorical delivery. The emphasis on sincerity in the culture of *Romanticism helped to discredit rhetoric, so that the usual modern sense of the term implies empty and ineffectual grandness in public speech. Modern critics sometimes refer to the rhetorical dimension of a literary work, meaning those aspects of the work that persuade or otherwise guide the responses of readers. A practitioner or theorist of rhetoric is called a **rhetorician**. For a fuller account, consult Peter Dixon, *Rhetoric* (1971).

rhetorical figure, *see* figure.

rhetorical question, a question asked for the sake of persuasive effect rather than as a genuine request for information, the speaker implying that the answer is too obvious to require a reply, as in Milton's line

> For what can war but endless war still breed?

rhyme, the identity of sound between syllables or paired groups of syllables, usually at the ends of verse lines; also a poem employing this device. Normally the last stressed vowel in the line and all sounds following it make up the rhyming element: this may be a monosyllable (*love/above*—known as '*masculine rhyme'), or two syllables (wh*ether*/ tog*ether*—known as '*feminine rhyme' or 'double rhyme'), or even three syllables (*glamorous / amorous*—known as '*triple rhyme'). Where a rhyming element in a feminine or triple rhyme uses more than one word (*famous*/sh*ame us*), this is known as a 'mosaic rhyme'. The rhyming pairs illustrated so far are all examples of 'full rhyme' (also called 'perfect rhyme' or 'true rhyme'); departures from this norm take three main forms: (i) *rime riche*, in which the consonants preceding the rhyming elements are also identical, even if the spellings and meanings of the words differ (*made/maid*); (ii) *eye rhyme, in which the spellings of the rhyming elements match, but the sounds do not (*love/prove*); (iii) *half-rhyme or 'slant rhyme', where the vowel sounds do not match (*love/have*, or, with rich *consonance, *love/leave*). Half-rhyme is known by several other names: 'imperfect rhyme', 'near rhyme', 'pararhyme', etc. Although rhyme is most often used at the ends of verse lines, *internal rhyme between syllables within the same line is also found (*see also* crossed rhyme, leonine rhyme). Rhyme is not essential to poetry: many languages rarely use it, and in English it finally replaced *alliteration as the usual patterning device of verse only in the late 14th century. A writer of rhyming verse may sometimes be referred to disparagingly as a **rhymester** or **rhymer**.

rhyme royal, a *stanza form consisting of seven 5-stress lines (iambic *pentameters) rhyming *ababbcc*, first used by Chaucer and thus also known as the Chaucerian stanza. Following Chaucer's use of rhyme royal in his *Troilus and Criseyde*, *The Parlement of Fowles*, and some of the *Canterbury Tales*, it continued to be an important form of English verse in the 15th and 16th centuries, being used by Dunbar, Henryson, Spenser, and Shakespeare (in his *Lucrece*, 1594); William Morris's *The Earthly Paradise* (1868–70) is a rare example of its use in later periods. The name of this stanza seems to come from its use in _The Kingis Quair_ (c.1424), a poem uncertainly attributed to King James I of Scotland.

rhyme scheme, the pattern in which the rhymed line-endings are arranged in a poem or *stanza. This may be expressed as a sequence of recurrences in which each line ending on the same rhyme is given the same alphabetic symbol: thus the rhyme scheme of a *limerick is given the notation _aabba_. Rhyme schemes may follow a fixed pattern, as in the *sonnet and several other forms, or they may be arranged freely according to the poet's requirements. The simplest rhyme schemes are those of rhyming *couplets (_aabbcc_, etc.) and of the common *quatrain forms (_abab, abcb, abba_), while those of *_ottava rima_, *rhyme royal, the *Spenserian stanza, and the French *fixed forms are far more intricate.

rhythm, the patern of sounds perceived as the recurrence of equivalent 'beats' at more or less equal intervals. In most English poetry, an underlying rhythm (commonly a sequence of four or five beats) is manifested in a metrical pattern (_see_ metre)—a sequence of measured beats and 'offbeats' arranged in verse lines and governing the alternation of stressed and unstressed syllables. While metre involves the recurrence of measured sound units, rhythm is a less clearly structured principle: one can refer to the unmeasured rhythms of everyday speech, or of *prose, and to the rhythms or *cadences of non-metrical verse (i.e. *free verse). _See also_ falling rhythm, rising rhythm, sprung rhythm.

riddle, a puzzlingly indirect description of some thing, person, or idea, framed in such a way as to challenge the reader to identify it. Riddles, usually in verse, are found as a popular literary form in most cultures and periods. An important Old English collection is preserved in the 10th-century Exeter Book.

rime riche [reem reesh], a kind of *rhyme (also called 'identical rhyme') in which the rhyming elements include matching consonants before the stressed vowel sounds. Often this means the rhyming of two words with the same sound and sometimes the same spelling but different meanings, e.g _seen/scene_. The term also covers word-endings where the consonant preceding the stressed vowel sound is the same: com_pare_/des_pair_. An even more excessive kind of rhyme is _rime très riche_, in which not only the preceding consonant but also the vowel sound before that remains the same: _allowed/aloud_. Usually avoided in English, _rimes riches_ are found far more often in French verse. The normal kind of English rhyme, in which the rhyming element begins only with the stressed vowel sound nearest to the end of the line, is referred to in French as *rime suffisante*.

rising rhythm, a rhythmic effect often found in metrical verse in which the unstressed syllables are perceived as being linked with the succeeding stressed syllables rather than with those preceding them. In terms of classical *prosody, lines composed of *iambs or *anapaests may show this rising rhythm, although this is not inevitable. Rising rhythm in English verse is far more common than its opposite, *falling rhythm.

rococo [rŏ-koh-koh], an 18th-century style of architecture and furnishing characterized by elaborately playful decoration, and regarded by stern classical purists as 'effeminate' or tastelessly pretty. As applied to literature, the term is unhelpfully vague, but usually suggests a cheerful lightness and intimacy of tone, and an elegant playfulness: Pope's *The Rape of the Lock* (1712–14) and Sterne's *Tristram Shandy* (1759–67) have been cited as English examples.

rodomontade [rod-ŏ-mon-**tayd**], a blusteringly boastful speech, or any arrogantly inflated manner of speaking or writing. *See also* bombast.

rogatio, a rhetorical *figure in which a question is posed and then answered by the same speaker or writer, as in Blake's famous couplet:

> What is it men in women do require?
> The lineaments of gratified desire.

See also rhetorical question.

roman à clef [roh-mah^n a klay], the French term ('novel with a key') for a kind of novel in which the well-informed reader will recognize identifiable persons from real life thinly disguised as fictional characters. A significant English example is Thomas Love Peacock's satirical novel *Nightmare Abbey* (1818), in which 'Mr Flosky' is clearly the poet Samuel Taylor Coleridge, 'Mr Cypress' is Lord Byron, and 'Scythrop' is Percy Bysshe Shelley. Very many novels based upon their authors' own lives are to some degree *romans à clef*.

roman à thèse [roh- mah^n a tez], the French term for a 'thesis novel', that is, a *didactic novel that puts forward an argument or proposes a solution to some problem of politics, morality, or philosophy. The most celebrated example in English is Harriet Beecher Stowe's *Uncle Tom's Cabin* (1852), which powerfully urged the abolition of slavery. A more philosophical kind of thesis novel is Jean-Paul Sartre's *La Nausée* (1938), which embodies many of the principles of his *existentialism. *See also* propagandism, thesis.

roman à tiroirs [roh-mahⁿ a tee-rwah], the French term for an *episodic novel, such as Alain-René Lesage's *Gil Blas* (1715–35)—a *tiroir* being a drawer in a desk or chest. *See also* picaresque novel.

romance, a fictional story in verse or prose that relates improbable adventures of idealized characters in some remote or enchanted setting; or, more generally, a tendency in fiction opposite to that of *realism. The term now embraces many forms of fiction from the *Gothic novel and the popular escapist love story to the 'scientific romances' of H. G. Wells, but it usually refers to the tales of King Arthur's knights written in the late Middle Ages by Chrétien de Troyes (in verse), Sir Thomas Malory (in prose), and many others (*see* chivalric romance). Medieval romance is distinguished from *epic by its concentration on *courtly love rather than warlike heroism. Long, elaborate romances were written during the *Renaissance, including Ludovico Ariosto's *Orlando Furioso* (1532), Edmund Spenser's *The Faerie Queene* (1590–6), and Sir Philip Sidney's prose romance *Arcadia* (1590), but Cervantes's *parody of romances in *Don Quixote* (1605) helped to undermine this tradition. Later prose romances differ from novels in their preference for *allegory and psychological exploration rather than realistic social observation, especially in American works like Nathaniel Hawthorne's *The Blithedale Romance* (1852). Several modern literary *genres, from *science fiction to the detective story, can be regarded as variants of the romance (*see also* fantasy, marvellous). In modern criticism of Shakespeare, the term is also applied to four of his last plays—*Pericles, Cymbeline, The Winter's Tale*, and *The Tempest*—which are distinguished by their daring use of magical illusion and improbable reunions. The **Romance languages** are those languages originating in southern Europe that are derived from Latin: the most important of these are Spanish, French, Italian, and Portuguese. In Spanish literature, the term has a special sense, the *romance* [ro-**mahn**-thay] being a *ballad composed in *octosyllabic lines. For a fuller account, consult Gillian Beer, *The Romance* (1970).

roman-feuilleton, a serialized novel: see *feuilleton*.

roman-fleuve [roh-mahⁿ flerv], a continuous sequence of novels through which are traced the fortunes of the same character or group of characters; literally a 'river-novel' that flows through from one book to the next. The most celebrated example is Marcel Proust's seven-novel sequence *A la recherche du temps perdu* (1913–27). In English, significant examples are Anthony Trollope's five Barsetshire novels (1855–67), Anthony Powell's *A Dance to the Music of Time* (12 novels, 1951–75), and Doris Lessing's *Children of Violence* sequence (5 novels, 1952–69). *See also* cycle, saga.

romantic comedy, a general term for *comedies that deal mainly with the follies and misunderstandings of young lovers, in a light-hearted and happily concluded manner which usually avoids serious *satire. The best-known examples are Shakespeare's comedies of the late 1590s, *A Midsummer Night's Dream, Twelfth Night*, and *As You Like It* being the most purely romantic, while *Much Ado About Nothing* approaches the *comedy of manners and *The Merchant of Venice* is closer to *tragicomedy. *See also* New Comedy.

romantic irony, a kind of literary self-consciousness in which an author signals his or her freedom from the limits of a given work by puncturing its fictional illusion and exposing its process of composition as a matter of authorial whim. This is often a kind of protective self-mockery involving a playful attitude towards the conventions of the (normally narrative) genre. Byron's narrative poem *Don Juan* (1819–24) is a sustained exercise in romantic irony, as is Laurence Sterne's novel *Tristram Shandy* (1759–67), but the effect may also be found in Chaucer and many other authors of different periods. For a fuller account, consult Anne K. Mellor, *English Romantic Irony* (1980).

Romanticism, a sweeping but indispensable modern term applied to the profound shift in Western attitudes to art and human creativity that dominated much of European culture in the first half of the 19th century, and that has shaped most subsequent developments in literature—even those reacting against it. In its most coherent early form, as it emerged in the 1790s in Germany and Britain, and in the 1820s in France and elsewhere, it is known as the **Romantic Movement** or **Romantic Revival**. Its chief emphasis was upon freedom of individual self-expression: sincerity, spontaneity, and originality became the new standards in literature, replacing the decorous imitation of classical models favoured by 18th-century *neoclassicism. Rejecting the ordered rationality of the *Enlightenment as mechanical, impersonal, and artificial, the **Romantics** turned to the emotional directness of personal experience and to the boundlessness of individual imagination and aspiration. Increasingly independent of the declining system of aristocratic patronage, they saw themselves as free spirits expressing their own imaginative truths; several found admirers ready to hero-worship the artist as a genius or prophet. The restrained balance valued in 18th-century culture was abandoned in favour of emotional intensity, often taken to extremes of rapture, nostalgia (for childhood or the past), horror, melancholy, or sentimentality. Some—but not all—Romantic writers cultivated the appeal of the exotic, the bizarre, or the macabre; almost all showed a new interest in the irrational realms of dream and delirium or of folk superstition and legend. The creative imagination occupied the centre of Romantic views of art, which replaced the 'mechanical' rules of conventional form with an 'organic' principle of natural growth and free development.

The emergence of Romanticism has been attributed to several developments in late 18th-century culture (*see* preromanticism), including a strong antiquarian interest in *ballads and medieval *romances (from which Romanticism takes its name). The immediate inspiration for the first self-declared Romantics—the German group including the Schlegel brothers and Novalis—was the transcendental philosophy of Kant and Fichte, which stressed the creative power of the mind and allowed nature to be seen as a responsive mirror of the soul. This new German thinking spread via S. T. Coleridge to Britain and via Mme de Staël to France, eventually shaping American *Transcendentalism. English Romanticism had emerged independently with William Blake's then little-known anti-Enlightenment writings of the 1790s and with the landmark of William Wordsworth's 1800 Preface to *Lyrical Ballads*. In a second wave after the Napoleonic wars, Romanticism established itself in France and across Europe; by the 1830s the movement extended from Pushkin in Russia to Poe in the USA. Romanticism drew some of its energies from the associated revolutionary movements of democracy and nationalism, although the 'classical' culture of the French Revolution actually delayed the arrival of French Romanticism, and a strong element of conservative nostalgia is also evident in many Romantic writers.

The literary rebellion of Wordsworth in England and Victor Hugo in France declared an end to the artificiality of older *conventions, breaking up the 18th-century system of distinct *genres and of *poetic diction. *Lyric poetry underwent a major revival led by Wordsworth, Keats, Shelley, Pushkin, Leopardi, Heine, and others; *narrative verse took on a new subjective dimension in the work of Wordsworth and Byron, but the theatre tended towards the sensationalism of *melodrama. In fiction, Hoffmann and Poe pioneered the tale of terror in the wake of the *Gothic novel, while the *historical novels of Walter Scott, Alessandro Manzoni, Victor Hugo, and James Fenimore Cooper combined bold action with nostalgic sentiment. A new wave of women novelists led by Mary Shelley, George Sand, and the Brontë sisters broke the imposed restraints of modesty in works of powerful imaginative force. The astonishing personality of Byron provided Alfred de Musset, Mikhail Lermontov, and other admirers throughout Europe with a model of the Romantic poet as tormented outcast. The growing international cult of Shakespeare also reflected the Romantic hero-worship which, in the writings of Thomas Carlyle and R. W. Emerson, became a 'heroic' view of history as the product of forceful personalities like Napoleon.

Although challenged in the second half of the 19th century by the rise of *realism and *naturalism, Romanticism has in some ways maintained a constant presence in Western literature, providing the basis for several schools and movements from the *Pre-Raphaelites and *Symbolists to *expressionism and *Surrealism. In a broader sense, the term 'romantic' may be applied to works and authors of other periods, by explicit or implicit comparison with a 'classical' standard: thus Shakespeare is more romantic than Molière or Ben Jonson, both because he disregards the structural models of Greek drama and because he exploits freely the supernatural elements of folk legend; and in a different way, W. B. Yeats and D. H. Lawrence are more romantic than W. H. Auden and E. M. Forster, because they assert the absolute primacy of their personal visions, rejecting common norms of objectivity. For a fuller account, consult Aidan Day, *Romanticism* (1996).

rondeau, a medieval French verse form also used by some late 19th-century poets in English. It normally consists of 13 *octosyllabic lines, grouped in *stanzas of five, three, and five lines. The whole poem uses only two rhymes, and the first word or phrase of the first line recurs twice as a *refrain after the second and third stanzas. The standard *rhyme scheme (with the unrhymed refrain indicated as R) is *aabba aabR aabbaR*. Variant forms of the rondeau include those using 10-syllable lines and those having only 12 lines, but in all cases the refrain and the restriction to two rhymes are retained. An even more complicated form is the *rondeau redoublé*, a 24-line poem also using only two rhymes in its six *quatrains, with each line of the first stanza recurring in turn as the final line of the following stanzas until the poem's opening phrase recurs after the last line. *See also* rondel, roundel.

rondel, a medieval French verse form related to the *triolet and the *rondeau. In its usual modern form, it is a 13-line poem using only two rhymes in its three *stanzas. It employs a two-line *refrain which opens the poem and recurs at lines 7 and 8, the first line (or, in a 14-line variant, both opening lines) also completing the poem. The *rhyme scheme— with the repeated lines given in capitals—is thus *ABba abAB abbaA(B)*. There is no fixed *metre. This form was adopted by some poets in England in the late 19th century, including Austin Dobson and W. E. Henley.

roundel, an English version of the *rondeau, devised by A. C. Swinburne for his collection *A Century of Roundels* (1883). It is a poem of eleven lines using only two rhymes in its three *stanzas of 4, 3, and 4 lines. Lines 4 and 11 are formed by the repetition of the poem's opening word or phrase as a *refrain, which may be rhymed with lines 2, 5, 7, and 9. The rhyme scheme (with the refrain represented as R) is thus *abaR bab abaR*, or, with a rhyming refrain, *abaB bab abaB*. The term was at one time a *synonym for a rondeau or *rondel.

roundelay, a short dancing song with a *refrain. The term covers the *rondeau, the *rondel, and various simpler forms, but commonly refers to such works as they are set to music.

rune, a letter belonging to an old Germanic alphabet thought to have been used from the 2nd century AD, which is found in inscriptions on stones, coins, etc. The **runic** alphabet came to be associated with magical powers, and so the term has sometimes been used to refer to any inscription, sign, or written message having magical properties or secret power.

Russian Formalism, a school of literary theory and analysis that emerged in Russia around 1915, devoting itself to the study of *literariness, i.e. the sum of 'devices' that distinguish literary language from ordinary language. In reaction against the vagueness of previous literary theories, it attempted a scientific description of literature (especially poetry) as a special use of language with observable features.

This meant deliberately disregarding the contents of literary works, and thus inviting strong disapproval from Marxist critics, for whom *formalism was a term of reproach. With the consolidation of Stalin's dictatorship around 1929, Formalism was silenced as a heresy in the Soviet Union, and its centre of research migrated to Prague in the 1930s. Along with 'literariness', the most important concept of the school was that of *defamiliarization: instead of seeing literature as a 'reflection' of the world, Victor Shklovsky and his Formalist followers saw it as a linguistic dislocation, or a 'making strange'. In the period of Czech Formalism, Jan Mukařovský further refined this notion in terms of *foregrounding. In their studies of *narrative, the Formalists also clarified the distinction between *plot (*sjuzet*) and *story (*fabula*). Apart from Shklovsky and his associate Boris Eikhenbaum, the most prominent of the Russian Formalists was Roman Jakobson, who was active both in Moscow and in Prague before introducing Formalist theories to the United States (*see* function). A somewhat distinct Russian group is the 'Bakhtin school' comprising Mikhail Bakhtin, Pavlev Medvedev, and Valentin Voloshinov; these theorists combined elements of Formalism and Marxism in their accounts of verbal *multi-accentuality and of the *dialogic text. Rediscovered in the West in the 1960s, the work of the Russian Formalists has had an important influence on *structuralist theories of literature, and on some of the more recent varieties of Marxist literary criticism. For a fuller account, consult Peter Steiner, *Russian Formalism* (1984).

S

S & F, a discreet abbreviation for a category of popular modern fiction known among cynics in the book trade as 'Shopping and Fucking'. This kind of *romance, usually written by and for women, is distinguished by its shamelessly explicit descriptions of expensive clothes, jewellery, perfumes, cars, and other accessories of the very rich, naming actual brand names; several sexual encounters are also described in graphic detail. The genre established itself in the 1980s, following the huge commercial success of Judith Krantz's *Scruples* (1978).

saga, the Norse name for various kinds of prose tales composed in medieval Scandinavia and Iceland and written down from the 12th century to the 14th. These usually tell of heroic leaders—early Norse kings or 13th-century bishops—or of the heroic settlers of Iceland in the 9th and 10th centuries; others, like the *Vǫlsunga saga*, relate earlier legends. The emphasis on feuds and family histories in some famous sagas like *Njáls saga* has led to the term's application in English to any long family story spanning two or more generations: this may take the form of a lengthy novel like D. H. Lawrence's *The Rainbow* (1915) or of a novel-sequence (see *roman-fleuve*) such as John Galsworthy's *The Forsyte Saga* (1922).

salon, a French cultural institution consisting of a weekly social gathering at the private house of an aristocratic lady, at which social, artistic, and scientific questions are discussed. From the early 17th century to the early 19th, several important literary and philosophical salons provided a social base for French writers. The term can also refer to an exhibition of paintings by living artists, so that in a second literary sense the title *Salon* has been given to an essay on contemporary art and related matters: Diderot in the 18th century and Baudelaire in the 19th both wrote important *Salons*. See also *cénacle*.

samizdat, a Russian word meaning 'self-publishing', applied since the 1960s to a clandestine mode of publication by which 'dissident' writings and other banned works have been secretly circulated, usually in typed carbon copies or photocopies. Novels by Alexander Solzhenitsyn and articles by Andrei Sakharov were among the important *samizdat* works of the 1960s and 1970s.

Sapphics, *lyric verses written in a Greek *metre named after Sappho, the legendary woman poet of Lesbos (7th/6th centuries BCE). Sapphic verse uses *stanzas of four lines, the first three having eleven syllables, the last having five. In the first three lines, the sequence of five metrical feet is: *trochee; trochee or *spondee; *dactyl; trochee; trochee or spondee. In the fourth line, a dactyl is followed by a trochee or a spondee. The metre was used frequently in Latin by Horace, but it is difficult to adapt to the stress-patterns of English. Sidney, Swinburne, and Pound are among the poets who have attempted English Sapphics.

satire, a mode of writing that exposes the failings of individuals, institutions, or societies to ridicule and scorn. Satire is often an incidental element in literary works that may not be wholly satirical, especially in *comedy. Its tone may vary from tolerant amusement, as in the verse satires of the Roman poet Horace, to bitter indignation, as in the verse of Juvenal and the prose of Jonathan Swift (*see* Juvenalian). Various forms of literature may be satirical, from the plays of Ben Jonson or of Molière and the poetry of Chaucer or Byron to the prose writings of Rabelais and Voltaire. The models of Roman satire, especially the verse satires of Horace and Juvenal, inspired some important imitations by Boileau, Pope, and Johnson in the greatest period of satire—the 17th and 18th centuries—when writers could appeal to a shared sense of normal conduct from which vice and folly were seen to stray. In this classical tradition, an important form is 'formal' or 'direct' satire, in which the writer directly addresses the reader (or recipient of a verse letter) with satiric comment. The alternative form of 'indirect' satire usually found in plays and novels allows us to draw our own conclusions from the actions of the characters, as for example in the novels of Evelyn Waugh or Chinua Achebe. *See also* lampoon. For a fuller account, consult Arthur Pollard, *Satire* (1970).

satyr play (or satyric drama), a humorous performance presented in Athenian dramatic contests, following a *trilogy of tragedies. The satyr play had a *chorus of satyrs (men with horses' tails and ears), and its action was a *burlesque of some mythical story appropriate to the foregoing tragedies, involving obscene language and gestures. Although fragments of satyr plays by Aeschylus and Sophocles have been found, the only complete example to have survived is the *Cyclops* (*c.*412 BC) of Euripides. Tony Harrison's *The Trackers of Oxyrhynchus* (1988) is a modern satyr play adapted from the fragmentary *Ichneutae* of Sophocles.

scansion, the analysis of poetic *metre in verse lines, by displaying *stresses, pauses, and rhyme patterns with conventional visual symbols. The simplest system, known as graphic scansion, marks stressed syllables (′ or – or ●), unstressed syllables (ˣ or ‿ or ○), divisions between metrical units or 'feet' (*see* foot) (|), and major pauses or *caesuras (‖) in a verse line, determining whether its metre is, for example, *iambic or *dactylic, and how many feet make up the line. In Greek and Latin *quantitative verse, the symbols – and ‿ indicate long and short syllables respectively. Scansion also analyses the *rhyme scheme in a poem or *stanza, giving alphabetical symbols to the rhymes: *abcb* or *abab* in most *quatrains, *aabba* in *limericks, for instance. The verb **scan** is applied not only to the activity of analysing metre, but also to the lines analysed: of a line with an irregular or inconsistent metrical pattern it is said that it does not scan. *See also* diacritic, prosody.

scatology, the study of excrement, e.g. in medicine or palaeontology. In the literary sense it means repeated reference to excrement and related matters, as in the coarse humour of François Rabelais or Jonathan Swift, whose works have passages of a scatological nature.

scenario [sin-ar-i-oh], a brief outline of the *plot, characters, and scene-changes of a play; or the script of a film. In the cinematic sense, a scenario is usually more detailed, whereas the theatrical scenarios of the *commedia dell' arte* were 'skeleton' summaries used as the basis for improvisations. A writer of scenarios, usually for the cinema, is sometimes called a **scenarist**.

scene, in a drama, a subdivision of an *act or of a play not divided into acts. A scene normally represents actions happening in one place at one time, and is marked off from the next scene by a curtain, a black-out, or a brief emptying of the stage. In the study of *narrative works, 'scene' is also the name given to a 'dramatic' method of narration that presents events at roughly the same pace as that at which they are supposed to be occurring, i.e. usually in detail and with substantial use of *dialogue. In this sense the scenic narrative method is contrasted with 'summary', in which the duration of the story's events is compressed into a brief account. *Adjective*: **scenic**.

scène à faire [sen a fair], a French term for the kind of *scene within a drama towards which the preceding action seems inevitably to tend, such as the crucial encounter between hero and villain. It usually provides an emotional *climax. The term is sometimes rendered in English as 'obligatory scene'. *See also* anagnorisis, catastrophe, crisis, dénouement, well-made play.

Schauerroman [show-er-roh-man] (plural *-mane*), the German term for a *Gothic novel or similar horror story, literally a 'shudder-novel'.

scheme, a term once used for a rhetorical *figure (or figure of speech), usually one that departs from the normal order or sound of words but does not extended their meanings as a *trope does. Some rhetoricians, however, have used the term to cover tropes as well.

scholasticism, the methods and doctrines of the leading academic philosophers and theologians of the late Middle Ages in Europe. The **schoolmen** of the 12th, 13th, and 14th centuries attempted to reconcile Christian theology with the Greek philosophy of Aristotle. The leading figures of scholasticism included Peter Abelard, Albertus Magnus, Duns Scotus, and above all Thomas Aquinas, whose *Summa Theologica* (mid-13th century) is the most ambitious of scholastic works; his followers are called Thomists. During the *Renaissance, the deductive logic of scholasticism was superseded by the inductive methods of modern science, while its theological concerns were challenged by the emergence of *humanism.

school drama, *see* academic drama.

science fiction, a popular modern branch of prose fiction that explores the probable consequences of some improbable or impossible transformation of the basic conditions of human (or intelligent non-human) existence. This transformation need not be brought about by a technological invention, but may involve some mutation of known biological or physical reality, e.g. time travel, extraterrestrial invasion, ecological catastrophe. Science fiction is a form of literary *fantasy or *romance that often draws upon earlier kinds of *utopian and *apocalyptic writing. The term itself was first given general currency by Hugo Gernsback, editor of the American magazine *Amazing Stories* from 1926 onwards, and it is usually abbreviated to **SF** (the alternative form 'sci-fi' is frowned upon by devotees); before this, such works were called 'scientific romances' by H. G. Wells and others. Several early precedents have been claimed for the genre—notably Mary Shelley's *Frankenstein* (1818)—but true modern science fiction begins with Jules Verne's *Voyage au centre de la terre* (1864) and H. G. Wells's *The Time Machine* (1895). Once uniformly dismissed as pulp trash, SF gained greater respect during the 1950s, as writers like Isaac Asimov, Ray Bradbury, and Arthur C. Clarke expanded its range. SF has also had an important influence on *postmodernist fiction by writers not devoted to this *genre alone: Thomas Pynchon, Kurt Vonnegut, Doris Lessing, and Italo Calvino are significant examples.

Scottish Chaucerians, the name given to a group of 15th- and 16th-century Scottish poets who wrote under the influence of Geoffrey Chaucer (or of his follower John Lydgate), often using his seven-line *rhyme royal stanza. The most important poets of this group were Robert Henryson, whose *Testament of Cresseid* continues and reinterprets the story of Chaucer's *Troilus and Criseyde*, and William Dunbar, whose *Lament for the Makaris* briefly pays tribute to Chaucer. Other figures are Gavin Douglas, Sir David Lyndsay, and (if his authorship of *The Kingis Quair* be accepted) King James I of Scotland. The term unfortunately diverts attention from the genuinely original character of these poets, and is thus not much favoured in Scotland.

screenplay, the script of a film, comprising *dialogue (and/or *narration) with instructions for sets and camera positions.

scriptible [scrip-teebl], a term used by the French critic Roland Barthes in his book *S/Z* (1970), and usually translated as 'writerly'. In contrast with the easily readable or 'readerly' text (*texte *lisible*), the writerly text does not have a single 'closed' meaning; instead, it obliges each reader to produce his or her own meanings from its fragmentary or contradictory hints. Ideally—and the concept is very much a theoretical ideal rather than a description—the writerly text is challengingly 'open', giving the reader an active role as co-writer, rather than as passive consumer. The nearest actual equivalents of this ideal would seem to be the more difficult works of *modernism and *postmodernism. *See also* indeterminacy, *jouissance*.

self-reflexive, a term applied to literary works that openly reflect upon their own processes of artful composition. Such self-referentiality is frequently found in modern works of fiction that repeatedly refer to their own fictional status (*see* metafiction). The *narrator in such works, and in their earlier equivalents such as Sterne's *Tristram Shandy*

(1759–67), is sometimes called a 'self-conscious narrator'. Self-reflexivity may also be found often in poetry. See also *mise-en-abyme*, romantic irony.

semantics, the philosophical or linguistic study of meanings in language. The semantic aspect of any expression is its meaning as opposed to its form.

seme, an elementary unit of meaning, usually a defining feature or characteristic of something. A basic description of a person as, e.g., 'white, male, grey-haired, clean-shaven' is a listing of semes. Some *structuralist studies of fiction have analysed fictional characters in terms of the presence or absence of given semes. *Adjective*: **semic**.

semiology, *see* semiotics.

semiotic, the, a term used by Julia Kristeva in *La Révolution du langage poétique* (1974) to designate the flow of pre-linguistic rhythms or 'pulsions' that is broken up by the child's entry into the *Symbolic order of language. The unconscious energies of the semiotic are repressed and marginalized by patriarchal logic and rationality, but they may still disrupt the Symbolic order, transgressing its rigid categories (including those of identity and sexual difference). In Kristeva's psychoanalytic theory, the semiotic is associated with the mother's body, but she detects the anarchic energies of the semiotic in the writings of both female and male authors, especially those of the *Symbolist and *modernist *avant-garde*.

semiotics or **semiology,** the systematic study of *signs, or, more precisely, of the production of meanings from sign-*systems*, linguistic or non-linguistic. As a distinct tradition of inquiry into human communications, semiotics was founded by the American philosopher C. S. Peirce (1839–1914) and separately by the Swiss linguist Ferdinand de Saussure (1857–1913), who proposed that linguistics would form one part of a more general science of signs: 'semiology'. Peirce's term 'semiotics' is usually preferred in English, although Saussure's principles and concepts—especially the distinctions between *signifier and *signified and between *langue* and *parole*—have been more influential as the basis of *structuralism and its approach to literature. Semiotics is concerned not with the relations between signs and things but with the interrelationships between signs themselves, within their structured systems or *codes of signification (*see* paradigm, syntagm). The semiotic approach to literary works stresses the production of literary meanings from shared *conventions and codes; but the scope of semiotics goes beyond spoken or written language to other kinds of communicative systems such as cinema, advertising, clothing, gesture, and cuisine. A practitioner of semiotics is a **semiotician.** The term **semiosis** is sometimes used to refer to the process of signifying. For a fuller account, consult Terence Hawkes, *Structuralism and Semiotics* (1977).

Senecan tragedy, a form of *tragedy developed by the Roman philosopher-poet Lucius Annaeus Seneca (*c*.4 BCE–65 CE) in his nine plays based on Greek drama (especially that of Euripides), and further adapted by playwrights of the Italian, French, and English *Renaissance. Seneca's plays were almost certainly *closet dramas intended for recitation rather than stage performance. Composed in five acts with intervening *choruses, they employ long rhetorical speeches, with important actions being recounted by messengers. Their bloodthirsty *plots, including ghosts and horrible crimes, appealed to the popular English dramatists of the late 16th century, who presented such horrors on stage in their *revenge tragedies. These were preceded by a purer form of English Senecan tragedy, notably in Thomas Norton and Thomas Sackville's *Gorboduc* (1561), the first English tragedy. The conventional five-act structure of Renaissance drama owes its origin to the influence of Seneca.

sensation novel, a kind of *novel that flourished in Britain in the 1860s, exploiting the element of suspense in stories of crime and mystery. The most successful examples are Wilkie Collins's *The Woman in White* (1860), Mary Elizabeth Braddon's *Lady Audley's Secret* (1862), and J. Sheridan Le Fanu's *Uncle Silas* (1864).

sensibility, an important 18th-century term designating a kind of sensitivity or responsiveness that is both aesthetic and moral, showing a capacity to feel both for others' sorrows and for beauty. The term is also used in a different sense in modern *criticism, the sensibility of a given writer being his or her characteristic way of responding—intellectually and emotionally—to experience (*see also* dissociation of sensibility). Its major significance, though, is as a concept or mood of 18th-century culture. In terms of moral philosophy, it signalled a reaction against Thomas Hobbes's view of human behaviour as essentially selfish: the 3rd Earl of Shaftesbury and other 18th-century thinkers argued that human beings have an innate 'benevolence' or sympathy for others. In literature, the quality of sensibility was explored and displayed in the 'novel of sensibility' (*see* sentimental novel), in *sentimental comedy, in *graveyard poetry, and in the poems of William Cowper among others. The cult of sensibility is also apparent in late 18th-century *primitivism and in the new interest in the *sublime. At its self-indulgent extremes— later criticized by Jane Austen in *Sense and Sensibility* (1811)—it is called sentimentalism. It was one of the cultural trends that gave rise to *Romanticism (*see* preromanticism). For a fuller account, consult Janet Todd, *Sensibility: An Introduction* (1986).

sententia (plural *-tiae*), a Latin term for an *aphorism or *maxim. Its English adjective, **sententious**, usually has a pejorative sense, referring to a style or statement that is condescending or self-important in giving advice; but it may be used neutrally to mean 'aphoristic'.

sentimental comedy, a kind of *comedy that achieved some popularity with respectable middle-class audiences in the 18th century. In contrast with the aristocratic cynicism of English *Restoration comedy, it showed virtue rewarded by domestic bliss; its plots, usually involving unbelievably good middle-class couples, emphasized *pathos rather than humour. Pioneered by Richard Steele in *The Funeral* (1701) and more fully in *The Conscious Lovers* (1722), it flourished in mid-century with the French *comédie larmoyante* ('tearful comedy') and in such plays as Hugh Kelly's *False Delicacy* (1768). The pious moralizing of this tradition, which survived into 19th-century *melodrama, was opposed in the 1770s by Sheridan and Goldsmith, who attempted a partial return to the *comedy of manners.

sentimental novel (also called novel of sentiment or novel of *sensibility), an emotionally extravagant *novel of a kind that became popular in Europe in the late 18th century. Partly inspired by the emotional power of Samuel Richardson's *Pamela, or Virtue Rewarded* (1740), the sentimental novels of the 1760s and 1770s exhibit the close connections between virtue and sensibility, in repeatedly tearful scenes; a character's feeling for the beauties of nature and for the griefs of others is taken as a sign of a pure heart. An excessively sentimental example is Henry Mackenzie's *The Man of Feeling* (1771), but Oliver Goldsmith's *The Vicar of Wakefield* (1766) and Laurence Sterne's *A Sentimental Journey* (1768) are more ironic. In Europe, the most important sentimental novels were J.-J. Rousseau's *La Nouvelle Héloïse* (1761) and J. W. von Goethe's *The Sorrows of Young Werther* (1774; *see* Wertherism). The fashion lingered on in the early *Gothic novels of Ann Radcliffe in the 1790s.

septenary, a verse line of seven feet (*see* foot) or of seven metrical stresses, more commonly known as a *heptameter.

septet, a *stanza of seven lines, such as the English *rhyme royal stanza.

sestet, a group of six verse lines forming the second part of a *sonnet (in its Italian or Petrarchan form), following the opening *octave. More rarely, the term may refer to a *stanza of six lines (also called a sexain, sextain, or sextet), such as the *Burns stanza or the stanza used in a *sestina.

sestina [ses-tee-nă], a poem of six 6-line *stanzas and a 3-line *envoi, linked by an intricate pattern of repeated line-endings. The most elaborate of the medieval French *fixed forms, it uses only six end-words (normally unrhymed), repeating them in a different order in each stanza so that the ending of the last line in each stanza recurs as the ending of the first line in the next. The *envoi* uses all six words, three of them as line-endings. The established pattern of repetition for the six stanzas is as follows: 1-ABCDEF, 2-FAEBDC, 3-CFDABE, 4-ECBFAD, 5-DEACFB, 6-BDFECA. The form was introduced into English by Sir Philip Sidney in his *Arcadia* (1590). A modern example is W. H. Auden's 'Paysage Moralisé' (1933). Even more remarkable as a technical feat is A. C. Swinburne's 'The Complaint of Lisa' (1878), a rhyming double sestina with twelve 12-line stanzas and a 6-line *envoi*.

Shakespearean sonnet, *see* sonnet.

Shavian [shay-vi-ăn], belonging to or characteristic of the work of the Irish playwright and controversialist Bernard Shaw (1856–1950). *See also* discussion play.

short measure or **short metre,** a form of verse *quatrain often used in *hymns. A variant of *common metre, it has four *stresses in its third line, but only three stresses in the other three, the metre usually being *iambic. The *rhyme scheme is usually *abcb*, or, as in this cheerful example from the children's hymn-writer Isaac Watts, *abab*:

> There is a dreadful Hell,
> And everlasting pains;
> There sinners must with devils dwell
> In darkness, fire, and chains.

The form has some similarity to *poulter's measure.

short story, a fictional prose tale of no specified length, but too short to be published as a volume on its own, as *novellas sometimes and *novels usually are. A short story will normally concentrate on a single event with only one or two characters, more economically than a novel's sustained exploration of social background. There are similar fictional forms of greater antiquity—*fables, *lais, *folktales, and *parables—but the short story as we know it flourished in the magazines of the 19th and early 20th centuries, especially in the USA, which has a particularly strong tradition. For a fuller account, consult Ian Reid, *The Short Story* (1977).

sibilance, the marked recurrence of the 'hissing' sounds known as sibilants (usually spelt *s*, *sh*, *zh*, *c*). The effect, also known as sigmatism after the Greek letter *sigma*, is often exploited in poetry, as in Long-fellow's lines

> Ships that pass in the night, and speak each other in passing;
> Only a signal shown and a distant voice in the darkness

See also alliteration.

sigmatism, *see* sibilance.

sign, a basic element of communication, either linguistic (e.g. a letter or word) or non-linguistic (e.g. a picture, or article of dress); or anything that can be construed as having a meaning. According to the influential theory of the Swiss linguist Ferdinand de Saussure, every sign has two inseparable aspects: the *signifier, which is the materially perceptible component such as a sound or written mark, and the *signified, which is the conceptual meaning. In a linguistic sign, according to Saussure, the relationship between signifier and signified is 'unmotivated' or *arbitrary; that is, it is based purely on social convention rather than on natural necessity: there is nothing about a horse which demands that it be called 'horse', since the French call the same thing *un cheval*. Saussure's theory deliberately leaves out the *referent or real external object referred to by a sign. The alternative theory of the American philosopher C. S. Peirce has more room for referents and for 'motivated' signs. Peirce calls the unmotivated sign a *symbol, while identifying two further kinds of sign: the *icon, which resembles its referent (e.g. a photograph), and the *index, which is caused by its referent (e.g. a medical symptom). *Verb*: **signify.** *See also* semiotics.

signified, the conceptual component of a *sign, as distinct from its material form, the *signifier. The signified, also known in French as the *signifié*, is the *idea* conventionally indicated by the signifier, rather than the actual external object or *referent (if any).

signifier, the concretely perceptible component of a *sign, as distinct from its conceptual meaning (the *signified). In language, this may be a meaningful sound, or a written mark such as a letter or sequence of letters making up a word. The term often appears in its French form, *significant*.

silver-fork novel, a kind of *novel that was popular in Britain from the 1820s to the 1840s, and was marked by concentration upon the fashionable etiquette and manners of high society. The term was used mockingly by critics of the time, and has been applied to works by Theodore Hook, Catherine Gore, Frances Trollope, Lady Caroline Lamb, Benjamin Disraeli, and Susan Ferrier.

simile [sim-ĭ-li], an explicit comparison between two different things, actions, or feelings, using the words 'as' or 'like', as in Wordsworth's line:

I wandered lonely as a cloud

A very common *figure of speech in both prose and verse, simile is more tentative and decorative than *metaphor. A lengthy and more elaborate kind of simile, used as a digression in a narrative work, is the *epic simile.

sjuzet [syuu-*zhet*] (also spelt *suzet, syuzhet*) the term used in *Russian Formalism to denote the *plot of a narrative work, as opposed to the events of its *story (called the **fabula*). The *sjuzet* is the finished arrangement of narrated events as they are presented to the reader, rather than the sequence of such events as reconstructed in their 'true' sequence and duration.

skald (or **scald**), an Old Norse word for a poet, usually applied to a Norwegian or Icelandic court poet or *bard of the period from the 9th century to the 13th. Skaldic verse is marked by its elaborate patterns of *metre, rhyme, and *alliteration, and by its use of *kennings.

Skeltonics, verses written in the manner favoured by John Skelton (*c.*1460–1529), whose lively satirical poems use irregular short lines of two or three *stresses, and often extend the same rhyme over several consecutive lines. A similar effect of vivid colloquial word-play is often found in modern *dub poetry.

sketch, a short composition, dramatic, narrative, or descriptive. In the theatre, a sketch is a brief, self-contained dramatic scene, usually comic. As a kind of prose narrative, a sketch is more modest than a *short story, showing less development in *plot or *characterization. The term is also applied to brief descriptions of people (the 'character sketch') or places.

slant rhyme, *see* half-rhyme.

slave narrative, a written account by an escaped or freed slave of his or her experiences of slavery. A special American form of autobiography, the slave narrative appeared as an important kind of abolitionist literature in the period preceding the Civil War. The outstanding example is the *Narrative of the Life of Frederick Douglass* (1845).

socialist realism, a slogan adopted by the Soviet cultural authorities in 1934 to summarize the requirements of Stalinist dogma in literature: the established techniques of 19th-century *realism were to be used to represent the struggle for socialism in a positive, optimistic light, while the allegedly 'decadent' techniques of *modernism were to be avoided as bourgeois deviations. The approved model was Maxim Gorky's novel *The Mother* (1907). A few outstanding novels have conformed to this official prescription, including Mikhail Sholokhov's *Virgin Soil Upturned* (1932) and Lewis Grassic Gibbon's *Grey Granite* (1934), but the doctrine acted chiefly to stifle imaginative experiment, and has been rejected as such by many leading socialist writers, notably Bertolt Brecht. *See also* proletcult, propagandism.

sociology of literature, a branch of literary study that examines the relationships between literary works and their social contexts, including patterns of literacy, kinds of audience, modes of publication and dramatic presentation, and the social class positions of authors and readers. Originating in 19th-century France with works by Mme de Staël and Hippolyte Taine, the sociology of literature was revived in the English-speaking world with the appearance of such studies as Raymond Williams's *The Long Revolution* (1961), and is most often associated with Marxist approaches to cultural analysis.

Socratic [sŏ-krat-ik], pertaining to the Greek philosopher Socrates (469–399 BCE). His manner of feigning ignorance in order to expose the self-contradictions of his interlocutors through cross-examination is known as Socratic irony. His method of seeking the truth by such processes of question-and-answer is illustrated in the Socratic *Dialogues* of his follower, Plato.

solecism [sol-ĭ-sizm], a grammatical error; or, more loosely, any mistake that exposes the perpetrator's ignorance. *Adjective*: **solecistic.**

soliloquy [sŏl-il-ŏ-kwi], a dramatic speech uttered by one character speaking aloud while alone on the stage (or while under the impression of being alone). The **soliloquist** thus reveals his or her inner thoughts and feelings to the audience, either in supposed self-communion or in a consciously direct address. Soliloquies often appear in plays from the age of Shakespeare, notably in his *Hamlet* and *Macbeth*. A poem supposedly uttered by a solitary speaker, like Robert Browning's 'Soliloquy of the Spanish Cloister' (1842), may also be called a soliloquy. Soliloquy is a form of *monologue, but a monologue is not a soliloquy if (as in the *dramatic monologue) the speaker is not alone. *Verb*: **soliloquize.**

sonnet, a *lyric poem comprising 14 rhyming lines of equal length: iambic *pentameters in English, *alexandrines in French, *hendeca- syllables in Italian. The *rhyme schemes of the sonnet follow two basic patterns.

(1) The Italian sonnet (also called the *Petrarchan sonnet after the most influential of the Italian sonneteers) comprises an 8-line 'octave' of two *quatrains, rhymed *abbaabba*, followed by a 6-line 'sestet' usually rhymed *cdecde* or *cdcdcd*. The transition from octave to sestet usually coincides with a 'turn' (Italian, *volta*) in the argument or mood of the poem. In a variant form used by the English poet John Milton, however, the 'turn' is delayed to a later position around the tenth line. Some later poets—notably William Wordsworth—have employed this feature of the 'Miltonic sonnet' while relaxing the rhyme scheme of the octave to *abbaacca*. The Italian pattern has remained the most widely used in English and other languages.

(2) The English sonnet (also called the Shakespearean sonnet after its foremost practitioner) comprises three quatrains and a final couplet, rhyming *ababcdcdefefgg*. An important variant of this is the Spenserian sonnet (introduced by the Elizabethan poet Edmund Spenser), which links the three quatrains by rhyme, in the sequence *ababbabccdcdee*. In either form, the 'turn' comes with the final couplet, which may sometimes achieve the neatness of an *epigram.

Originating in Italy, the sonnet was established by Petrarch in the 14th century as a major form of love poetry, and came to be adopted in Spain,

France, and England in the 16th century, and in Germany in the 17th. The standard subject-matter of early sonnets was the torments of sexual love (usually within a *courtly love convention), but in the 17th century John Donne extended the sonnet's scope to religion, while Milton extended it to politics. Although largely neglected in the 18th century, the sonnet was revived in the 19th by Wordsworth, Keats, and Baudelaire, and is still widely used. Some poets have written connected series of sonnets, known as sonnet sequences or sonnet cycles: of these, the outstanding English examples are Sir Philip Sidney's *Astrophel and Stella* (1591), Spenser's *Amoretti* (1595), and Shakespeare's *Sonnets* (1609); later examples include Elizabeth Barrett Browning's *Sonnets from the Portuguese* (1850) and W. H. Auden's 'In Time of War' (1939). A group of sonnets formally linked by repeated lines is known as a *crown of sonnets. Irregular variations on the sonnet form have included the 12-line sonnet sometimes used by Elizabethan poets, G. M. Hopkins's *curtal sonnets of 10½ lines, and the 16-line sonnets of George Meredith's sequence *Modern Love* (1862). For an extended introductory account, consult John Fuller, *The Sonnet* (1972).

soubrette, the *stock character of the heroine's maidservant in French comedy of the 17th and 18th centuries. The soubrette usually protests against the delusions of her master, ingeniously scheming on behalf of her young mistress. The character of Dorine in Molière's *Le Tartuffe* (1664) is a model for the type, which originated in the *commedia dell' arte*.

Spasmodic School, a title applied mockingly by the Scottish poet and critic W. E. Aytoun in 1854 to a group of poets who had lately achieved some popularity in Britain: P. J. Bailey, Sydney Dobell, Alexander Smith, and others. Their work is marked by extravagant attempts to represent emotional turmoil, sometimes in a manner derived from Byron. Dobell's dramatic poem *Balder* (1853) includes the notorious line:

Ah! Ah! Ah! Ah! Ah! Ah! Ah! Ah! Ah! Ah!

The term has sometimes been extended to the comparable emotional intensities of Tennyson's *Maud* (1855), and of some poems by Elizabeth Barrett Browning.

speech act theory, a modern philosophical approach to language, which has challenged the long-standing assumption of philosophers that human utterances consist exclusively of true or false statements about the world. Initiated by the English philosopher J. L. Austin in lectures

published posthumously as *How to Do Things with Words* (1962), speech act
theory begins with the distinction between 'constative' utterances
(which report truly or falsely on some external state of affairs) and
*performatives (which are verbal actions in themselves—such as
promising—rather than true or false statements). Further analysis
reveals that a single utterance may comprise three distinct kinds of
speech act: in addition to its simple 'locutionary' status as a grammatical
utterance, it will have an *illocutionary force (i.e. an active function
such as threatening, affirming, or reassuring), and probably a
*perlocutionary force (an effect on the listener or reader). Since
Austin's death in 1960, speech act theory has been developed further by
J. R. Searle in *Speech Acts* (1969) and other works, and applied to problems
of literary analysis by Mary Louise Pratt in *Toward a Speech Act Theory of
Literary Discourse* (1977).

Spenserian stanza, an English poetic *stanza of nine *iambic lines,
the first eight being *pentameters while the ninth is a longer line known
either as an iambic hexameter or as an *alexandrine. The rhyme scheme
is *ababbcbcc*. The stanza is named after Edmund Spenser, who invented
it—probably on the basis of the *ottava rima* stanza—for his long
allegorical *romance *The Faerie Queene* (1590–6). It was revived
successfully by the younger English Romantic poets of the early 19th
century: Byron used it for *Childe Harold's Pilgrimage* (1812, 1816), Keats for
'The Eve of St Agnes' (1820), and Shelley for *The Revolt of Islam* (1818) and
Adonais (1821). For the Spenserian sonnet, *see* sonnet.

spondee, a metrical unit (*foot) consisting of two *stressed syllables
(or, in *quantitative verse, two long syllables). Spondees occur regularly
in several Greek and Latin metres, and as substitutes for other feet, as in
the dactylic *hexameter; but in English the spondee is an occasional
device of metrical variation. The normal alternation of stressed and
unstressed syllables in English speech makes it virtually impossible to
compose a complete line of true spondees. Some English compound
words like *childbirth* are **spondaic,** although even these do not have
exactly equal stresses. The occurrence of adjacent stressed syllables in
English verse may be accounted for more convincingly in terms of
*demotion, rather than in the doubtfully applicable terms of classical
quantitative feet.

Spoonerism, a phrase in which the initial consonants of two words
have been swapped over, creating an amusing new expression. It takes

its name from the Revd W. A. Spooner (1844–1930), Warden of New College, Oxford. His reputed utterances, like the accusation that a student had 'hissed my mystery lectures', appear to have been inadvertent slips, but Spoonerisms may also be used for deliberately humorous effect: W. H. Auden referred dismissively to Keats and Shelley as 'Sheets and Kelly', while a feminist theatre group toured Britain in the 1970s under the name Cunning Stunts.

sprung rhythm, the term used by the English poet Gerard Manley Hopkins (1844–89) to describe his peculiar metrical system, based on the *accentual verse of nursery rhymes and on medieval *alliterative metres. It counts the number of strong stresses in a line, regardless of the number of unstressed syllables, and permits the juxtaposition of stressed syllables more frequently than normal English *duple or *triple metre (*see* metre). Hopkins saw his metre as having four kinds of *foot, each beginning with a stressed syllable: the stressed monosyllable (●), the *trochee (●○), the *dactyl (●○○), and the first *paeon (●○○○); additional unstressed syllables or 'outrides' were also permitted. Hopkins's aim was to make use of the energies of everyday speech, and his sprung rhythm may be regarded as a kind of *free verse based partly on accentual metres.

squib, another word for a *lampoon: a short satirical attack upon a person, work, or institution.

stanza, a group of verse lines forming a section of a poem and sharing the same structure as all or some of the other sections of the same poem, in terms of the lengths of its lines, its *metre, and usually its *rhyme scheme. In printed poems, stanzas are separated by spaces. Stanzas are often loosely referred to as 'verses', but this usage causes serious confusion and is best avoided, since a verse is, strictly speaking, a single line. Although some writers regard the *couplet and the *tercet as kinds of stanza, the term is most often applied to groups of four lines or more, the four-line *quatrain being by far the most common, in the *ballad metre and various other forms. Among the longer and more complex kinds of stanza used in English are the *Burns stanza, *ottava rima, *rhyme royal, and the *Spenserian stanza; but there are many others with no special names. The *fixed forms derived from medieval French verse have their own intricate kinds of stanza. Poems that are divided regularly into stanzas are **stanzaic,** whereas poems that form a continuous sequence of lines of the same length are referred to as being *stichic. In many poems which are divided up irregularly (usually those written in *blank verse, *heroic couplets, or *free verse), the sections are sometimes called *verse paragraphs, but in the irregular form of the *ode, these unmatched subdivisions are usually called stanzas or *strophes.

stave, another word for a *stanza, especially in a song.

stichic [stik-ik], composed as a continuous sequence of verse lines of the same length and *metre, and thus not divided into *stanzas. Poems written in *blank verse or in *heroic couplets are usually stichic; if divided up at all, their uneven subdivisions are called *verse paragraphs.

stichomythia [stik-oh-**mith**-iă], a form of dramatic *dialogue in which two disputing characters answer each other rapidly in alternating single lines, with one character's replies balancing (and often partially repeating) the other's utterances. This kind of verbal duel or 'cut and thrust' dialogue was practised more in ancient Greek and Roman tragedy than in later drama, although a notable English example occurs in the dialogue between Richard and Elizabeth in Shakespeare's *Richard III* (Act IV, scene iv). *See also* hemistich, repartee.

stock character, a stereotyped character easily recognized by readers or audiences from recurrent appearances in literary or folk tradition, usually within a specific *genre such as comedy or fairy tale. Common examples include the absent-minded professor, the country bumpkin, the damsel in distress, the old miser, the whore with a heart of gold, the bragging soldier, the villain of *melodrama, the wicked stepmother, the jealous husband, and the *soubrette. Similarly recognizable incidents or plot-elements which recur in fiction and drama are known as **stock situations**: these include the mistaken identity, the 'eternal triangle', the discovery of the birthmark, the last-minute rescue, the dying man's confession, and love at first sight. *See also* archetype, convention, type.

stock response, a routinely insensitive reaction to a literary work or to some element of it. A stock response perceives in a work only those meanings that are already familiar from a reader's or audience's previous experience, failing to recognize fresh or unfamiliar meanings. Writers may deliberately exploit stock responses (e.g. our sympathy for the hero or heroine), but often fall victim to them when attempting to reach beyond readers' habitual expectations.

story, in the everyday sense, any *narrative or tale recounting a series of events. In modern *narratology, however, the term refers more specifically to the sequence of imagined events that we reconstruct from the actual arrangement of a narrative (or dramatic) *plot. In this modern distinction between story and plot, derived from *Russian Formalism and its opposed terms *fabula and *sjuzet, the story is the full sequence of events as we assume them to have occurred in their likely order, duration, and frequency, while the plot is a particular selection and (re-)ordering of these. Thus the story is the abstractly conceived 'raw material' of events which we reconstruct from the finished arrangement of the plot: it includes events preceding and otherwise omitted from the perceived action, and its sequence will differ from that of the plot if the action begins *in medias res or otherwise involves an *anachrony. As an abstraction, the story can be translated into other languages and media (e.g. film) more successfully than the style of the *narration could be.

stream of consciousness, the continuous flow of sense-perceptions, thoughts, feelings, and memories in the human mind; or a literary method of representing such a blending of mental processes in fictional characters, usually in an unpunctuated or disjointed form of *interior monologue. The term is often used as a synonym for interior monologue, but they can also be distinguished, in two ways. In the first (psychological) sense, the stream of consciousness is the subject-matter while interior monologue is the technique for presenting it; thus Marcel Proust's novel A la recherche du temps perdu (1913–27) is *about* the stream of consciousness, especially the connection between sense-impressions and memory, but it does not actually use interior monologue. In the second (literary) sense, stream of consciousness is a special style of interior monologue: while an interior monologue always presents a character's thoughts 'directly', without the apparent intervention of a summarizing and selecting narrator, it does not necessarily mingle them with impressions and perceptions, nor does it necessarily violate the norms of grammar, syntax, and logic; but the stream-of-consciousness technique also does one or both of these things. An important device of *modernist fiction and its later imitators, the technique was pioneered by Dorothy Richardson in Pilgrimage (1915–35) and by James Joyce in Ulysses (1922), and further developed by Virginia Woolf in Mrs Dalloway (1925) and William Faulkner in The Sound and the Fury (1928). For a fuller account, consult Robert Humphrey, Stream of Consciousness in the Modern Novel (1968).

stress, the relative emphasis given in pronunciation to a syllable, in loudness, pitch, or duration (or some combination of these). The term is usually interchangeable with *accent, although some theorists of *prosody reserve it only for the emphasis occurring according to a metrical pattern (*see* metre). In English verse, the metre of a line is determined by the number of stresses in a sequence composed of stressed and unstressed syllables (also referred to as strongly stressed and weakly stressed syllables). In *quantitative verse, on the other hand, the metrical pattern is made up of syllables measured by their duration rather than by stress.

strong-stress metre, another term for the metre of *accentual verse, in which only the stressed syllables are counted while the unstressed syllables may vary in number. The term thus encompasses the Old Germanic *alliterative metre, various kinds of popular English metre, and G. M. Hopkin's *sprung rhythm.

strophe [stroh-fi], a *stanza, or any less regular subdivision of a poem, such as a *verse paragraph. In a special sense, the term is applied to the opening section (and every third succeeding section) of a Greek choral *ode. In the *Pindaric ode, sometimes imitated in English, the strophe is followed by an *antistrophe having the same number of lines and the same complex metrical arrangement; this is then followed by an *epode of differing length and structure, and the triadic pattern may then be repeated a number of times. In choral odes, the *chorus would dance in one direction while chanting the strophe, then back again during the antistrophe, standing still for the epode. *Adjective*: **strophic.**

structuralism, a modern intellectual movement that analyses cultural phenomena according to principles derived from linguistics, emphasizing the systematic interrelationships among the elements of any human activity, and thus the abstract *codes and *conventions governing the social production of meanings. Building on the linguistic concept of the *phoneme—a unit of meaningful sound defined purely by its differences from other phonemes rather than by any inherent features—structuralism argues that the elements composing any cultural phenomenon (from cooking to drama) are similarly 'relational': that is, they have meaning only by virtue of their contrasts with other elements of the system, especially in *binary oppositions of paired opposites. Their meanings can be established not by referring each element to any supposed equivalent in natural reality, but only by analysing its function within a self-contained cultural code. Accordingly, structuralist analysis seeks the underlying system or *langue* that governs individual utterances or instances. In formulating the laws by which elements of such a system are combined, it distinguishes between sets of interchangeable units (*paradigms) and sequences of such units in combination (*syntagms), thereby outlining a basic '*syntax' of human culture.

Structuralism and its 'science of signs' (*see* semiotics) are derived chiefly from the linguistic theories of Ferdinand de Saussure (1857–1913), and partly from *Russian Formalism and the related *narratology of Vladimir Propp's *Morphology of the Folktale* (1928). It flourished in France in the 1960s, following the widely discussed applications of structural analysis to mythology by the anthropologist Claude Lévi-Strauss. In the study of literary works, structuralism is distinguished by its rejection of those traditional notions according to which literature 'expresses' an author's meaning or 'reflects' reality. Instead, the '*text' is seen as an objective structure activating various codes and conventions which are independent of author, reader, and external reality. Structuralist criticism is less interested in interpreting what literary works mean than in explaining *how* they can mean what they mean; that is, in showing what implicit rules and conventions are operating in a given work. The structuralist tradition has been particularly strong in narratology, from Propp's analysis of narrative *functions to Greimas' theory of *actants. The French critic Roland Barthes was an outstanding practitioner of structuralist literary analysis notably in his book *S/Z* (1970)—and is famed for his witty analyses of wrestling, striptease, and other phenomena in *Mythologies* (1957): some of his later writings, however, show a shift to *post-structuralism, in which the over-confident 'scientific' pretensions of structuralism are abandoned. For more extended accounts of this enterprise, consult Terence Hawkes, *Structuralism and Semiotics* (1977), Jonathan Culler, *Structuralist Poetics* (1975), and Robert Scholes, *Structuralism in Literature: An Introduction* (1974).

Sturm und Drang [shtoorm uunt drang], the name—'Storm and Stress'—given to a short-lived but important movement in German literature of the 1770s. An early precursor of *Romanticism, it was passionately individualistic and rebellious, maintaining a hostile attitude to French *neoclassicism and the associated rationalism of the *Enlightenment. The term is taken from the title of a play by

F. M. Klinger (1776), but the leaders of the movement were J. G. Herder and J. W. von Goethe. Herder, inspired by the *primitivism of J.-J. Rousseau, encouraged the cult of *Ossianism and praised the 'natural' qualities of Shakespeare and of folk song. Goethe's play *Götz von Berlichingen* (1773), a Shakespearean *chronicle play about a leader in the 16th-century peasants' revolt, is the major dramatic work of the *Sturm und Drang* period, while his *sentimental novel of hopeless love and suicide, *The Sorrows of Young Werther* (1774), is its most significant novel. A belated product of the movement is Friedrich Schiller's play *Die Räuber* (1781), which influenced the later development of *melodrama.

style, any specific way of using language, which is characteristic of an author, school, period, or *genre. Particular styles may be defined by their *diction, *syntax, *imagery, *rhythm, and use of *figures, or by any other linguistic feature. Different categories of style have been named after particular authors (e.g. Ciceronian), periods (e.g. Augustan), and professions (e.g. journalistic), while in the *Renaissance a scheme of three stylistic 'levels' was adopted, distinguishing the high or 'grand' style from the middle or 'mean' style and the low or 'base' style. The principle of *decorum held that certain subjects required particular levels of style, so that an *epic should be written in the grand style whereas *satires should be composed in the base style. Since the literary revolution of *Romanticism, however, this hierarchy has been replaced by the notion of style as an expression of individual personality. *Adjective*: **stylistic.**

stylistics, a branch of modern linguistics devoted to the detailed analysis of literary *style, or of the linguistic choices made by speakers and writers in non-literary contexts. For an introductory account, consult Mick Short, *Exploring the Language of Poems, Plays and Prose* (1996).

subgenre [sub-zhah^{n}r], any category of literary works that forms a specific class within a larger *genre: thus the *pastoral elegy may be regarded as a subgenre of *elegy, which is in turn a subgenre of *lyric poetry.

sublime, the, a quality of awesome grandeur in art or nature, which some 18th-century writers distinguished from the merely beautiful. An anonymous Greek critical treatise of the 1st century CE, *Peri hypsous* ('On the Sublime', mistakenly attributed to the 3rd-century rhetorician Longinus), provided the basis for the 18th-century interest in sublimity, after Boileau's French translation in 1672. 'Longinus' refers to the sublime as a loftiness of thought and feeling in literature, and associates it with terrifyingly impressive natural phenomena such as mountains, volcanoes, storms, and the sea. These associations were revived in Edmund Burke's influential *Philosophical Enquiry into the Origin of our Ideas of the Sublime and Beautiful* (1757), which argues that the sublime is characterized by obscurity, vastness, and power, while the beautiful is light, smooth, and delicate. The 18th-century enthusiasm for the sublime in landscape and the visual arts was one of the developments that undermined the restraints of *neoclassicism and thus prepared the way for *Romanticism.

subplot, a secondary sequence of actions in a dramatic or narrative work, usually involving characters of lesser importance (and often of lower social status). The subplot may be related to the main plot as a parallel or contrast, or it may be more or less separate from it. Subplots are especially common in Elizabethan and Jacobean drama, a famous example being that of Gloucester and his sons in Shakespeare's *King Lear*; but they are also found in long novels such as those of Dickens.

substitution, a term used in traditional *prosody to denote the use of one kind of *foot in place of the foot normally required by the metrical pattern of a verse line. In English verse, the kind of substitution most commonly referred to by prosodists is the replacement of the first *iamb in an iambic line by a *trochee; this 'initial trochaic *inversion', as it is called, appears in Tennyson's line:

> Far on the ringing plains of windy Troy.

The substitution of an *anapaest for an iamb, or of a *dactyl for a trochee, is called trisyllabic substitution, since it increases the number of syllables from two to three. The feet known as the *spondee (●●) and the *pyrrhic (○○) are sometimes invoked as substitute feet where stressed or unstressed syllables occur in pairs. Thus Keats's line

> O for a beaker full of the warm South

shows, in addition to its initial trochaic inversion, a metrical variation at the end, which would be described in traditional prosody as the substitution of a pyrrhic and a spondee for the final two iambs. Some more modern theories of versification, however, have rejected the concept of the foot and along with it that of substitution, accounting for such metrical variations in terms of *demotion, *promotion, and the 'pairing' of stressed and unstressed syllables. In this view, the ending of

Keats's line illustrates a permissible variation in English iambic verse, whereby the occurrence of two stressed syllables together can be compensated (in certain positions) by the pairing of two unstressed syllables. In Greek and Latin *quantitative verse, some kinds of substitution are governed by the principle of 'equivalence' whereby one long syllable is equal to two short syllables, so that under certain conditions a spondee, for example, can stand in for a dactyl.

subtext, any meaning or set of meanings which is implied rather than explicitly stated in a literary work, especially in a play. Modern plays such as those of Harold Pinter, in which the meaning of the action is sometimes suggested more by silences and pauses than by dialogue alone, are often discussed in terms of their hidden subtexts.

succès d'estime [suuk-sed est-eem] a high reputation enjoyed by a work on the basis of critics' favourable judgements; thus a critical success rather than a merely commercial one. Another kind of reputation for which the French have a phrase is the *succès de scandale*: a success based on notoriety, when a work becomes famous because of some public excitement or outrage not directly arising from its actual merits. Some works have both kinds of success: Vladimir Nabokov's novel *Lolita* (1956) enjoyed a *succès de scandale* based on its notorious paedophilic subject-matter, but still ranks as a *succès d'estime* on the strengths of its widely admired use of English prose.

surface structure, *see* deep structure.

surfiction, a term coined in 1973 by the American experimental writer Raymond Federman to designate a new kind of fiction which is now more often referred to as *postmodernist. Rather than attempt to mirror some pre-existing reality, surfiction abandons *realism in favour of *metafiction, self-consciously advertising its own fictional status. Federman proposed that 'the new fiction will not attempt to be meaningful, truthful, or realistic'. He reprinted his 1973 manifesto 'Surfiction—A Position' in a volume of essays, *Surfiction: Fiction Now . . . and Tomorrow* (1975), which also included contributions from Ronald Sukenick and John Barth. The term's reference is broadly similar to that of Robert Scholes's *fabulation, although it has not been so widely adopted.

Surrealism, an anti-rational movement of imaginative liberation in European (mainly French) art and literature in the 1920s and 1930s, launched by André Breton in his *Manifeste du Surréalisme* (1924) after his break from the *Dada group in 1922. The term *surréaliste* had been used by the French poet Guillaume Apollinaire in 1917 to indicate an attempt to reach beyond the limits of the 'real'. Surrealism seeks to break down the boundaries between rationality and irrationality, exploring the resources and revolutionary energies of dreams, hallucinations, and sexual desire. Influenced both by the *Symbolists and by Sigmund Freud's theories of the unconscious, the surrealists experimented with *automatic writing and with the free association of random images brought together in surprising juxtaposition. Although surrealist painting is better known, a significant tradition of surrealist poetry established itself in France, in the work of Breton, Paul Éluard, Louis Aragon, and Benjamin Péret. Surrealism also attempted to become an international revolutionary movement, associated for a while with the Communist International. Although dissolved as a coherent movement by the end of the 1930s, its tradition has survived in many forms of post-war experimental writing, from the theatre of the *absurd to the songs of Bob Dylan. The adjectives **surreal** and **surrealistic** are often used in a loose sense to refer to any bizarre imaginative effect.

syllabic verse [si-**lab**-ik], verse in which the lines are measured according to the number of syllables they contain, regardless of the number of *stresses. This syllabic principle operates in the poetry of the Romance languages (French, Italian, Spanish etc.) and of Chinese and Japanese; but in English, purely syllabic verse occurs only in rare experiments such as those of Marianne Moore, W. H. Auden, and Thom Gunn. The counting of syllables in the line is one element of English *prosody, but not the dominant principle, English verse being either purely *accentual, in which case the number of syllables per line does not matter, or **accentual-syllabic,** in which case the number of stresses is counted as well as the total number of syllables. English accentual-syllabic verse can tend towards either the syllabic or the accentual principle: thus Alexander Pope and other poets of the early 18th century were quite strict in counting the ten syllables of their *pentameters, which can therefore be called decasyllabic lines; but other English poets like Shakespeare and Keats allowed themselves more variation in the syllable-count (especially in the use of *feminine endings, which add an eleventh syllable), so that it is more accurate to call their pentameters five-stress lines. The conventions of European syllabic verse give us the names of certain standard lines: the *hendecasyllable is important in

Italian verse, as the 12-syllable *alexandrine is in French, while *octo-syllabic verse is very common in many languages including English (where it is composed in four-stress lines). *See also* metre.

syllepsis, a construction in which one word (usually a verb or preposition) is applied to two other words or phrases, either ungrammatically or in two differing senses. In the first case, the verb or preposition agrees grammatically with only one of the two elements which it governs, e.g. 'He works his work, I mine' (Tennyson). In the second case, the word also appears only once but is applied twice in differing senses (often an abstract sense and a concrete sense), as in Pope's *The Rape of the Lock*:

> Here, thou, great Anna! whom three realms obey
> Dost sometimes counsel take—and sometimes tea.

A more far-fetched instance occurs in Dickens's *Pickwick Papers* when it is said of a character that she 'went home in a flood of tears and a sedan chair'. There is usually a kind of *pun involved in this kind of syllepsis. The term is frequently used interchangeably with *zeugma, attempts to distinguish the two terms having foundered in confusion: some rhetoricians place the ungrammatical form under the heading of syllepsis while others allot it to zeugma. It seems preferable to keep zeugma as the more inclusive term for syntactic 'yoking' and to reserve syllepsis for its ungrammatical or punning varieties. *Adjective*: **sylleptic.**

syllogism [sil-ŏ-jizm], a form of logical argument that derives a conclusion from two propositions ('premises') sharing a common term, usually in this form: all x and y (major premise); z is x (minor premise); therefore z is y (conclusion). For example: all poets are alcoholics; Jane is a poet; therefore Jane is an alcoholic. In this deductive logic, the conclusion is of course reliable only if both premises are true. Syllogistic reasoning was cultivated in medieval *scholasticism, and is sometimes found in Chaucer and Shakespeare. *Verb*: **syllogize.**

symbol, in the simplest sense, anything that stands for or represents something else beyond it—usually an idea conventionally associated with it. Objects like flags and crosses can function symbolically; and words are also symbols. In the *semiotics of C. S. Peirce, the term denotes a kind of *sign that has no natural or resembling connection with its referent, only a conventional one: this is the case with words. In literary usage, however, a symbol is a specially evocative kind of image (*see* imagery); that is, a word or phrase referring to a concrete object,

scene, or action which also has some further significance associated with
it: roses, mountains, birds, and voyages have all been used as common
literary symbols. A symbol differs from a *metaphor in that its
application is left open as an unstated suggestion: thus in the sentence
She was a tower of strength, the metaphor ties a concrete image (the
'vehicle': tower) to an identifiable abstract quality (the *tenor: strength).
Similarly, in the systematically extended metaphoric parallels of
*allegory, the images represent specific meanings: at the beginning of
Langland's allegorical poem *Piers Plowman* (*c*.1380), the tower seen by the
dreamer is clearly identified with the quality of Truth, and it has no
independent status apart from this function. But the symbolic tower in
Robert Browning's poem ' "Childe Roland to the Dark Tower Came" '
(1855), or that in W. B. Yeat's collection of poems *The Tower* (1928),
remains mysteriously indeterminate in its possible meanings. It is
therefore usually too simple to say that a literary symbol 'stands for'
some idea as if it were just a convenient substitute for a fixed meaning; it
is usually a substantial image in its own right, around which further
significances may gather according to differing interpretations. The
term **symbolism** refers to the use of symbols, or to a set of related
symbols; however, it is also the name given to an important movement
in late 19th-century and early 20th-century poetry: for this sense, *see*
Symbolists. One of the important features of *Romanticism and
succeeding phases of Western literature was a much more pronounced
reliance upon enigmatic symbolism in both poetry and prose fiction,
sometimes involving obscure private codes of meaning, as in the poetry
of Blake or Yeats. A well-known early example of this is the albatross in
Coleridge's 'The Rime of the Ancient Mariner' (1798). Many novelists—
notably Herman Melville and D. H. Lawrence—have used symbolic
methods: in Melville's *Moby-Dick* (1851) the White Whale (and indeed
almost every object and character in the book) becomes a focus for many
different suggested meanings. Melville's extravagant symbolism was
encouraged partly by the importance which American
*Transcendentalism gave to symbolic interpretation of the world. *Verb*:
symbolize. *See also* motif.

Symbolic, the, a term used by the French psychoanalyst Jacques Lacan
and by the literary theorist Julia Kristeva to designate the objective order
(sometimes called the Symbolic Order) of language, law, morality,
religion, and all social existence, which is held to constitute the identity
of any human subject who enters it. Drawing on Freud's theory of the

Oedipus complex and on the *structuralist anthropology of Claude Lévi-Strauss, Lacan developed an opposition between the 'Imaginary' state enjoyed by the infant who has no distinct sense of a self opposed to the world, and the Symbolic Order in which the child then becomes a separate subject within human culture. The Symbolic is the realm of distinctions and differences—between self and others, subject and object—and of absence or 'lack', since in it we are exiled from the completeness of the Imaginary, and can return to it only in fantasized identifications. The infant's entry into the Symbolic is associated with the 'splitting' of the subject by language, which allots distinct 'subject-positions' ('I' and 'you') for us to occupy in turn. In Kristeva's literary theory, the Symbolic is opposed to the disruptive energies of the *semiotic, which have their source in the Imaginary state.

Symbolists, an important group of French poets who, between the 1870s and the 1890s, founded the modern tradition in Western poetry. The leading Symbolists—Paul Verlaine, Arthur Rimbaud, and Stephane Mallarmé—wrote in reaction against *realism and *naturalism, and against the objectivity and technical conservatism of the *Parnassians. Among the minor Symbolist poets were Jules Laforgue and Tristan Corbière. The Symbolists aimed for a poetry of suggestion rather than of direct statement, evoking subjective moods through the use of private *symbols, while avoiding the description of external reality or the expression of opinion. They wanted to bring poetry closer to music, believing that sound had mysterious affinities with other senses (*see* synaesthesia). Among their influential innovations were *free verse and the *prose poem. Their chief inspiration was the work of the poet Charles Baudelaire (1821–67), especially his theory of the 'correspondences' between physical and spiritual realms and between the different senses; Baudelaire had also promoted Edgar Allan Poe's doctrine of 'pure' poetry, which the Symbolists attempted to put into practice. As a self-conscious movement, French symbolism declared itself under that name only in 1886, forming part of the so-called *decadence of that period. It appeared in drama too, notably in the works of the Belgian playwright Maurice Maeterlinck in the 1890s; and some of its concerns were reflected in novels by J.-K. Huysmans and Édouard Dujardin. The influence of symbolism on European and American literature of the early 20th century was extensive: Paul Valéry in French, Rainer Maria Rilke in German, and W. B. Yeats in English carried the tradition into the 20th century, and hardly any major figure of *modernism was unaffected by it. *See also* hermeticism, impressionism, *poète maudit*.

synaeresis or **syneresis** [sin-eer-ĭsis], a form of contraction or *elision in which two adjacent vowel sounds are run together into a single *diphthong or vowel: thus 'the effect' becomes *th'effect*, and 'seëst' becomes *seest*. The device is used in poetry for the sake of conformity to the *metre, especially in *syllabic and accentual-syllabic verse. A distinction is sometimes made between synaeresis, which creates diphthongs, and **sinizesis**, which creates simple vowels. *See also* diaeresis, syncope.

synaesthesia [sin-ĕs-**thee**-ziă], a blending or confusion of different kinds of sense-impression, in which one type of sensation is referred to in terms more appropriate to another. Common synaesthetic expressions include the descriptions of colours as 'loud' or 'warm', and of sounds as 'smooth'. This effect was cultivated consciously by the French *Symbolists, but is often found in earlier poetry, notably in Keats. *See also* catachresis.

synchronic [sin-**kron**-ik], concerned only with the state of something at a given time, rather than with its historical development. In modern linguistics, the synchronic study of language as it is has generally been preferred to the *diachronic study of changes in language that dominated the concerns of 19th-century *philology. *Noun*: **synchrony**.

syncope [**sink**-ŏ-pi], a kind of verbal contraction by which a letter or syllable is omitted from within a word (rather than from the beginning or end of the word, as in *elision). Obvious cases are *heav'n* for 'heaven' and *o'er* for 'over'; but the term also covers the omission of sounds without indication in the spelling (e.g. the word *extraordinary*, commonly pronounced as four or five syllables instead of six). The device is especially common in *syllabic and accentual-syllabic verse, where it keeps the word within the metrical scheme. *Adjective*: **syncopal** or **syncopic**.

synecdoche [si-**nek**-dŏki], a common *figure of speech (or *trope) by which something is referred to indirectly, either by naming only some part or constituent of it (e.g. 'hands' for manual labourers) or—less often—by naming some more comprehensive entity of which it is a part (e.g. 'the law' for a police officer). Usually regarded as a special kind of *metonymy, synecdoche occurs frequently in political journalism (e.g. 'Moscow' for the Russian government) and sports commentary (e.g. 'Liverpool' for one of that city's football teams), but also has literary uses like Dickens's habitual play with bodily parts: the character of Mrs Merdle in *Little Dorrit* is referred to as 'the Bosom'. *Adjective*: **synecdochic**.

synizesis, *see* synaeresis.

synonym, a word that has the same—or virtually the same—meaning as another word, and so can substitute for it in certain contexts. This identity of meaning is called **synonymy**. *Adjective*: **synonymous**.

synopsis, a brief summary or précis of a work's *plot or argument. *Adjective*: **synoptic**.

syntagm [sin-tam] or **syntagma** [sin-**tag**-mă], a linguistic term designating any combination of units (usually words or *phonemes) which are arranged in a significant sequence. A sentence is a syntagm of words. Language is said to have two distinct dimensions: the **syntagmatic** or 'horizontal' axis of combination in which sequences of words are formed by combining them in a recognized order, and the *paradigmatic or 'vertical' axis of selection, from which particular words are chosen to fill given functions within the sequence. The syntagmatic dimension is therefore the 'linear' aspect of language. *See also* syntax.

syntax, the way in which words and clauses are ordered and connected so as to form sentences; or the set of grammatical rules governing such word-order. Syntax is a major determinant of literary *style: while simple English sentences usually have the structure 'subject-verb-object' (e.g. *Jane strangled the cat*), poets often distort this syntax through *inversion, while prose writers can exploit elaborate **syntactic** structures such as the *periodic sentence.

synthesis [sin-thĕ-sis], any compound produced by uniting two or more elements; or the process of combining things into one. Synthesis, which brings elements into combination, is the opposite of analysis, which breaks something down into its constituent parts. In philosophical *dialectic, the synthesis is the product of the opposition between a *thesis and its *antithesis. *Adjective*: **synthetic**.

syuzhet, see *sjuzet*.

tableau [tab-loh] (plural **-leaux** or **-leaus**), a 'picture' formed by living persons caught in static attitudes. Tableaux were sometimes used at the ends of *acts in 19th-century *melodrama and *farce. The parlour-game of *tableaux vivants* ('living pictures'), in which living people adopt the postures of characters in a famous painting, was also a popular diversion in the 19th century, and is sometimes found in modern *pageants. In a story or poem, a description of some group of people in more or less static postures is sometimes called a tableau.

Tagelied, *see* aubade.

tail-rhyme stanza, a *stanza that combines longer lines with two or more short lines or 'tails'. Several English verse *romances of the late Middle Ages use a twelve-line stanza rhyming *aabccbddbeeb* or *aabaabccbddb*, with the lines ending in the *b*-rhyme having three stresses, the other lines having four. Chaucer's *parody, the *Tale of Sir Thopas*, uses a six-line version of this, rhyming *aabaab* in some stanzas, *aabccb* in others. Tail-rhyme is also known as caudate rhyme (the tail being a 'cauda' or 'coda'), and in French as *rime couée*.

tall tale or **tall story,** a humorously exaggerated story of impossible feats. Several tall stories attributed to the German Baron Münchhausen appeared in the 1780s, but the form flourished in the *oral tradition of the American frontier in the 19th century, several tall tales being published by Mark Twain, George Washington Harris, and others.

tanka, a traditional form of Japanese *lyric poem consisting of 31 syllables arranged in lines of 5, 7, 5, 7, and 7 syllables. It has had fewer Western imitators than the *haiku.

tenor, the subject to which a metaphorical expression is applied. In a *metaphor like *the ship of state*, the state is the tenor, while the metaphorical term *ship* is called the 'vehicle'. This distinction between tenor and vehicle was formulated by the critic I. A. Richards in *The*

Philosophy of Rhetoric (1936), where he argues that the total meaning of a metaphor is the product of a complex interaction between them.

tercet [ter-**set** *or* **ter**-sit], a unit of three verse lines, usually rhyming either with each other or with neighbouring lines. The three-line *stanzas of *terza rima* and of the *villanelle are known as tercets. The *sestet of an Italian *sonnet is composed of two tercets. *See also* triplet.

terza rima [**ter**-tsă **ree**-mă] a verse form consisting of a sequence of interlinked *tercets rhyming *aba bcb cdc ded* etc. Thus the second line of each tercet provides the rhyme for the first and third lines of the next; the sequence closes with one line (or in a few cases, two lines) rhyming with the middle line of the last tercet: *yzy z(z)*. The form was invented by Dante Alighieri for his *Divina Commedia* (c.1320), using the Italian *hendecasyllabic line. It has been adopted by several poets in English *pentameters, notably by P. B. Shelley in his 'Ode to the West Wind' (1820).

tetralogy [tet-**ral**-ŏji], a group of four connected plays or novels. Ancient Greek dramatic festivals presented tetralogies comprising three related tragedies and a *satyr play. Shakespeare's major *history plays fall into two tetralogies, the first comprising the three parts of *Henry VI* and *Richard III*, the second comprising *Richard II*, *Henry IV* Parts 1 and 2, and *Henry V*. Lawrence Durrell's *Alexandria Quartet* (1957–60) is a tetralogy of novels.

tetrameter [tet-**ram**-it-er], a verse line of four feet (*see* foot). In English verse, this means a line of four *stresses, usually *iambic or *trochaic—a very common form.

text, the actual wording of a written work, as distinct from a reader's (or theatrical director's) interpretation of its *story, *theme, *subtext etc.; or a specific work chosen as the object of analysis. *Adjective*: **textual**.

textual criticism, a branch of literary scholarship that attempts to establish the most accurate version of a written work by comparing all existing manuscript and/or printed versions so as to reconstruct from them the author's intention, eliminating copyists' and printers' errors and any corrupt *interpolations. *See also* bibliography, higher criticism, redaction.

texture, a term used in some modern criticism (especially in *New

Criticism) to designate those 'concrete' properties of a literary work that cannot be subjected to *paraphrase, as distinct from its paraphrasable 'structure' or abstract argument. The term is applied especially to the particular pattern of sounds used in a poem: its *assonance, *consonance, *alliteration, *euphony, and related effects. Often, though, the term also covers *diction, *imagery, *metre, and *rhyme.

theatre in the round, a form of theatrical presentation in which the audience is placed around a central acting area or stage, as in a circus or boxing match.

theatre of cruelty, a term introduced by the French actor Antonin Artaud in a series of manifestos in the 1930s, collected as *Le Théâtre et son double* (1938). It refers to his projected revolution in *drama, whereby the rational 'theatre of psychology' was to be replaced by a more physical and primitive rite intended to shock the audience into an awareness of life's cruelty and violence. The idea, derived partly from *Surrealism, was that the audience should undergo a *catharsis through being possessed by a 'plague' or epidemic of irrational responses. Artaud's own attempts to put this theory into dramatic practice failed, and he was locked up for some time as a lunatic. Some later dramatists, though, have developed these principles more successfully: a celebrated instance was Peter Brook's production in 1964 of Peter Weiss's *Marat/Sade*.

theatre of the absurd, *see* absurd.

theme, a salient abstract idea that emerges from a literary work's treatment of its subject-matter; or a topic recurring in a number of literary works. While the subject of a work is described concretely in terms of its action (e.g. 'the adventures of a newcomer in the big city'), its theme or themes will be described in more abstract terms (e.g. love, war, revenge, betrayal, fate, etc.). The theme of a work may be announced explicitly, but more often it emerges indirectly through the recurrence of *motifs. *Adjective*: **thematic.**

thesis, an argument or proposition, which may be opposed by an *anti-thesis; or a scholarly essay defending some proposition, usually a dissertation submitted for an academic degree. The thesis of a literary work is its abstract doctrinal content, that is, a proposition for which it argues. For 'thesis novel', see *roman à thèse*; for 'thesis play', *see* problem play.

third-person narrative, a *narrative or mode of storytelling in which the *narrator is not a character within the events related, but stands 'outside' those events. In a third-person narrative, all characters within the story are therefore referred to as 'he', 'she', or 'they'; but this does not, of course, prevent the narrator from using the first person 'I' or 'we' in commentary on the events and their meaning. Third-person narrators are often *omniscient or 'all-knowing' about the events of the story, but they may sometimes appear to be restricted in their knowledge of these events. Third-person narrative is by far the most common form of storytelling. *See also* point of view.

threnody, a *dirge or lament for the dead. A writer or speaker of threnodies is a **threnodist**. *Adjective*: **threnodic** or **threnodial**. *See also* elegy, monody.

tone, a very vague critical term usually designating the mood or atmosphere of a work, although in some more restricted uses it refers to the author's attitude to the reader (e.g. formal, intimate, pompous) or to the subject-matter (e.g. ironic, light, solemn, satiric, sentimental). *Adjective*: **tonal**. *See also* voice.

topographical poetry, poetry devoted to the description of specific places, usually with additional meditative passages. Following John Denham's poem 'Cooper's Hill' (1642), topographical poetry became a significant genre of English verse throughout the 18th century, culminating in the poems of Wordsworth, notably his 'Lines Composed a few miles above Tintern Abbey, on revisiting the banks of the Wye during a tour. July 13, 1798' (usually called 'Tintern Abbey'). This kind of poetry is sometimes called loco-descriptive verse.

topos [top-oss] (plural **topoi**), an older term for a *motif commonly found in literary works, or for a stock device of *rhetoric.

touchstone, a short quotation from a recognized poetic masterpiece, employed as a standard of instant comparison for judging the value of other works. The term was used by the English poet and critic Matthew Arnold in his essay 'The Study of Poetry' (1880), in which he recommends certain lines of Homer, Dante, Shakespeare, and Milton as touchstones for testing 'the presence or absence of high poetic quality' in samples chosen from other poets. Arnold's claim that this procedure is 'objective' has not been accepted by many modern critics. Literally, a touchstone is a hard stone of the kind once used for testing the quality of gold or silver. *See also* criterion.

tract, a short pamphlet or essay presenting some religious (or political) argument or doctrine.

tradition, any body of works, styles, conventions, or beliefs which are represented as having been 'handed down' from the past to the present. In practice, this means a specific selection of works arranged according to a certain interpretation of the past, usually made in order to lend authority to present critical arguments. Thus T. S. Eliot re-invented the tradition of English poetry by aligning it with the work of John Donne rather than John Milton; while F. R. Leavis in *The Great Tradition* (1948) excluded several major novelists from 'the' tradition of English fiction.

tragedy, a serious play (or, by extension, a novel) representing the disastrous downfall of a central character, the *protagonist. In some ancient Greek tragedies such as the *Eumenides* of Aeschylus, a happy ending was possible, provided that the subject was mythological and the treatment dignified, but the more usual conclusion, involving the protagonist's death, has become the defining feature in later uses of the term. From the works of the Greek tragedians Aeschylus, Euripides, and Sophocles, the philosopher Aristotle arrived at the most influential definition of tragedy in his *Poetics* (4th century BCE): the imitation of an action that is serious and complete, achieving a *catharsis ('purification') through incidents arousing pity and terror. Aristotle also observed that the protagonist is led into a fatal calamity by a *hamartia* ('error') which often takes the form of *hubris (excessive pride leading to divine retribution or *nemesis). The tragic effect usually depends on our awareness of admirable qualities—manifest or potential—in the protagonist, which are wasted terribly in the fated disaster. The most painfully tragic plays, like Shakespeare's *King Lear*, display a disproportion in scale between the protagonist's initial error and the overwhelming destruction with which it is punished. English tragedy of Shakespeare's time was not based directly on Greek examples, but drew instead upon the more rhetorical Roman precedent of *Senecan tragedy (*see also* revenge tragedy). Shakespearean tragedy thus shows an 'irregular' construction in the variety of its scenes and characters, whereas classical French tragedy of the 17th century is modelled more closely on Aristotle's observations, notably in its observance of the *unities of time, place, and action. Until the beginning of the 18th century, tragedies were written in verse, and usually dealt with the fortunes of royal families or other political leaders. Modern tragic drama, however, normally combines the socially inferior protagonist of *domestic tragedy with the use of prose, as in the plays of Henrik Ibsen and Arthur Miller. Some novels, like Thomas Hardy's *The Mayor of Casterbridge* (1886) and Malcolm Lowry's *Under the Volcano* (1947) can be described as tragedies, since they describe the downfall of a central character.

tragedy of blood, *see* revenge tragedy.

tragic flaw, the defect of character that brings about the protagonist's downfall in a *tragedy: Othello's jealousy is a famous example. The idea of the tragic flaw involves a narrowing and personalizing of the broader Greek concept of *hamartia* ('error' or 'failure'). *See also* hubris.

tragic irony, *see* irony.

tragicomedy, a play that combines elements of tragedy and comedy, either by providing a happy ending to a potentially tragic story or by some more complex blending of serious and light moods. In its broadest sense, the term may be applied to almost any kind of drama that does not conform strictly to comic or tragic conventions—from the medieval *mystery play to the *epic theatre of Brecht—but it is associated more specifically with a dramatic tradition that emerged from Italy in the 16th century, notably in Battista Guarini's *pastoral play *Il Pastor Fido* (1583). Guarini mixed 'high' and 'low' characters who had usually been kept apart in the separate genres, and he aimed for a 'middle' style between the tragic and the comic. The English playwrights Francis Beaumont and John Fletcher followed his example in their *Philaster* (*c*.1609), creating a new fashion for dramatic 'romances' that turned threatening situations into improbably happy conclusions through surprising reversals of fortune. This kind of tragicomedy appears to have influenced Shakespeare's later plays, including *The Winter's Tale* and *Cymbeline*, although the tragicomic pattern of sudden release from deadly danger had appeared before in his *Measure for Measure* and *The Merchant of Venice*. Shakespeare's *Troilus and Cressida* is also known as a tragicomedy for different reasons, primarily the lack of any other term to describe it (*see* problem play). The conventions of *poetic justice came to be associated with later kinds of tragicomedy, including the French *drame* and the English *heroic drama. In modern dramatic criticism, the term has come to be attached to the theatre of the *absurd: Samuel Beckett applied it to his own play *En attendant Godot* (1952), while the plays of Harold Pinter are often seen as tragicomic. *See also* black comedy, comic relief.

transcendental signified, *see* logocentrism.

Transcendentalism, an idealist philosophical tendency among writers in and around Boston in the mid-19th century. Growing out of Christian Unitarianism in the 1830s under the influence of German and British *Romanticism, Transcendentalism affirmed Kant's principle of intuitive knowledge not derived from the senses, while rejecting organized religion for an extremely individualistic celebration of the divinity in each human being. The leading Transcendentalist Ralph Waldo Emerson issued what was virtually the movement's manifesto in his essay *Nature* (1836), which presents natural phenomena as symbols of higher spiritual truths. The nonconformist individualism of the Transcendentalists is expressed in Emerson's essay 'Self-Reliance' (1841) and in Henry David Thoreau's *Walden* (1854)—a kind of autobiographical sermon against modern materialism. Others involved in the Transcendental Club in the late 1830s and with its magazine *The Dial* (1840–4) included Amos Bronson Alcott, Margaret Fuller, and William Ellery Channing. The Transcendentalists' manner of interpreting nature in symbolic terms had a profound influence on American literature of this period, notably in the works of Nathaniel Hawthorne, Herman Melville, and Walt Whitman. *See also* American Renaissance.

transferred epithet, *see* epithet, hypallage.

travesty, a mockingly undignified or trivializing treatment of a dignified subject, usually as a kind of *parody. Travesty may be distinguished from the *mock epic and other kinds of *burlesque in that it treats a solemn subject frivolously, while they treat frivolous subjects with mock solemnity. Cervantes' *Don Quixote* (1605) is a travesty of chivalric *romances, and James Joyce's *Ulysses* (1922) is partly a travesty of Homer's *Odyssey*. Verb: **travesty.**

treatise [tree-tiz], a written work devoted to the systematic examination of a particular subject, usually philosophical or scientific.

trilogy, a group of three connected plays or novels. Ancient Greek tragedies were presented at Athenian festivals in groups of three, but the *Oresteia* of Aeschylus is the only such trilogy to have survived. Shakespeare's *Henry VI* is a later dramatic example. There are several examples in modern prose fiction, including Samuel Beckett's trilogy of novels, *Molloy* (1950), *Malone Meurt* (*Malone Dies*, 1951), and *L'Innommable* (*The Unnamable*, 1952).

trimeter [trim-it-er], a verse line of three feet (*see* foot). In English verse, this means a line of three *stresses.

triolet, a poem of eight lines using only two rhymes, the first two lines being repeated as the final two lines, the first line also recurring as the fourth. The rhyme scheme—with repeated lines given in capitals—is *ABaAabAB*. The triolet is one of the medieval French *fixed forms, and may be considered as a simplified form of the *rondel. A few English poets, including Austin Dobson and W. E. Henley, revived it in the late 19th century.

triple metre, a term covering poetic *metres based on a *foot of three syllables (a **triple foot**), as opposed to the much more common *duple metre in which the predominant foot has two syllables. English verse in triple metres thus displays a more or less regular alternation of single stressed syllables with pairs of unstressed syllables, the feet being described traditionally as *anapaests or *dactyls.

triple rhyme, a rhyme on three syllables, the first stressed and the others unstressed: *beautiful/dutiful*. Triple rhymes are used chiefly for comic purposes in *light verse, as in Edward Lear's *limerick beginning

> There was an old man of Thermopylae
> Who never did anything properly.

Byron's *Don Juan* has some ludicrous examples. *See also* rhyme.

triplet, a sequence of three verse lines sharing the same *rhyme, sometimes appearing as a variation among the *heroic couplets of Dryden and some 18th-century poets: or any group or *stanza of three lines. Triplets occurring among heroic couplets are sometimes indicated by a brace, as in Pope's *Essay on Criticism* (1711):

> Musick resembles Poetry, in each
> Are nameless Graces which no Methods teach, $\Big\}$
> And which a Master-Hand alone can reach.

The three-line units used in *terza rima* and those composing the *sestet of an Italian sonnet are more often referred to as *tercets.

trochee [troh-ki], a metrical unit (*foot) of verse, having one stressed syllable followed by one unstressed syllable, as in the word 'tender' (or, in Greek and Latin *quantitative verse, one long syllable followed by one short syllable). Lines of verse made up predominantly of trochees are referred to as **trochaic verse** or **trochaics**. Regular trochaic lines are quite rare in English, Longfellow's *Song of Hiawatha* (1855) being a celebrated example of their extended use:

> Ye whose hearts are fresh and simple

Far more common in English is the truncated or *catalectic line that drops the final unstressed syllable, as in Emily Brontë's lines:

> Long neglect has worn away
> Half the sweet enchanting smile.

Since the trochee is often found as a variation at the beginning of *iambic lines (*see* substitution), this sort of trochaic line beginning and ending with a stressed syllable can be difficult to distinguish from iambic verse.

trope, a *figure of speech, especially one that uses words in senses beyond their *literal meanings. The theory of *rhetoric has involved several disputed attempts to clarify the distinction between tropes (or 'figures of thought') and *schemes (or 'figures of speech'). The most generally agreed distinction in modern theory is that tropes change the meanings of words, by a 'turn' of sense, whereas schemes merely rearrange their normal order. The major figures that are agreed upon as being tropes are *metaphor, *simile, *metonymy, *synecdoche, *irony, *personification, and *hyperbole; *litotes and *periphrasis are also sometimes called tropes. The figurative sense of a word is sometimes called its **tropological** sense, tropology being the study of tropes—and especially of the spiritual meanings concealed behind the literal meanings of religious scriptures (*see* typology). In a second sense, the term was applied in the Middle Ages to certain additional passages introduced into church services. The most important of these, the *quem quaeritis* trope in the Easter Introit, is thought to have been the origin of *liturgical drama. *Adjective*: **tropical.**

troubadour, a poet of southern France (or sometimes northern Italy) writing in Provençal in the late Middle Ages. The troubadours, mostly aristocratic poets rather than wandering *minstrels or *jongleurs, flourished in the period 1100–1350, composing elaborate *lyrics of *courtly love which had an extensive influence on Western poetry and culture. Among the best known are Guillaume d'Aquitaine, Arnaut Daniel, and Betran de Born. Their favoured poetic forms included the *aubade, the *chanson, and the *pastourelle. From the late 12th century onwards they found imitators in northern France (the *trouvères) and in Germany (the *Minnesänger).

trouvère [troo-**vair**], a poet of northern France in the late Middle Ages. The *trouvères* flourished in the late 12th and early 13th centuries, and were in many respects the followers of the Provençal *troubadours, although their repertoire extended beyond love *lyrics into *narrative verse, especially the *chanson de geste and the verse *romance. The term covers some of the professional entertainers known as *jongleurs, but applies mainly to poets of higher rank. The most important was Chrétien de Troyes, who established the Arthurian romance of *courtly love with his *Lancelot* (*c.*1170); other notable *trouvères* include Conon de Béthune, Thibaud de Champagne, and Blondel de Nesle—who, according to legend, discovered the imprisoned Richard the Lionheart by singing under his window.

truncation, the shortening of a metrical verse line by omitting a syllable or syllables (usually unstressed) from the full complement expected in the regular metrical pattern. This may occur at the beginning of the line (acephalexis: *see* acephalous) or, more usually, at the end (catalexis: *see* catalectic). In English verse, truncation is most often found in trochaic verse (see *trochee), where the final unstressed syllable is commonly not employed.

turn, the English term for an abrupt change in the mood or argument of a poem, especially in a *sonnet (see *volta*); also an older word for a *trope.

two-hander, a play written for only two speaking parts, such as Samuel Beckett's *Happy Days* (1961).

type, a fictional character who stands as a representative of some identifiable class or group of people. Although some uses of the term equate it with the stereotyped *stock character of literary and folk *tradition, other uses distinguish between this 'two-dimensional' stock character and the more individualized type: in the work of the Hungarian Marxist critic Georg Lukács, 'typicality' is a quality combining uniquely individualized with historically representative features. Lukács found this typicality in the characters of early 19th-century *realist novels like those of Balzac; similarly, the realist fiction of George Eliot and Henry James is inhabited by such types, who are certainly not mere stock characters. In two other senses, the term is used in reference to literary *forms as a synonym for *genre, and in reference to religious *allegory as another word for emblem or *symbol (*see* typology).

typography, the arrangement of printed words on the page. Typographical factors—most obviously the lack of a right-hand margin in most verse, and the spaces between *stanzas—have some influence on readers' understanding of literary works. The exploitation of typography for special effects is found in *pattern poetry and modern *concrete poetry, and in some experimental prose works like those of the Scottish novelist Alasdair Gray.

typology, a system of interpretation applied by early Christian theologians to the Hebrew scriptures (the 'Old Testament'), by which certain events, images, and personages of pre-Christian *legend could be understood as prophetic 'types' or 'figures' foreshadowing the life of Christ. Typology—literally the study of types—is thus a method of re-reading the Old Testament anachronistically in terms of the New Testament, so that Adam, Isaac, Jonah, and other characters are pre-figurings of Christ, the Tree of Knowledge in Eden is a type of the Cross, and so on. By the 13th century an elaborate system of *allegory had been constructed, dividing the sense of anything in the Old Testament into four levels of meaning: the literal, the allegorical (referring to the New Testament or the Christian Church), the moral or tropological (referring to the fate of the individual soul), and the *anagogical (referring to universal history and *eschatology). In the standard illustration of this scheme, Jerusalem is literally a city, allegorically the Church, tropologically the soul of the believer, and anagogically the heavenly City of God. Typological allegory is an important element in many literary works of medieval Christianity, including Dante's *Divina Commedia* (*c*.1320), and in some later sermons and religious verse.

U

ubi sunt [uubi suunt], a Latin phrase ('where are ... ?') often used in medieval Latin poems on the transitoriness of life and beauty, usually as an opening line or *refrain referring to the dead who are listed in the poem. The phrase serves as the name for a common *motif in medieval (and some later) poetry, Latin and *vernacular, in which the speaker asks what has become of various heroes and beautiful ladies. The most celebrated example of the motif is François Villon's 'Ballade des dames du temps jadis' (*c*.1460), with its refrain:

> Mais ou sont les neiges d'antan?

In D. G. Rossetti's translation, this is rendered 'But where are the snows of yester-year?'

uncanny, the, a kind of disturbing strangeness evoked in some kinds of horror story and related fiction. In Tzvetan Todorov's theory of the *fantastic, the uncanny is an effect produced by stories in which the incredible events can be explained as the products of the *narrator's or *protagonist's dream, hallucination, or delusion. A clear case of this is Edgar Allan Poe's tale 'The Tell-Tale Heart' (1843), in which the narrator is clearly suffering from paranoid delusions. In tales of the *marvellous, on the other hand, no such psychological explanation is offered, and strange events are taken to be truly supernatural.

undecidable, *see* aporia, indeterminacy.

unities, the, principles of dramatic structure proposed by critics and dramatists of the 16th and 17th centuries, claiming the authority of Aristotle's *Poetics* (4th century BCE). The three unities were the unity of time, the unity of place, and the unity of action. In fact Aristotle in his discussion of *tragedy insists only on unity of action, mentioning unity of time in passing, and says nothing about place. Italian and French critics of the 16th century attempted to codify his views into rules, but with little effect on dramatic practice until Jean Mairet's *Sophonisbe* (1634), the first French tragedy to observe the unities. As formulated by Mairet and later by Boileau in *L'Art poétique* (1674), the unities required that any serious play should have a unified action, without the distractions of a *subplot, representing events of a single day (24 hours, or 12, or ideally the same time as the duration of the performance itself) within a single setting—which could include different parts of the same city. The tragedies of Pierre Corneille—apart from his controversial play *Le Cid* (1637)—and those of Jean Racine were the outstanding examples of this mode of dramatic composition. In England, however the French rules never established themselves in dramatic practice, although they were much debated by critics. The influence of Shakespeare is usually believed to be the reason for this resistance: apart from *The Tempest* and *The Two Gentlemen of Verona*, all of his plays violate the unities. The rise of *Romanticism involved a rebellion against *neoclassicism and its rules, including the unities; the example of Shakespeare was again invoked to support freely structured drama.

university wits, the name given by some modern literary historians to a group of English poets and playwrights who established themselves in London in the 1580s and 1590s after attending university at either Oxford or Cambridge. The most important member of the group was Christopher Marlowe, whose powerful *blank-verse plays prepared the way for Shakespeare. Others included George Peele, Robert Greene, Thomas Nashe, John Lyly, and Thomas Lodge. There seems to have been some rivalry between this group and the newcomers Shakespeare and Jonson, who did not have university educations.

univocal [yoo-ni-**voh**-kăl], having only one meaning; unmistakeable in sense. The term **univocality** is sometimes employed in contrasts with the *ambiguity of literary works; for other contrasting terms, *see* polysemy, multi-accentuality.

unreliable narrator, a *narrator whose account of events appears to be faulty, misleadingly biased, or otherwise distorted, so that it departs from the 'true' understanding of events shared between the reader and the *implied author. The discrepancy between the unreliable narrator's view of events and the view that readers suspect to be more accurate creates a sense of *irony. The term does not necessarily mean that such a narrator is morally untrustworthy or a habitual liar (although this may be true in some cases), since the category also includes harmlessly naïve, 'fallible', or ill-informed narrators. A classic case is Huck in Mark Twain's *Adventures of Huckleberry Finn* (1884): this 14-year-old narrator does not understand the full significance of the events he is relating and commenting on. Other kinds of unreliable narrator seem to be falsifying their accounts from motives of vanity or malice. In either case, the reader is offered the pleasure of picking up 'clues' in the narrative that betray the true state of affairs. This kind of *first-person narrative is particularly favoured in 20th-century fiction: a virtuoso display of its use is William Faulkner's *The Sound and the Fury* (1928), which employs three unreliable narrators—an imbecile, a suicidal student, and an irritable racist bigot. *See also* point of view.

Urtext, the German term for an original version of a text, usually applied to a version that is lost and so has to be reconstructed by *textual criticism. Some scholars believe that Shakespeare's *Hamlet* is based on an earlier play that has not survived even in name; this hypothetical work is referred to as the *Ur-Hamlet*.

ut pictura poesis [uut pik-**too**-ră poh-**ees**-is] a phrase used by the Roman poet Horace in his *Ars Poetica* (*c*.20 BCE), meaning 'as painting is, so is poetry'. The phrase has come to stand for the principle of similarity between the two arts, an idea shared by many writers and artists of different periods and found in common metaphors of literary 'depiction' or 'portrayal'. It held an important place in aesthetic debates of the late *Renaissance and in the theories of *neoclassicism, but was subjected to an important *critique by the German dramatist and critic G. E. Lessing in his essay *Laokoon* (1766). The relationship between the two 'sister arts' is usually said to lie in their imitation of nature (*see* mimesis).

utopia, an imagined form of ideal or superior (thus usually communist) human society; or a written work of *fiction or philosophical speculation describing such a society. Utopias may be distinguished from mythological Golden Ages or religious paradises in that they are the products of human (i.e. political) arrangement for human benefit. The word was coined by Sir Thomas More in his Latin work *Utopia* (1516), as a pun on two Greek words, *eutopos* ('good place') and *outopos* ('no place'). More's account of an ideal commonwealth was followed by several others including Francis Bacon's *New Atlantis* (1627); later examples include Edward Bellamy's *Looking Backward* (1888), and William Morris's *dream vision of socialism in *News from Nowhere* (1890). Utopian fiction has often been used as the basis of *satire on contemporary life, as in Samuel Butler's *Erewhon* (1872); it is also closely related to some kinds of *science fiction. For the inverted or undesirable equivalent of a utopia, the term *dystopia is often used, as it is for works describing such a 'bad place'.

variorum edition, originally an *edition of an author's works (or of a single work) containing explanatory notes by various commentators and editors. In recent usage, however, the term has come to mean an edition that includes all the variant readings from manuscript and other versions. Many modern variorum editions answer both descriptions.

Varronian satire, *see* Menippean satire.

vatic, inspired by powers of prophecy, or relating to a divinely inspired poet or *bard, such a poet being called in Latin a *vates*.

vaudeville, a form of variety show popular in the USA in the late 19th and early 20th centuries, and more respectable than the American *burlesque show. In Britain, this form of entertainment with various songs, dances, sketches, acrobatics, ventriloquisms, and other 'acts' is more often called music hall. In 18th- and 19th-century France, however, vaudeville was a more coherent form of light-hearted comedy interspersed with satirical songs; it evolved into the comic opera.

vehicle, *see* tenor.

Verfremdungseffekt, *see* alienation effect.

verisimilitude, the semblance of truth or reality in literary works; or the literary principle that requires a consistent illusion of truth to life. The term covers both the exclusion of improbabilities (as in *realism and *naturalism) and the careful disguising of improbabilities in non-realistic works. As a critical principle, it originates in Aristotle's concept of *mimesis or imitation of nature. It was invoked by French critics (as *vraisemblance*) to enforce the dramatic *unities in the 17th and 18th centuries, on the grounds that changes of scene or time would break the illusion of truth to life for the audience. *Adjective*: **verisimilar.**

verismo [ve-**riz**-moh], an Italian form of *naturalism, best exemplified by the novels and stories written in the 1880s by the Sicilian writer Giovanni Verga; these document the harsh lives of the Sicilian poor.

Another notable **verist** of this period is the short-story writer Federico de Roberto. *Verismo*, through Verga's story *Cavalleria rusticana*, had a significant influence on Italian opera (notably on Puccini), and later upon the emergence of *neo-realism. In English, the term **verism** is sometimes applied to *realism as a critical doctrine. *Adjective*: **veristic.**

vernacular [ver-**nak**-yŭ-ler], the local language or *dialect of common speech; or (as an adjective) written in such a local language or dialect. The term distinguishes living languages from dead or priestly languages (e.g. French or English rather than Latin or Greek), the languages of the colonized from those of the colonists (e.g. Middle English rather than French; Welsh or Bengali rather than English), or the use of dialect rather than 'standard' forms of the same language; but in a looser sense it may refer to the use of a colloquial rather than a formal style.

vers de société [vaird sos-yay-tay], the French term ('society verse') for a kind of *light verse which deals with the frivolous concerns of upper-class social life, usually in a harmlessly playful vein of *satire and with some technical elegance. Some of Alexander Pope's minor poems fall into this category, while the modern master of *vers de société* in English is John Betjeman.

vers libre [vair leebr], *see* free verse.

verse, (1) *poetry, as distinct from *prose. The term is usually more neutral than 'poetry', indicating that the technical requirements of *rhythm and *metre are present, while poetic merit may or may not be. It is almost always reserved for metrical compositions, the looser non-metrical category of *free verse being a special case. (2) a line of poetry; or, in common usage, a *stanza, especially of a hymn or song. Strictly, the term should refer to a line rather than a stanza, although the battle to retain this distinction seems to have been lost. Even so, to avoid confusion it is preferable to call a line a line and a stanza a stanza. (3) a poem.

verse paragraph, a group of verse lines forming a subdivision of a poem, the length of this unit being determined by the development of the sense rather than by a formal *stanza pattern. Long *narrative poems in *blank verse or *heroic couplets are often divided into paragraphs of uneven lengths, the breaks being indicated either by indentation (as in prose) or by spaces. Some shorter poems like Matthew Arnold's 'Dover Beach' are also composed in irregular verse paragraphs rather than stanzas. The subdivisions of *free verse are necessarily non-stanzaic and are therefore also usually called verse paragraphs. Some critics have claimed that a stanza or even a complete short poem like a *sonnet should be considered as a verse paragraph, but this usage loses the valuable distinction between the terms. *See also* stichic, strophe.

versification, the techniques, principles, and practice of composing *verse, especially in its technical aspects of *metre, *rhyme, and *stanza form; or the conversion of a prose passage or work into metrical verse form. *Verb*: **versify.** *See also* prosody.

verso, the back of a printed sheet; thus the left-hand (and even-numbered) page in a book, as opposed to the *recto*, which is the right-hand, odd-numbered page on the other side.

Vice, the, a *stock character in medieval *morality plays; he is a cynical kind of fool in the service of the Devil, and tries to tempt others in a comical but often sinister manner. The Vice is believed to be the ancestor of some later dramatic villains like Shakespeare's Iago, and of some more comic characters like his Falstaff.

vignette [vin-yet], any brief composition or self-contained passage, usually a descriptive prose *sketch, *essay, or *short story. The term also refers to a kind of decorative design sometimes found at the beginning or end of a chapter in a book; these were often based on vine-leaves.

villain, the principal evil character in a play or story. The villain is usually the *antagonist opposed to the *hero (and/or heroine), but in some cases he may be the *protagonist, as in Shakespeare's *Richard III*. The villains of English Elizabethan and *Jacobean drama, especially in *revenge tragedy, appear to be descended from the devils and the *Vice in earlier *morality plays. A more simplified villainous *stock character appears in 19th-century *melodrama, usually as a bewhiskered seducer. *See also* Machiavel.

villanelle, a poem composed of an uneven number (usually five) of *tercets rhyming *aba*, with a final *quatrain rhyming *abaa*. In this French *fixed form, the first and third lines of the opening tercet are repeated alternately as the third lines of the succeeding tercets, and together as the final couplet of the quatrain. Representing these repeated lines in capitals, with the second of them given in italic, the rhyme

scheme may be displayed thus: AbA abA abA abA abA abAA. The form was
established in France in the 16th century, and used chiefly for *pastoral
songs. In English, it was used for light *vers de société* by some minor poets
of the late 19th century; but it has been adopted for more serious use by
W. H. Auden, William Empson, and Derek Mahon. The best-known
villanelle in English, however, is Dylan Thomas's 'Do Not Go Gentle into
That Good Night' (1952).

virelay [vi-rĕ-lay] or *virelai*, a form of *lyric poem or song found in
medieval France, but hardly ever in English. It has various forms, usually
employing short lines and only two rhymes. In some a *refrain is used,
while in others a pattern of interlinked rhymes connects the *stanzas,
with the final rhyme of each stanza providing the main rhyme of the
next.

voice, a rather vague metaphorical term by which some critics refer to
distinctive features of a written work in terms of spoken utterance. The
voice of a literary work is then the specific group of characteristics
displayed by the *narrator or poetic 'speaker' (or, in some uses, the
actual author behind them), assessed in terms of *tone, *style, or
personality. Distinctions between various kinds of narrative voice tend
to be distinctions between kinds of narrator in terms of how they address
the reader (rather than in terms of their perception of events, as in the
distinct concept of *point of view). Likewise in non-narrative poems,
distinctions can be made between the personal voice of a private lyric
and the assumed voice (the *persona) of a *dramatic monologue.

volta or ***volte*,** the Italian term for the 'turn' in the argument or mood
of a *sonnet, occurring (in the Italian form of sonnet) between the octave
and the sestet, i.e. at the 9th line. In the Miltonic variant of the Italian
pattern, though, the *volta* comes later, about the 10th line; while in the
Shakespearean or English form of the sonnet—which does not observe
the octave/sestet division—it usually comes with the final couplet, i.e. at
the 13th line.

Vorticism, a short-lived artistic movement that announced itself in
London in 1914. It was led by the painter and writer Wyndham Lewis,
and attracted the support of the sculptors Jacob Epstein and Henri
Gaudier-Brzeska. Its literary significance is negligible except in that Ezra
Pound regarded it as an advance upon his previous phase of *Imagism.
The Vorticist manifestos that appeared in the two issues of Lewis's

magazine *Blast* (1914–15) celebrated the dynamic energies of the machine age while accusing *Futurism of having romanticized the machine. Vorticism called for an end to all sentimentality, and for a new abstraction that would, paradoxically, be both dynamic and static. For Pound the 'vortex' was the concentrated energy of the *avant-garde*, which was to blast away the complacency of the established culture. Vorticism was thus one of the minor currents of *modernism.

vraisemblance [vray-som-blah[n]s], the French word for the artistic illusion of truth, usually known in English as *verisimilitude. *Adjective*: *vraisemblable*.

vulgate, a commonly used version of a work; or the common form of a language (i.e. *vernacular prose). In *textual criticism, the vulgate is the version of a text most commonly used, as distinct from its most accurate version. The **Vulgate** is a version of the Bible in Latin, translated mainly by St Jerome in the late 14th century, and later adapted as the authorized Roman Catholic text. The **Vulgate Cycle** of *chivalric romances is a group of 13th-century French prose works dealing with King Arthur and his knights; it includes the accounts of the quest for the Holy Grail and of Arthur's death upon which Thomas Malory based his *Le Morte Darthur* (1485).

weak ending, the *promotion of a normally unstressed monosyllable (usually a conjunction, preposition, or auxiliary verb) to the position usually occupied by a stressed syllable at the end of an *iambic line, causing a wrenched *accent. In this quotation from Shakespeare's *Antony and Cleopatra*, both line-endings are weak:

> Friends, be gone. You shall
> Have letters from me to some friends that will
> Sweep your way for you.

The weak ending may be distinguished from the *feminine ending in that it places the unstressed syllable in a stress position (the 10th syllable in an iambic *pentameter) rather than adding an extra 11th syllable. *See also* enjambment.

well-made play, now a rather unfavourable term for a play that is neatly efficient in the construction of its plot but superficial in ideas and characterization. In 19th-century France, the term (*pièce bien faite*) at first had a more positive sense, denoting the carefully constructed suspense in comedies and *melodramas by Eugène Scribe (1791–1861) and his follower Victorien Sardou (1831–1908). As this tradition was displaced by the more serious concerns of dramatic *naturalism, the term acquired its dismissive sense, especially in the critical writings of Bernard Shaw. For a fuller account, consult John Russell Taylor, *The Decline and Fall of the Well-Made Play* (1967).

Weltanschauung [velt-an-show-uung], the German term for a 'world-view', that is, either the 'philosophy of life' adopted by a particular person or the more general outlook shared by people in a given period.

Weltschmerz [velt-shmairts], the German word for world-weariness (literally 'world-ache'), a vague kind of melancholy often associated with Romantic poetry.

Wertherism [ver-ter-izm], a fashion for morbid and self-indulgent

melancholy or *Weltschmerz* provoked by J. W. von Goethe's
*sentimental novel *Die Lieden des jungen Werthers* (*The Sorrows of Young
Werther*, 1774), in which the hero commits suicide because of his
hopeless love for a young married woman. The novel was a sensation
throughout Europe: Napoleon read it several times, and young men
copied Werther's distinctive costume of yellow breeches with a blue
coat. More alarmingly, one young woman drowned herself with a copy of
the novel in her pocket, and several other youthful suicides were blamed
on this craze.

West End, in theatrical parlance, the area of central London in and
around Shaftesbury Avenue where the major commercial theatres have
been concentrated since the 19th century. It has become associated with
polished but generally 'lighter' kinds of dramatic entertainment
(musicals, *farces, etc.) by contrast with the higher literary drama
offered at theatres located in less fashionable districts—such as the Old
Vic or the National Theatre, both south of the Thames.

wit, a much-debated term with a number of meanings ranging from the
general notion of 'intelligence' through the more specific 'ingenuity' or
'quickness of mind' to the narrower modern idea of amusing verbal
cleverness. In its literary uses, the term has gone through a number of
shifts: it was associated in the *Renaissance with intellectual keenness
and a capacity of 'invention' by which writers could discover surprisingly
appropriate *figures and *conceits, by perceiving resemblances between
apparently dissimilar things. It took on an additional sense of elegant
arrangement in the 17th and 18th centuries, as in Pope's famous
definition of true wit in his *Essay on Criticism* (1711):

What oft was Thought, but ne'er so well Exprest.

However, the advent of *Romanticism with its cult of *imagination
and genius tended to relegate wit, along with *fancy and ingenuity,
to an inferior position, transferring its older positive senses to the
imaginative faculty. The usual modern sense of wit, then, is one of light
cleverness and skill in *repartee or the composition of amusing
*epigrams. In 20th-century criticism, an attempt to restore a stronger
sense of wit was mounted by T. S. Eliot in his discussions of the
*metaphysical poets: he praised the wit of Andrew Marvell as a kind of
'tough reasonableness', while other critics have seen wit as a kind of
disposition towards *irony. The important point to note is that earlier
uses of the term included the positive sense of imaginative capacity,

which has since become rather detached from the weaker modern notion of what is witty.

wrenched accent, *see* accent.

writerly, see *scriptible*.

z

Zeitgeist [tsyt-gyst], the German word for 'time-spirit', more often translated as 'spirit of the age'. It usually refers to the prevailing mood or attitude of a given period.

zeugma [zewg-mă], a *figure of speech by which one word refers to two others in the same sentence. Literally a 'yoking', zeugma may be achieved by a verb or preposition with two objects, as in the final line of Shakespeare's 128th sonnet:

> Give them thy fingers, me thy lips to kiss.

Or it may employ a verb with two subjects, as in the opening of his 55th sonnet:

> Not marble nor the gilded monuments
> Of princes shall outlive this powerful rhyme.

However, the term is frequently used as a synonym for *syllepsis—a special kind of zeugma in which the yoking term agrees grammatically with only one of the terms to which it is applied, or refers to each in a different sense. In the confusion surrounding these two terms, some rhetoricians have reserved 'zeugma' for the ungrammatical sense of syllepsis. _Adjective_: **zeugmatic**.

Further Reference

Many terms lying beyond the scope of this dictionary are explained in other reference books, which are listed below under subject headings.

General

J. A. Cuddon, *A Dictionary of Literary Terms* (1977) is the most respected of the larger general dictionaries in this field. Revised by Cuddon himself, and after his death in 1996 by C. E. Preston, it is now available as *The Penguin Dictionary of Literary Terms and Literary Theory* (1999). C. Hugh Holman and William Harmon, *A Handbook to Literature* (1986) features longer entries on literary periods, with chronologies and lists of Nobel and Pulitzer prize-winners.

Literary and Cultural Theory

Many rather general topics such as *art*, *belief*, and *language* are discussed in Roger Fowler (ed.), *A Dictionary of Modern Critical Terms* (1973; revised 1987). A careful historical investigation into shifting senses of terms like *creative*, *culture*, and *ideology* is conducted in Raymond Williams, *Keywords* (1976).

There are now several other reference works on the terminology of modern literary theory. These include Michael Groden and Martin Kreiswirth (eds.), *The Johns Hopkins Guide to Literary Theory and Criticism* (1994), which offers lengthy essays on critical schools and movements across an international range; Joseph Childers and Gary Henzi (eds.), *The Columbia Dictionary of Modern Literary and Cultural Criticism* (1995), written by a large team and thus rather variable in the quality and relevance of its entries; Michael Payne (ed.), *A Dictionary of Cultural and Critical Theory* (1996); David Macey, *The Penguin Dictionary of Critical Theory* (2000), which, like the *Johns Hopkins Guide* and Payne's book, features entries on major theorists as well as on terms and concepts; and Jeremy Hawthorn, *A Glossary of Contemporary Literary Theory* (4th edn., 2000).

Poetry

Many of the more obscure poetic terms are covered by Cuddon and by Holman and Harmon (see above). The most extensive coverage of poetic terminology is to be found in Alex Preminger (ed.), *Princeton Encyclopedia of Poetry and Poetics* (1965; expanded 1974). A shorter selection of entries from this work has been published as the *Princeton Handbook of Poetic Terms* (1986). Some terms not found in the Princeton volume are explained in Jack Myers and Michael Simms, *Longman Dictionary and Handbook of Poetry* (1985).

Drama

A helpful guide to dramatic terms is Terry Hodgson, *The Batsford Dictionary of Drama* (1988). Some terms are also explained in Phyllis Hartnoll (ed.), *The Oxford Companion to the Theatre* (4th edition 1983). Fuller coverage of dramatic concepts is offered in Patrice Pavis, *Dictionary of the Theatre: Terms, Concepts, and Analysis* (1998).

Rhetoric

A convenient guide is Richard A. Lanham, *A Handlist of Rhetorical Terms* (1968). Many of the major rhetorical terms are discussed in more detail in the *Princeton Encyclopedia of Poetry and Poetics* (see under Poetry above).

Narratology

The now extensive vocabulary of modern narratology is explained in Gerald Prince, *A Dictionary of Narratology* (1987).

Linguistics

The standard guide to linguistic terms is David Crystal, *A Dictionary of Linguistics and Phonetics* (4th edition 1996). More helpful for literary terminology is Katie Wales, *A Dictionary of Stylistics* (2nd edition 2001). Helpful introductory glossaries are P. H. Matthews, *The Concise Oxford Dictionary of Linguistics* (1997) and Geoffrey Finch, *Linguistic Terms and Concepts* (2000).

Oxford Paperback Reference

The Concise Oxford Companion to English Literature
Margaret Drabble and Jenny Stringer

Based on the best-selling *Oxford Companion to English Literature*, this is an indispensable guide to all aspects of English literature.

Review of the parent volume
'a magisterial and monumental achievement'

Literary Review

The Concise Oxford Companion to Irish Literature
Robert Welch

From the ogam alphabet developed in the 4th century to Roddy Doyle, this is a comprehensive guide to writers, works, topics, folklore, and historical and cultural events.

Review of the parent volume
'Heroic volume ... It surpasses previous exercises of similar nature in the richness of its detail and the ecumenism of its approach.'

Times Literary Supplement

A Dictionary of Shakespeare
Stanley Wells

Compiled by one of the best-known international authorities on the playwright's works, this dictionary offers up-to-date information on all aspects of Shakespeare, both in his own time and in later ages.

Oxford Paperback Reference

The Concise Oxford Dictionary of English Etymology
T. F. Hoad

A wealth of information about our language and its history, this
reference source provides over 17,000 entries on word origins.

'A model of its kind'

Daily Telegraph

A Dictionary of Euphemisms
R. W. Holder

This hugely entertaining collection draws together euphemisms from all
aspects of life: work, sexuality, age, money, and politics.

Review of the previous edition
'This ingenious collection is not only very funny but extremely
instructive too'

Iris Murdoch

The Oxford Dictionary of Slang
John Ayto

Containing over 10,000 words and phrases, this is the ideal reference for
those interested in the more quirky and unofficial words used in the
English language.

'hours of happy browsing for language lovers'

Observer

More Literature titles from OUP

Shakespeare: An Oxford Guide
Stanley Wells and Lena Cowen Orlin

This comprehensive guide to Shakespeare comprises over 40 specially commissioned essays by an outstanding team of contemporary Shakespeare scholars.

Literature in the Modern World
Dennis Walder

A unique perspective for students on literary studies from the 1920s to the present day.

The Poetry Handbook
John Lennard

A lucid and entertaining guide to the poet's craft, and an invaluable introduction to practical criticism.

VISIT THE HIGHER EDUCATION LITERATURE WEB SITE AT
www.oup.com/uk/best.textbooks/literature

AskOxford.com
Oxford Dictionaries Passionate about language

For more information about the background to Oxford Quotations and Language Reference Dictionaries, and much more about Oxford's commitment to language exploration, why not visit the world's largest language learning site, www.AskOxford.com

Passionate about English?

What were the original 'brass monkeys'?   **Ask**Oxford.com

How do new words enter the dictionary?   **Ask**Oxford.com

How is 'whom' used?   **Ask**Oxford.com

Who said, 'For also knowledge itself is power?'   **Ask**Oxford.com

How can I improve my writing?   **Ask**Oxford.com

If you have a query about the English language, want to look up a word, need some help with your writing skills, are curious about how dictionaries are made, or simply have some time to learn about the language, bypass the rest and ask the experts at www.AskOxford.com.

Passionate about language?

If you want to find out about writing in French, German, Spanish, or Italian, improve your listening and speaking skills, learn about other cultures, access resources for language students, or gain insider travel tips from those   **Ask**Oxford.com
in the know, ask the experts at

OXFORD

Oxford Paperback Reference

The Concise Oxford Dictionary of Art & Artists
Ian Chilvers

Based on the highly praised *Oxford Dictionary of Art*, over 2,500 up-to-date entries on painting, sculpture, and the graphic arts.

'the best and most inclusive single volume available, immensely useful and very well written'

Marina Vaizey, *Sunday Times*

The Concise Oxford Dictionary of Art Terms
Michael Clarke

Written by the Director of the National Gallery of Scotland, over 1,800 entries cover periods, styles, materials, techniques, and foreign terms.

A Dictionary of Architecture
James Stevens Curl

Over 5,000 entries and 250 illustrations cover all periods of Western architectural history.

'splendid ... you can't have a more concise, entertaining, and informative guide to the words of architecture'

Architectural Review

'excellent, and amazing value for money ... by far the best thing of its kind'

Professor David Walker

Oxford Paperback Reference

The Kings of Queens of Britain
John Cannon and Anne Hargreaves

A detailed, fully-illustrated history ranging from mythical and pre-conquest rulers to the present House of Windsor, featuring regional maps and genealogies.

A Dictionary of Dates
Cyril Leslie Beeching

Births and deaths of the famous, significant and unusual dates in history – this is an entertaining guide to each day of the year.

'a dipper's blissful paradise ... Every single day of the year, plus an index of birthdays and chronologies of scientific developments and world events.'

Observer

A Dictionary of British History
Edited by John Cannon

An invaluable source of information covering the history of Britain over the past two millennia. Over 3,600 entries written by more than 100 specialist contributors.

Review of the parent volume
'the range is impressive ... truly (almost) all of human life is here'
Kenneth Morgan, *Observer*

Oxford Paperback Reference

The Concise Oxford Dictionary of Quotations
Edited by Elizabeth Knowles

Based on the highly acclaimed *Oxford Dictionary of Quotations*, this paperback edition maintains its extensive coverage of literary and historical quotations, and contains completely up-to-date material. A fascinating read and an essential reference tool.

The Oxford Dictionary of Humorous Quotations
Edited by Ned Sherrin

From the sharply witty to the downright hilarious, this sparkling collection will appeal to all senses of humour.

Quotations by Subject
Edited by Susan Ratcliffe

A collection of over 7,000 quotations, arranged thematically for easy look-up. Covers an enormous range of nearly 600 themes from 'The Internet' to 'Parliament'.

The Concise Oxford Dictionary of Phrase and Fable
Edited by Elizabeth Knowles

Provides a wealth of fascinating and informative detail for over 10,000 phrases and allusions used in English today. Find out about anything from the 'Trojan house' to 'ground zero'.

More Art Reference from Oxford

The Grove Dictionary of Art

The 34 volumes of *The Grove Dictionary of Art* provide unrivalled coverage of the visual arts from Asia, Africa, the Americas, Europe, and the Pacific, from prehistory to the present day.

'succeeds in performing the most difficult of balancing acts, satisfying specialists while ... remaining accessible to the general reader'

The Times

The Grove Dictionary of Art – Online
www.groveart.com

This immense cultural resource is now available online. Updated regularly, it includes recent developments in the art world as well as the latest art scholarship.

'a mammoth one-stop site for art-related information'

Antiques Magazine

The Oxford History of Western Art
Edited by Martin Kemp

From Classical Greece to postmodernism, *The Oxford History of Western Art* is an authoritative and stimulating overview of the development of visual culture in the West over the last 2,700 years.

'here is a work that will permanently alter the face of art history ... a hugely ambitious project successfully achieved'

The Times

The Oxford Dictionary of Art
Edited by Ian Chilvers

The Oxford Dictionary of Art is an authoritative guide to the art of the western world, ranging across painting, sculpture, drawing, and the applied arts.

'the best and most inclusive single-volume available'

Marina Vaizey, *Sunday Times*

Oxford Paperback Reference

The Oxford Dictionary of Dance
Debra Craine and Judith Mackrell

Over 2,500 entries on everything from hip-hop to classical ballet, covering dancers, dance styles, choreographers and composers, techniques, companies, and productions.

'A must-have volume ... impressively thorough'
Margaret Reynolds, *The Times*

Who's Who in Opera
Joyce Bourne

Covering operas, operettas, roles, perfomances, and well-known personalities.

'a generally scrupulous and scholarly book'
Opera

The Concise Oxford Dictionary of Music
Michael Kennedy

The most comprehensive, authoritative, and up-to-date dictionary of music available in paperback.

'clearly the best around ... the dictionary that everyone should have'
Literary Review

More History titles from OUP

The Oxford History of the French Revolution
William Doyle

'A work of breath-taking range ... It is the fullest history to appear of the Revolutionary era, of the events preceding it and of its impact on a wider world. Masterfully written.'

Observer

The Twentieth Century World
William R. Keylor

The complete guide to world history during the last century.

Tudor England
John Guy

'Lucid, scholarly, remarkably accomplished ... an excellent overview.'

The Sunday Times

**VISIT THE HIGHER EDUCATION HISTORY WEB SITE AT
www.oup.com/uk/best.textbooks/history**

Oxford Paperback Reference

The Concise Oxford Dictionary of World Religions
Edited by John Bowker

Over 8,200 entries containing unrivalled coverage of all the major world religions, past and present.

'covers a vast range of topics ... is both comprehensive and reliable'
The Times

The Oxford Dictionary of Saints
David Farmer

From the famous to the obscure, over 1,400 saints are covered in this acclaimed dictionary.

'an essential reference work'
Daily Telegraph

The Concise Oxford Dictionary of the Christian Church
E. A. Livingstone

This indispensable guide contains over 5,000 entries and provides full coverage of theology, denominations, the church calendar, and the Bible.

'opens up the whole of Christian history, now with a wider vision than ever'
Robert Runcie, former Archbishop of Canterbury

Oxford Paperback Reference

A Dictionary of Psychology
Andrew M. Colman

Over 10,500 authoritative entries make up the most wide-ranging
dictionary of psychology available.

'impressive ... certainly to be recommended'
Times Higher Educational Supplement

'Comprehensive, sound, readable, and up-to-date, this is probably the
best single-volume dictionary of its kind.'
Library Journal

A Dictionary of Economics
John Black

Fully up-to-date and jargon-free coverage of economics. Over 2,500
terms on all aspects of economic theory and practice.

A Dictionary of Law

An ideal source of legal terminology for systems based on English law.
Over 4,000 clear and concise entries.

'The entries are clearly drafted and succinctly written ... Precision for the
professional is combined with a layman's enlightenment.'
Times Literary Supplement

OXFORD